AF469936

The right of Edward Whitaker to be identified as the authors of this work has been
asserted by them in accordance with the Copyright, Designs and Patents Act 1988.

First published in Great Britain in 2018 by Racing Post Books
27 Kingfisher Court, Hambridge Road, Newbury, Berkshire, RG14 5SJ

10 9 8 7 6 5 4 3 2 1

A catalogue record for this book is available from the British Library.

ISBN 978-1-910497-78-4

Designed by Soapbox, www.soapbox.co.uk
Printed and bound in Slovenia by DZS Grafik

Every effort has been made to fulfil requirements with regard to copyright material.
The author and publisher will be glad to rectify any omissions at the earliest opportunity.

www.racingpost.com/shop

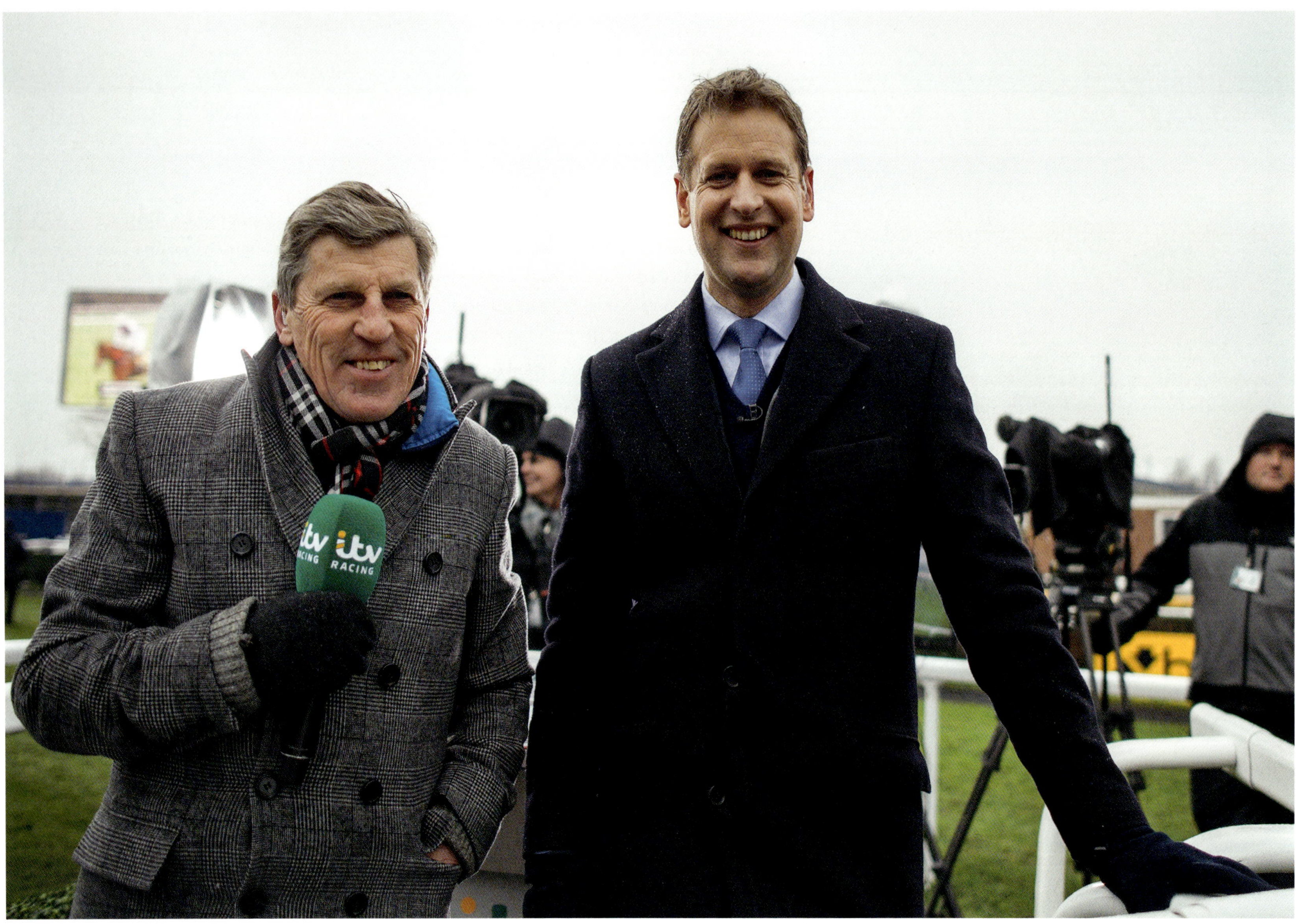

Foreword

On ITV our big mission is to try and get the viewer into the heart of the action. In this book Edward Whitaker delivers this in spades. That photograph of the Grand National start has the whole field coming at you.

He takes us on a wonderful journey capturing the magic of horseracing from St Moritz to Cheltenham, from Plumpton to Epsom, Longchamp, Punchestown and all stops to Del Mar. His pictures make you wonder, wince, laugh and cry.

His skill is to capture the memorable both human and equine. There's the awesome power of a 'chaser on Newbury take off, the punch-the-air thrill of a winner at Chester, that sensuous shot of New Approach being hosed down at Dalham, and that so poignant image of Henry Cecil in the shadows by the Al Bahathri gallops in Newmarket.

It's his attention to detail that makes Edward so special, that has won him awards not just in racing but across the whole photographic field. When I get to the press room early on TV days he is already there going over his plans. When I go off to rehearse I see him out and around looking for new angles, a bit like an animal stalking his prey. He'll be down by the rails, out by the fences; one time

I remember spotting him on an adjacent hill. I will say 'what on earth is he doing'? This book comes up with the answers and our understanding of how he thinks and operates is much enhanced by the pithiest of captions.

There is atmosphere as well as action: bookmakers boards glowing like harbour lights in the gloom, dawn coming up at Santa Anita, Richard Johnson hitting the ground at Wincanton and, one of my favourites, the dazzling shot of Might Bite jumping the water at Cheltenham with his reflection sharp beneath.

Most people have their talents blunted by facing the same challenges again and again. Edward's have only sharpened down the years. Enjoy.

ED CHAMBERLIN

January

The flying horseshoe
Plenty of horses lose shoes in a
race as Vyta Du Roc did this day at
Cheltenham. But I had never caught
one like this before, high above
the fence in the perfect shape of
a lucky horseshoe.

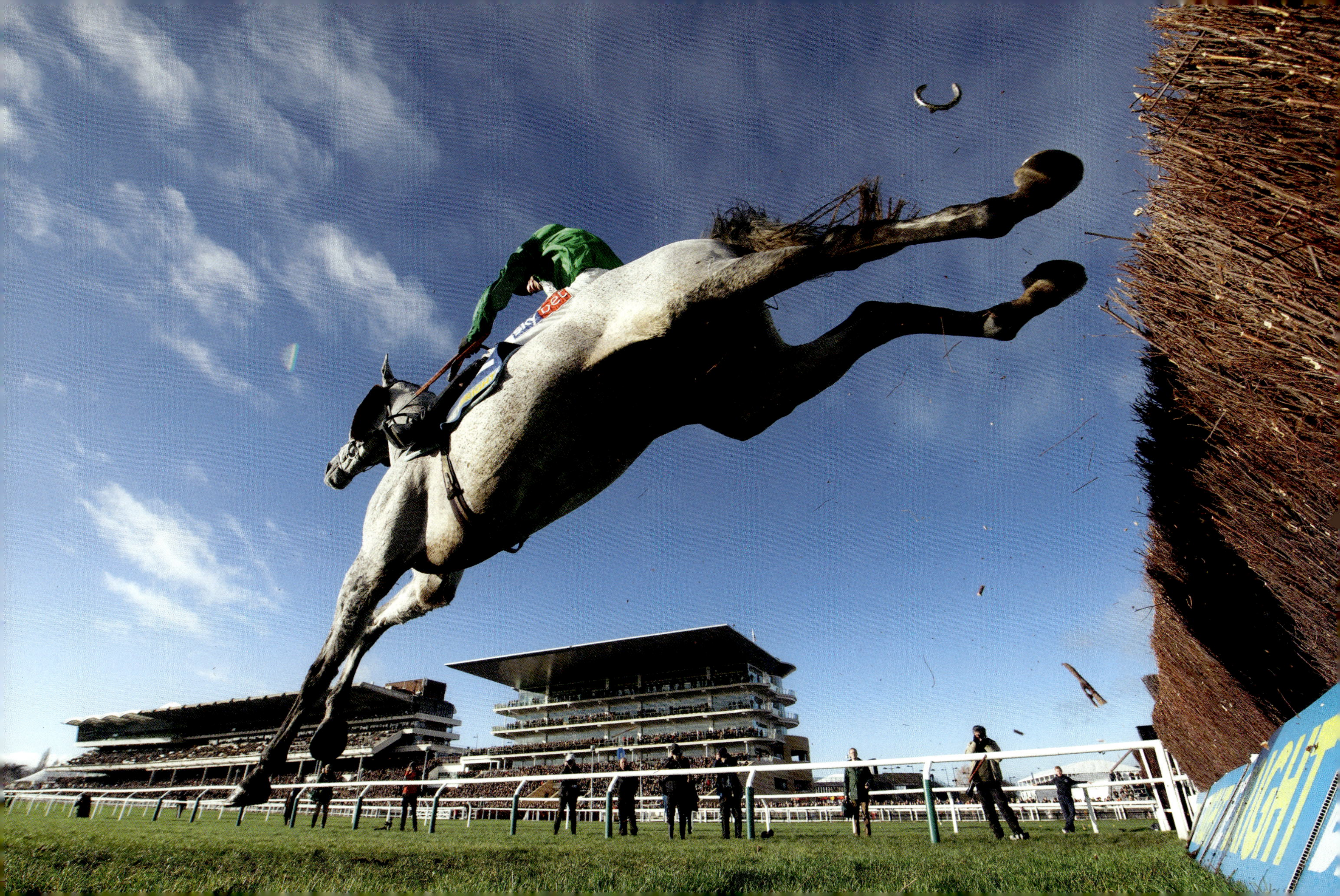

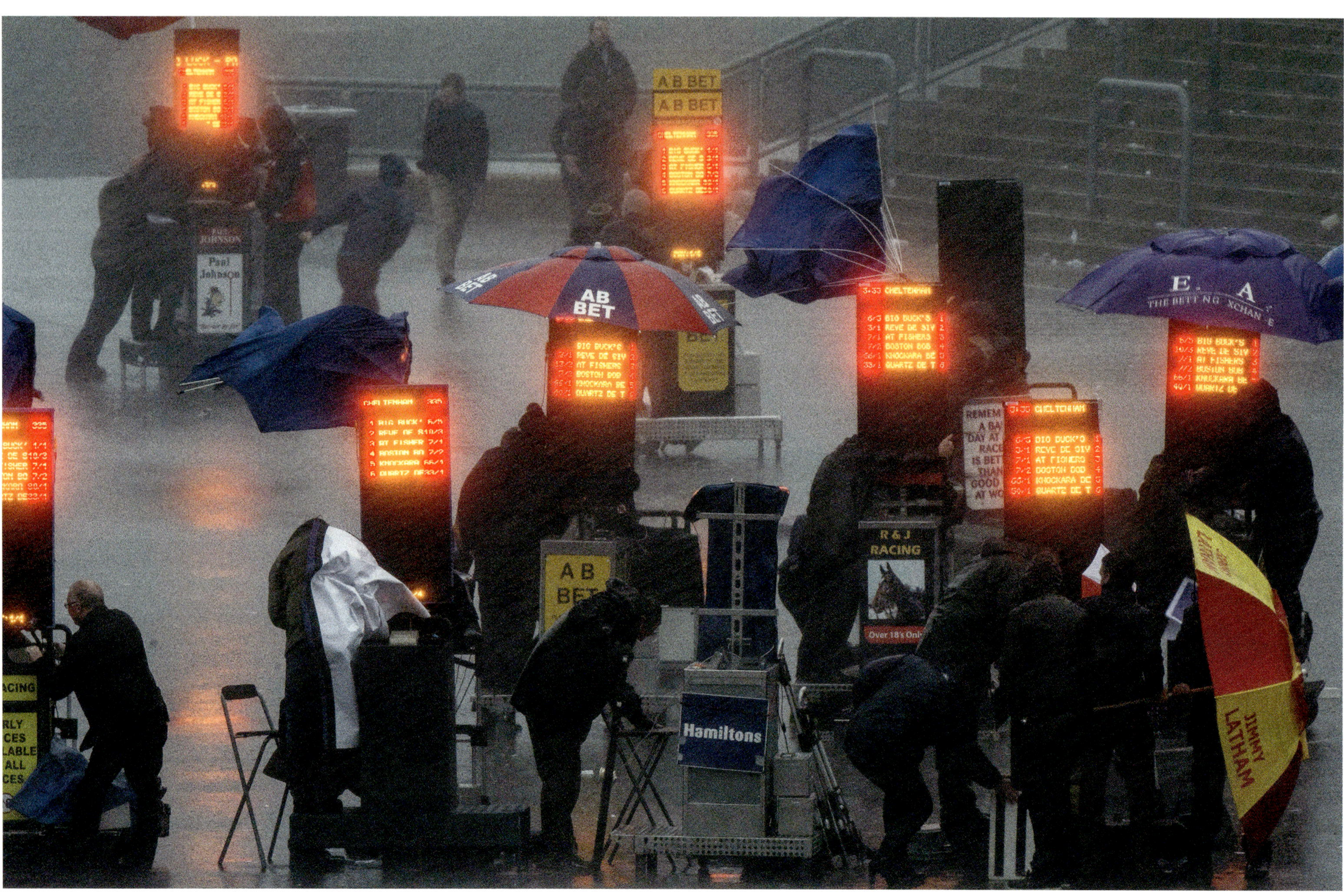

Camaraderie and contemplation
Before a race, jockeys tend to josh
with one another as Ruby Walsh and
AP McCoy do here, but there can
be deeper thoughts too. Penny for
them Barry Geraghty?

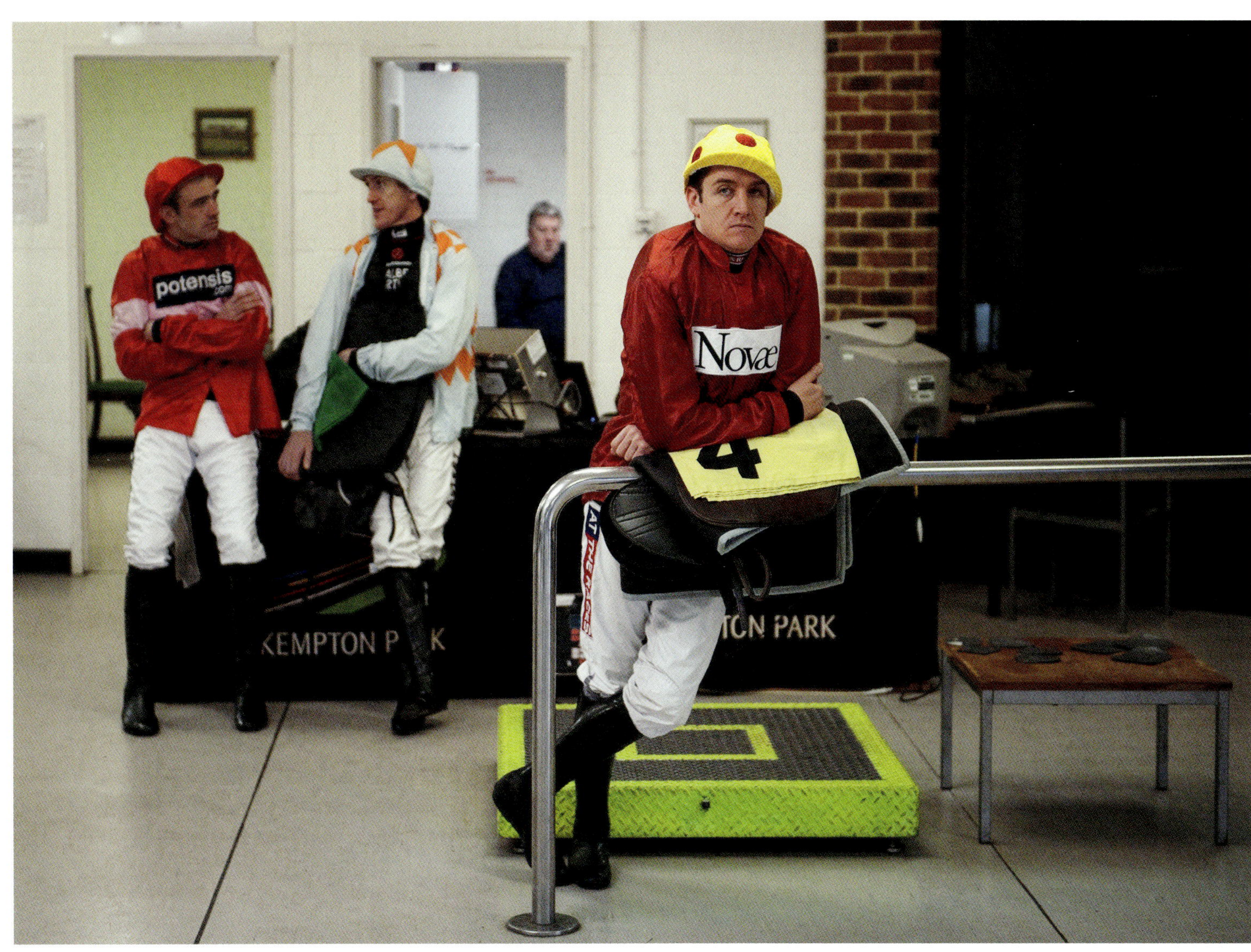

Lanterns in the gloom
A huge thunderstorm hits
Cheltenham and suddenly the
bookies' boards looked like boats
bobbing in a hurricane.

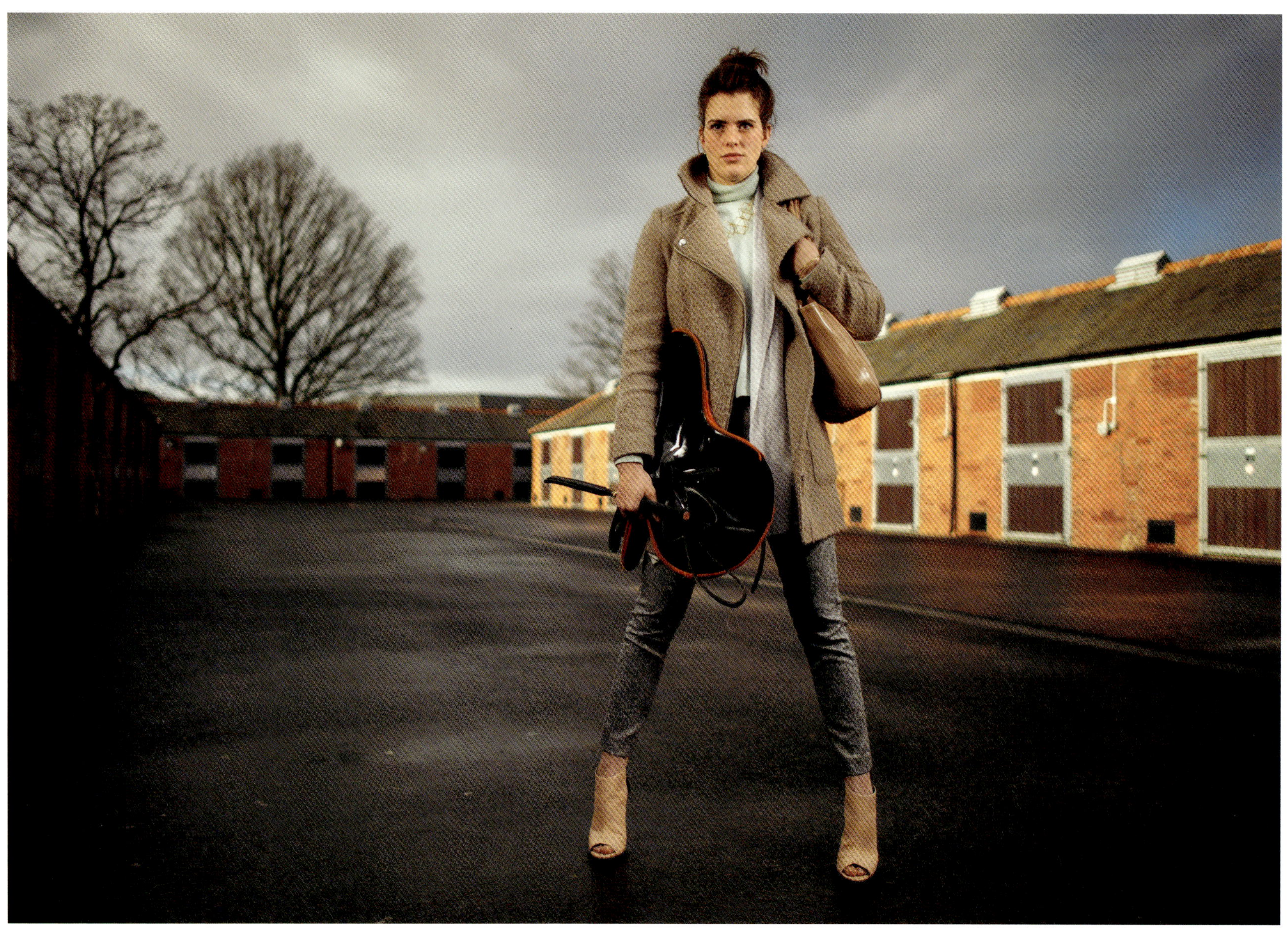

Power straddle
Lizzie Kelly had just won her first
Grade 1 chase at Kempton on Boxing
Day. I liked the idea of the power
straddle stance – she didn't need
any persuading.

Winter Wonderland 1
Snow is a challenge for racehorse
trainers and a great opportunity
for photographers. In this picture
of Harry Dunlop's string on the
Mandown gallops, Upper Lambourn
has a raw blue starkness about it.

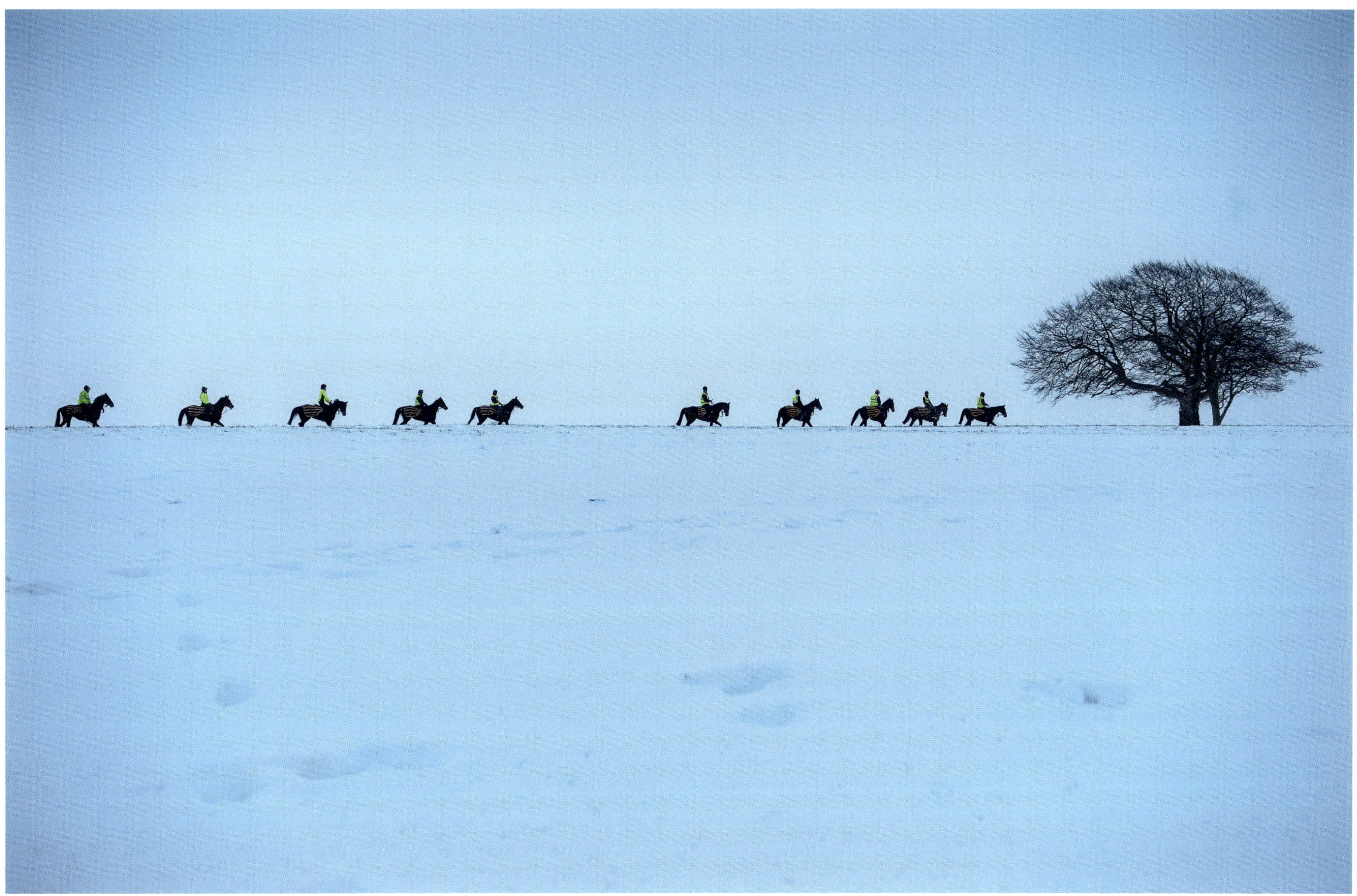

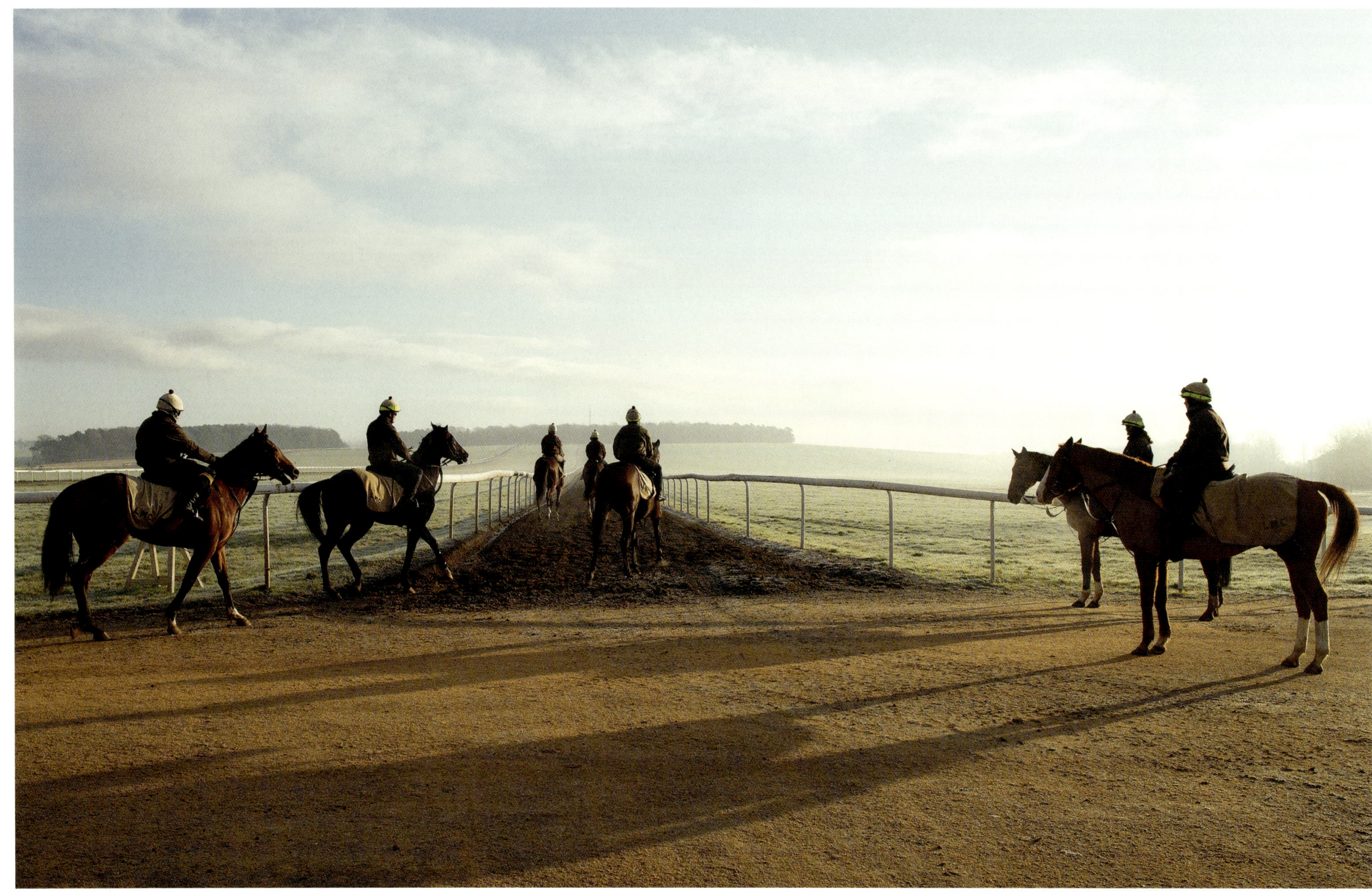

Winter Wonderland 2
Luca Cumani's string at the bottom
of Warren Hill, a tranquil look at what
over the year must be the busiest
exercising strip in the country.

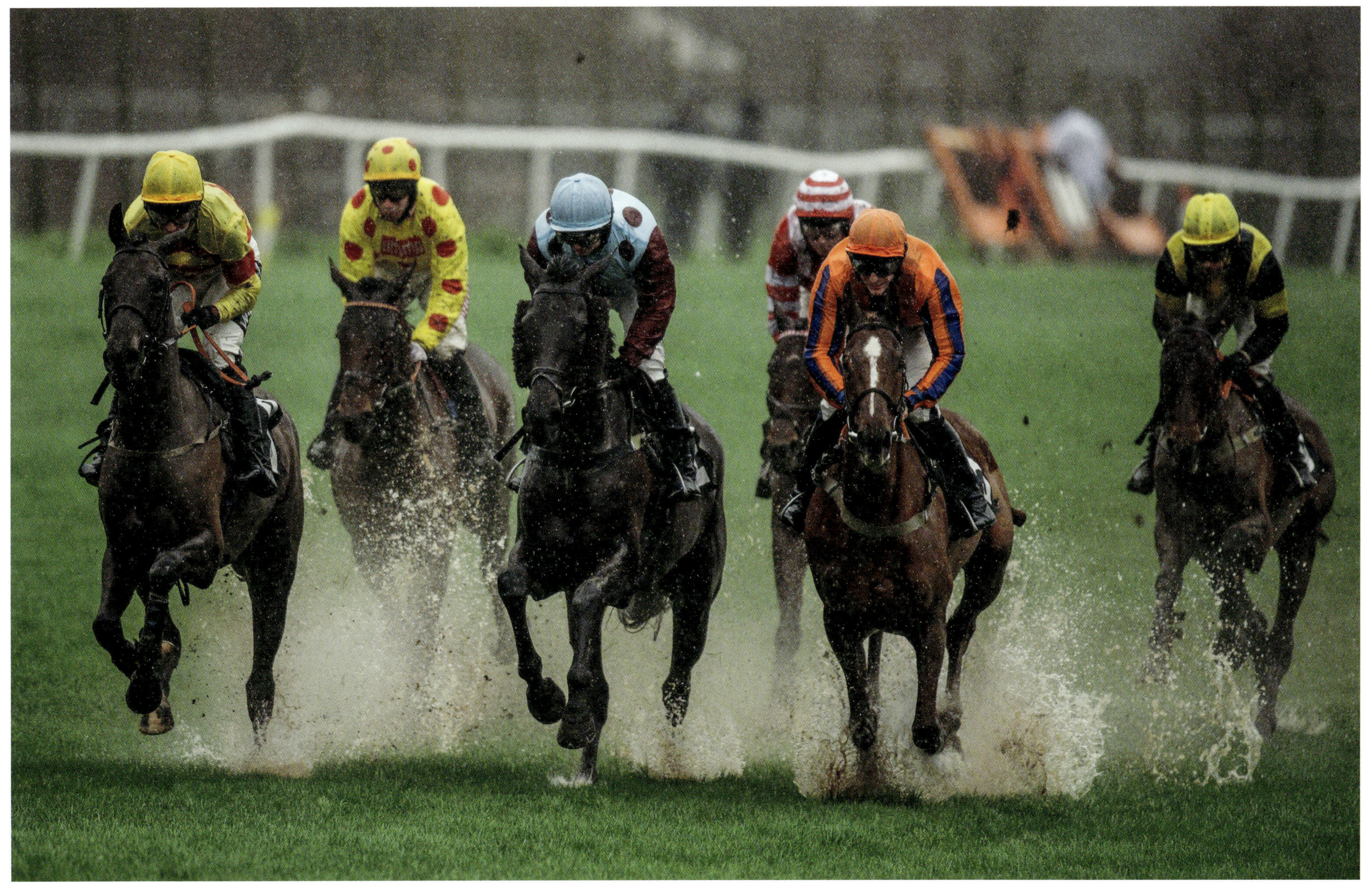

Water splash
After two races the rain won the battle on this soggiest of days at Plumpton. But not before we saw this full-on water splash before the final hurdle.

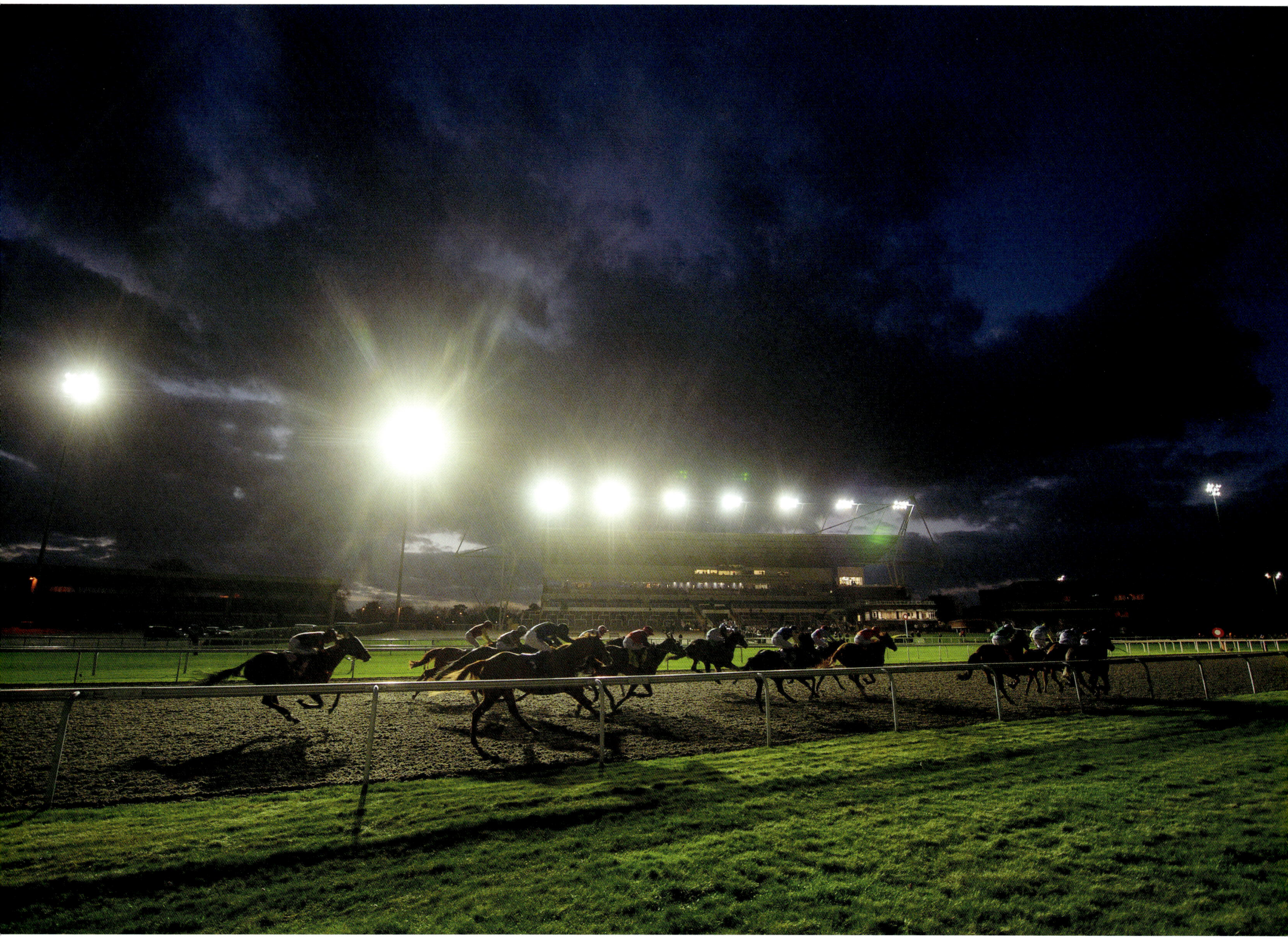

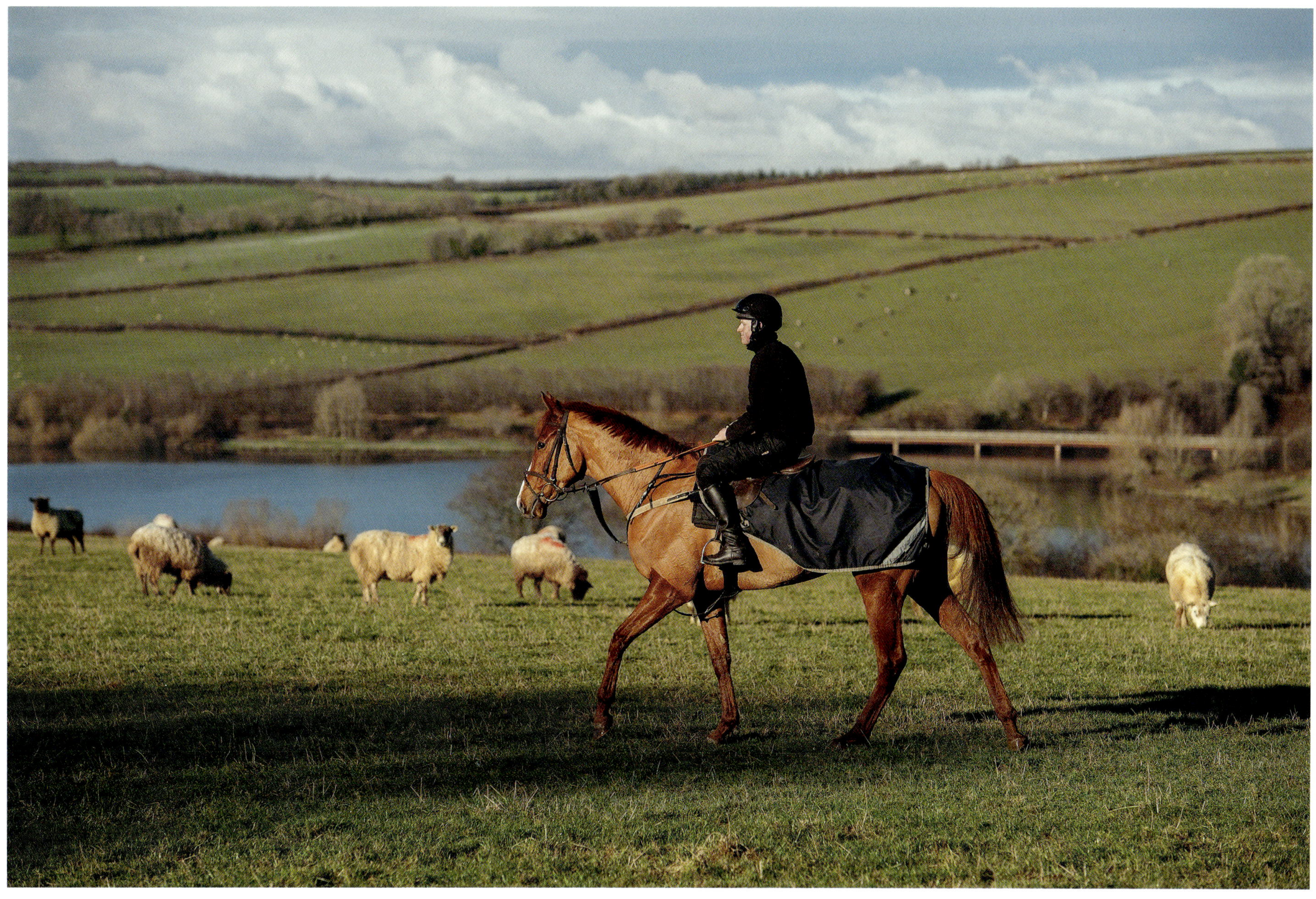

Fading lights?
Floodlights at dusk always add to
the drama at a racecourse and the
day before this the Jockey Club had
said that Kempton would be sold
for development. Well, it's my local
track and I love it there.

Rural roots
Stable star Melodic Rendezvous
and groom Steven Croft exercise
at trainer Jeremy Scott's farm on
the edge of Exmoor.

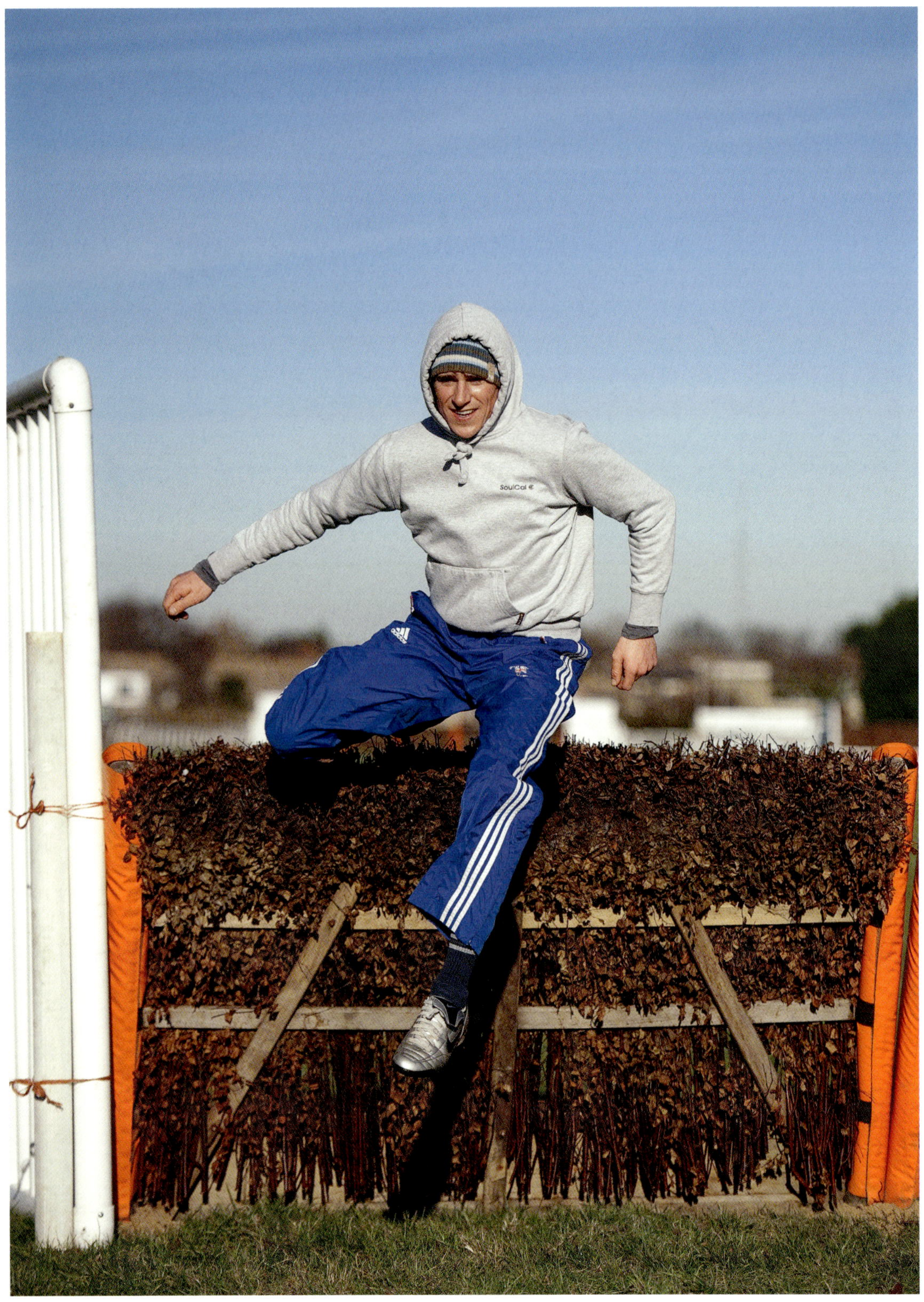

Who needs a horse?
Harry Skelton jumps the final flight while warming up at Plumpton. That's a lot higher than the athletes jump in the 3,000m steeplechase at the Olympics.

Picking a puddle
Swaddled up trainer's wife Jayne Moore on the grey Donna's Palm leads through the mud at their base in West Sussex. Was this the plan when she got a degree in American literature and a job offer from the *Chicago Sun-Times*?

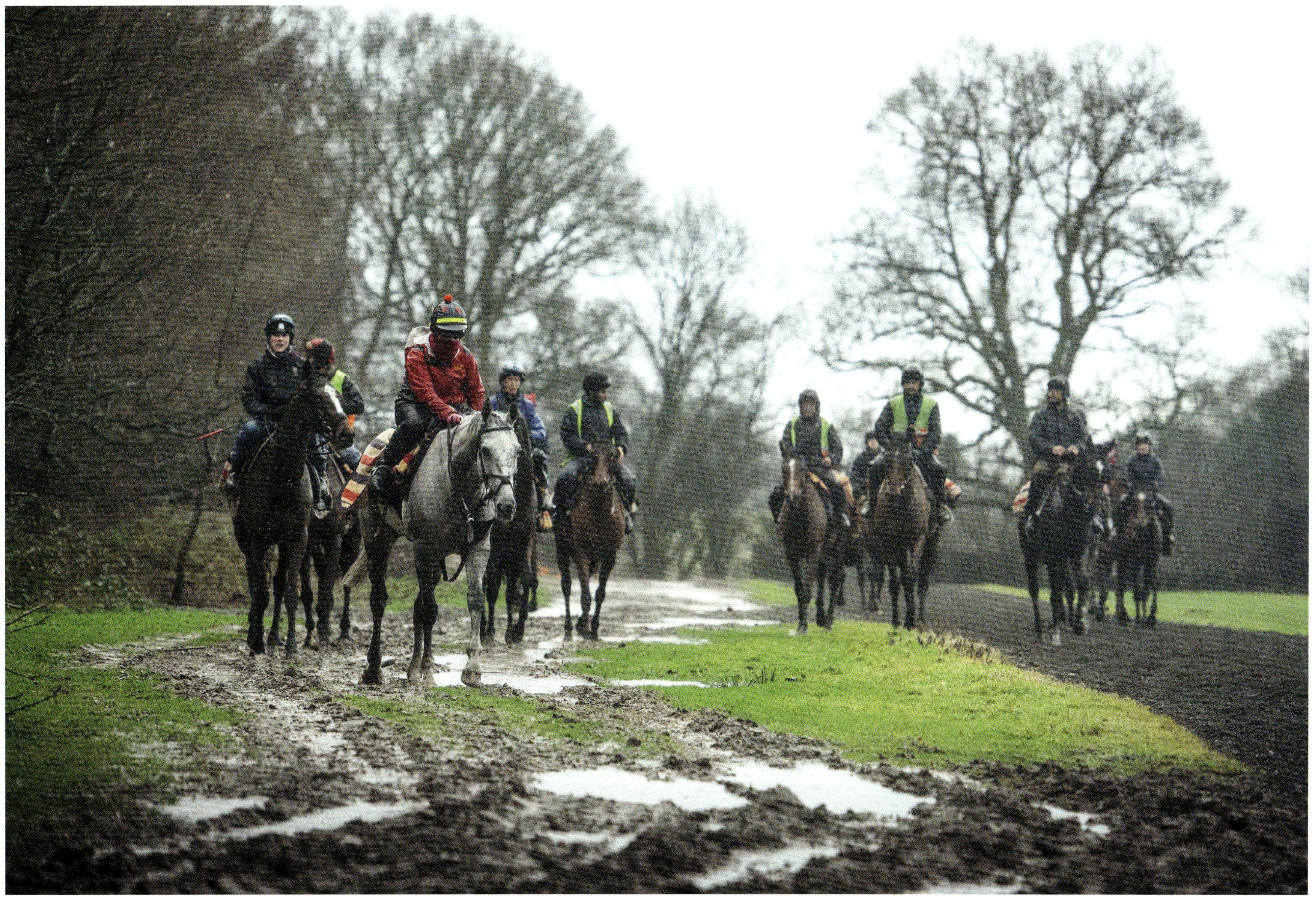

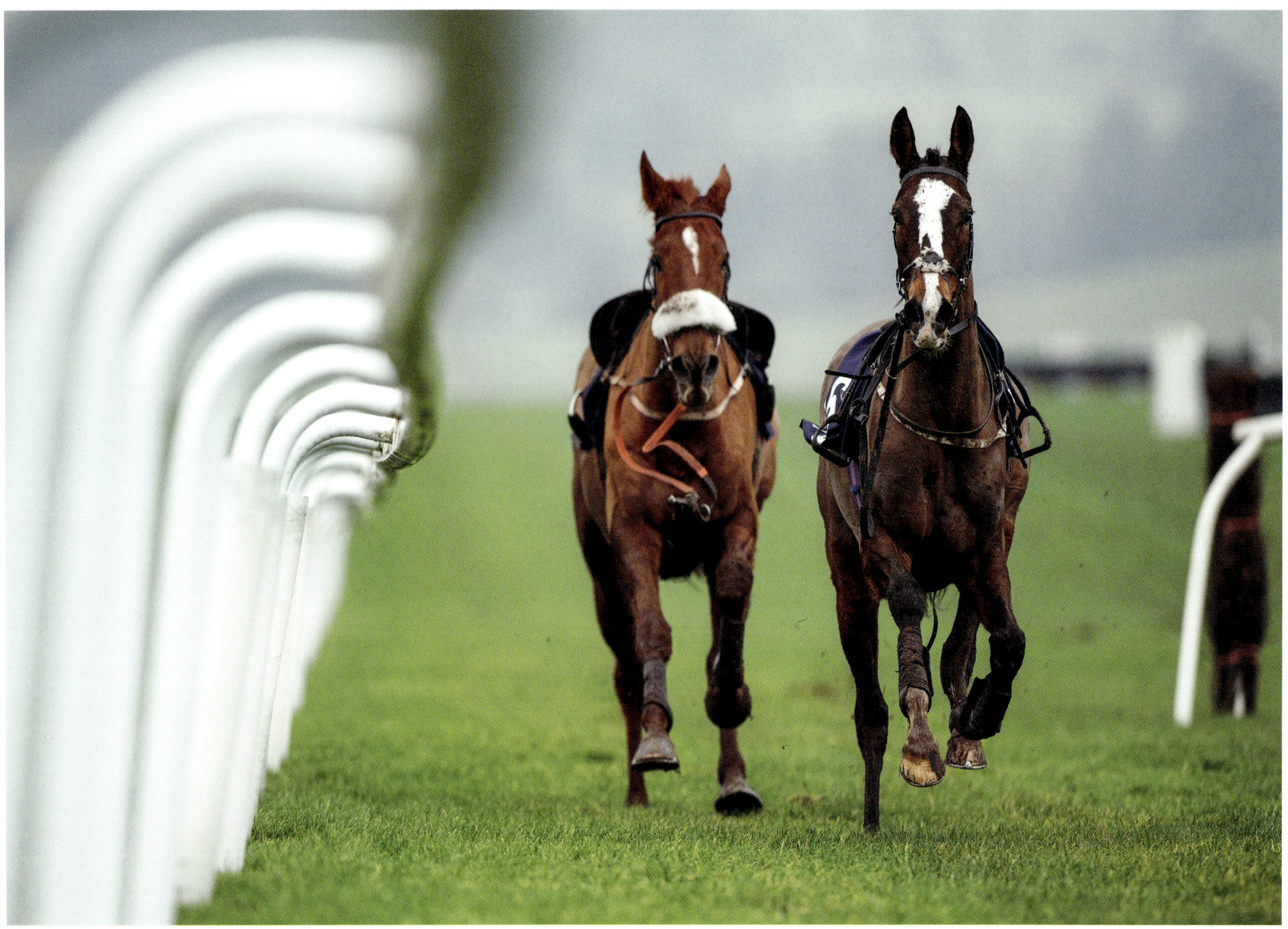

Naughty boys
I loved this pair's sense of freedom
as if celebrating the fun of galloping
without a jockey on a damp day
at Chepstow.

Light and shade at Plumpton
The single tree sets up the shot
as the runners spin around the top
of the hill in that sharp, bright light
that often comes in January.

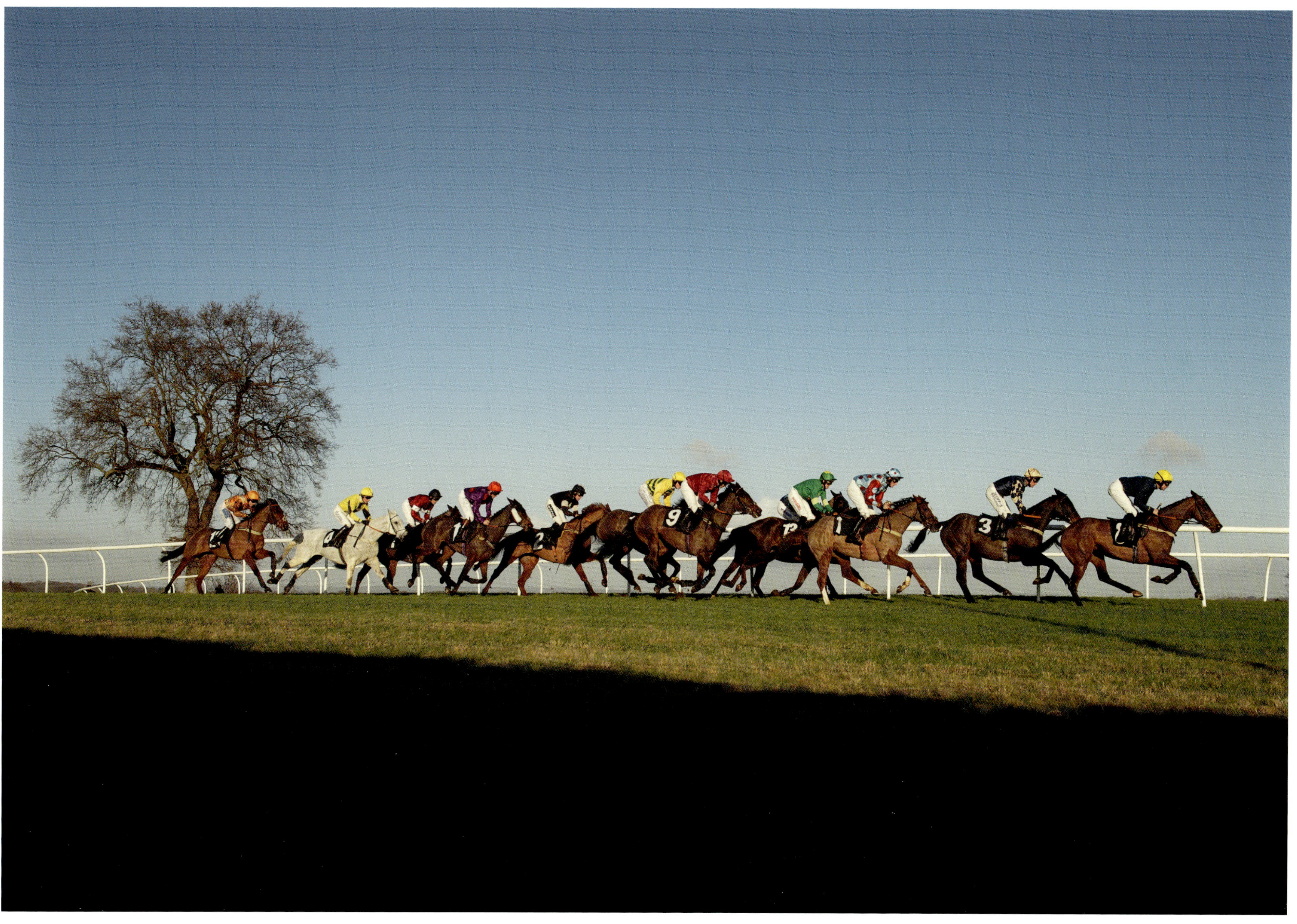

February

Super blue blood moon
The night of 31 January / 1 February
saw the rising and setting of the
'Super Blue Blood Moon' which only
happens every 150 years. Best of all
it was a clear night, so at 6am I was
on the gallops at Lambourn.

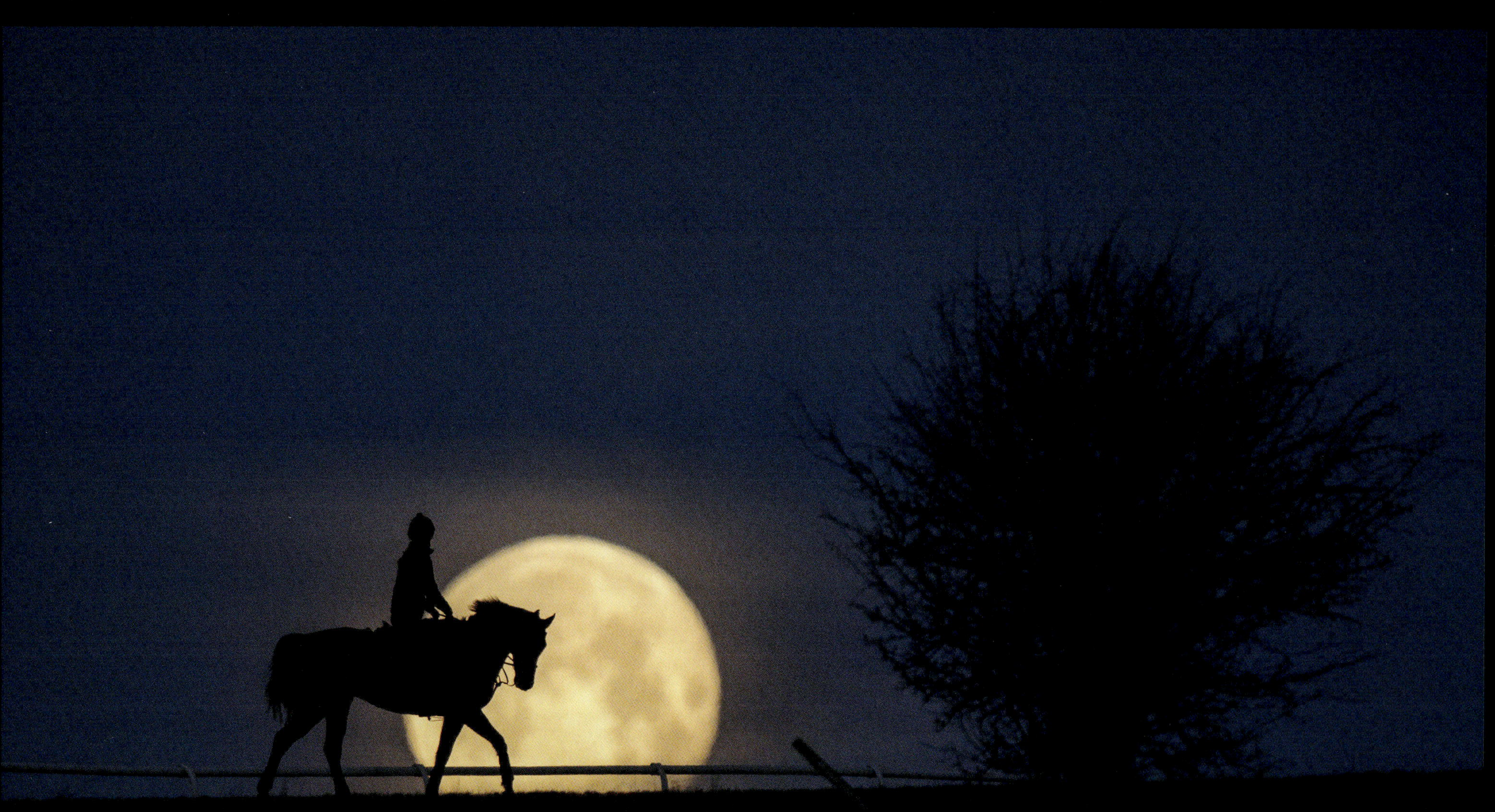

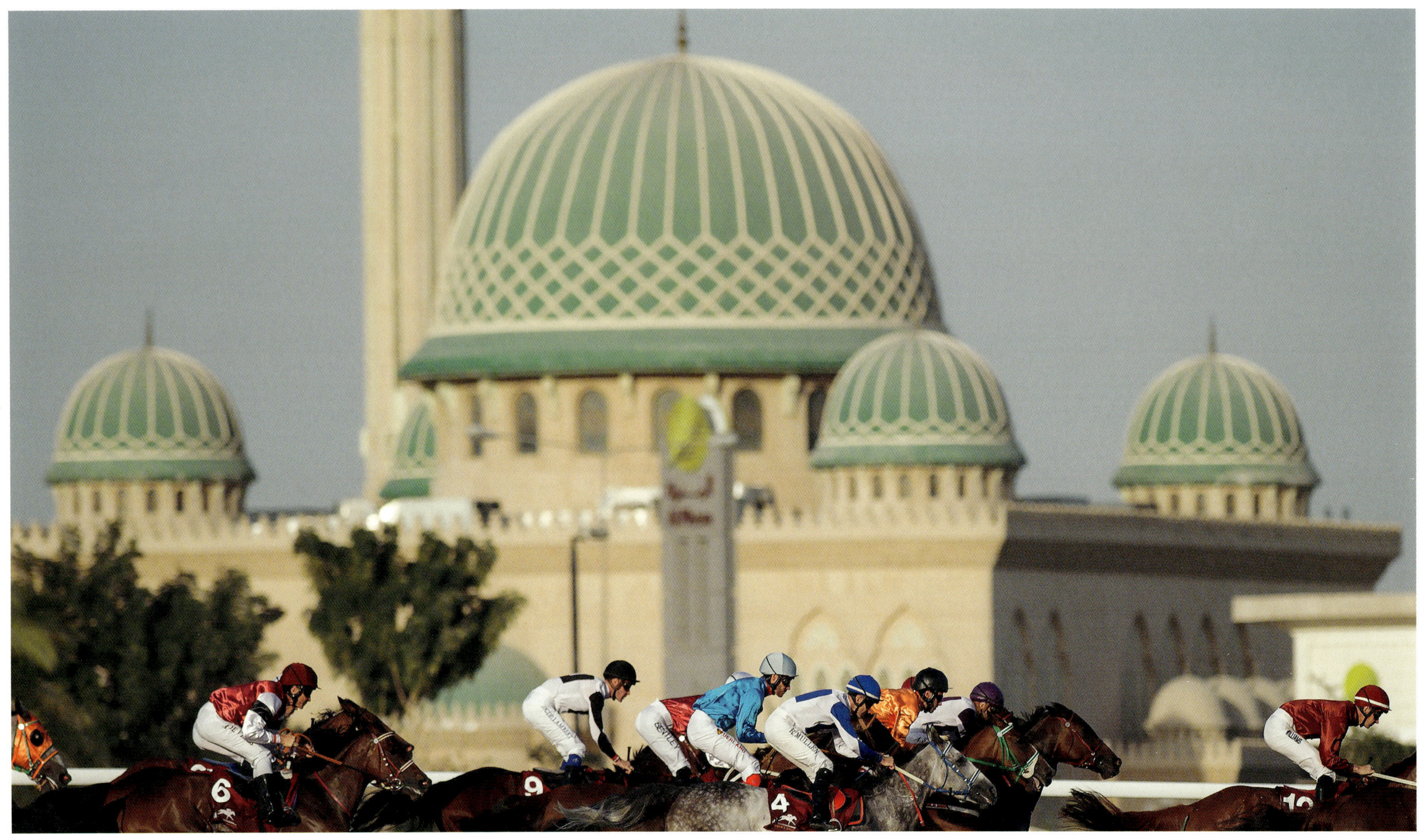

Mosque in Qatar
The qubba or dome on a mosque is a symbolic representation of the vault of heaven. Whether any of these horses or riders at Qatar's Al Rayyan racetrack in Doha are on their way there may be open to question.

Local rider in Qatar
Between races, entertainment at Al Rayyan features a series of traditional match races between local horsemen. Never mind the headgear, check out this guy's cufflinks.

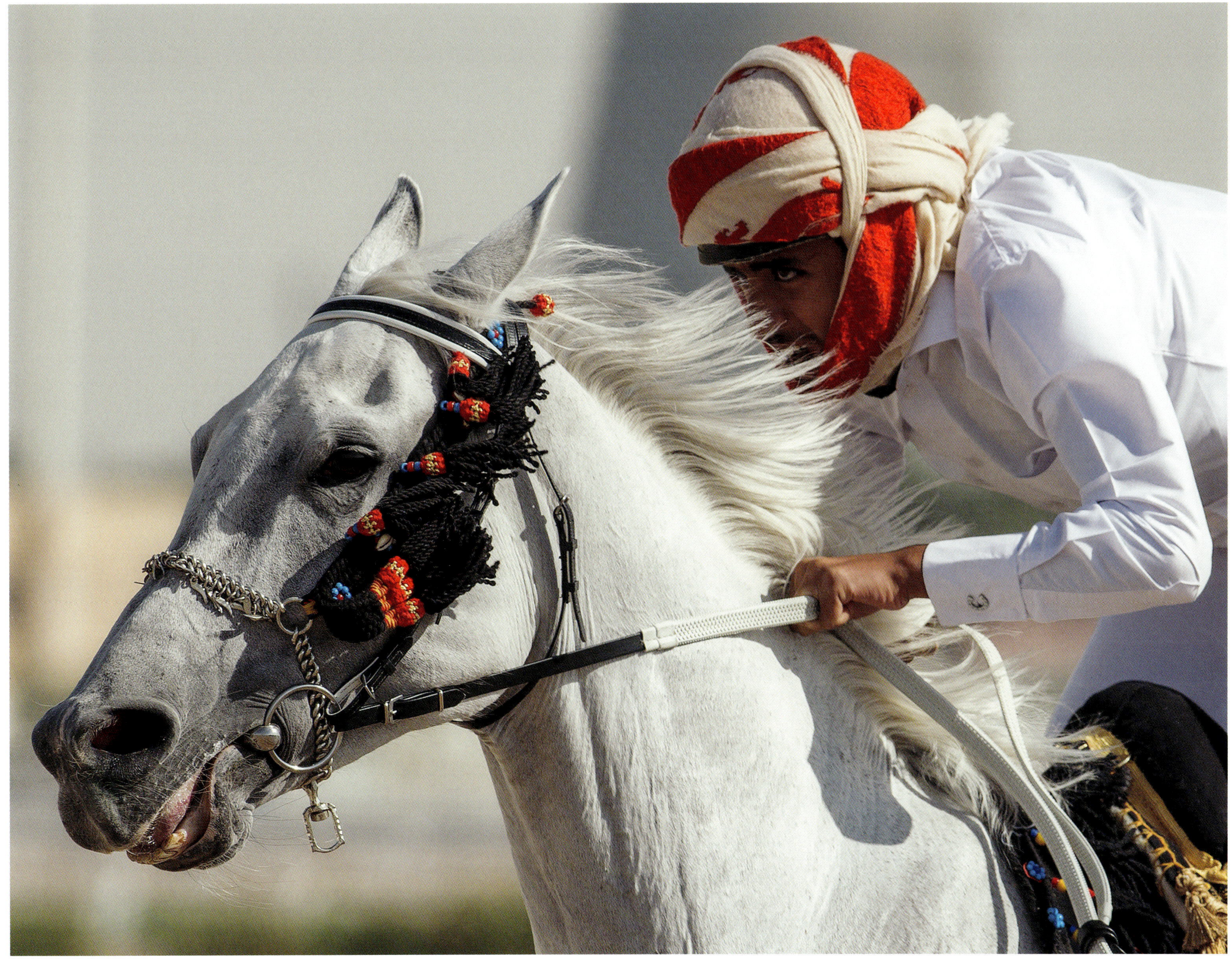

Through the trees
Winter trees sculpt lovely shapes
and these Nicky Henderson horses
passing through the copse above
Seven Barrows set them off perfectly.

Not so perfect dress rehearsal
In 2016, Olympic cycling star Victoria
Pendleton took to steeplechasing.
Pacha Du Polder was to carry her
around Cheltenham, but the first
attempt at Fakenham ended in this
synchronised unseating alongside
Carey Williamson (on the right).

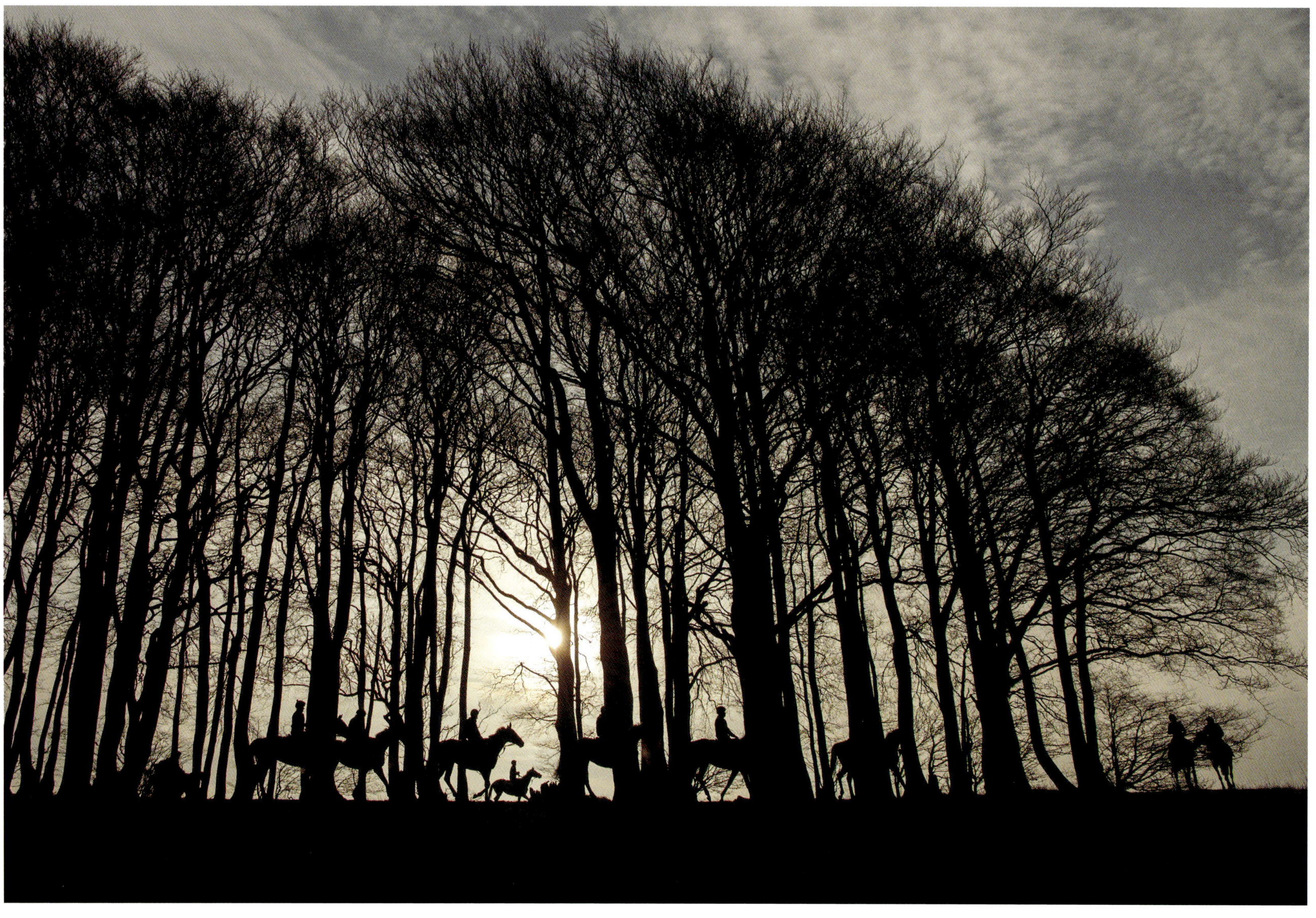

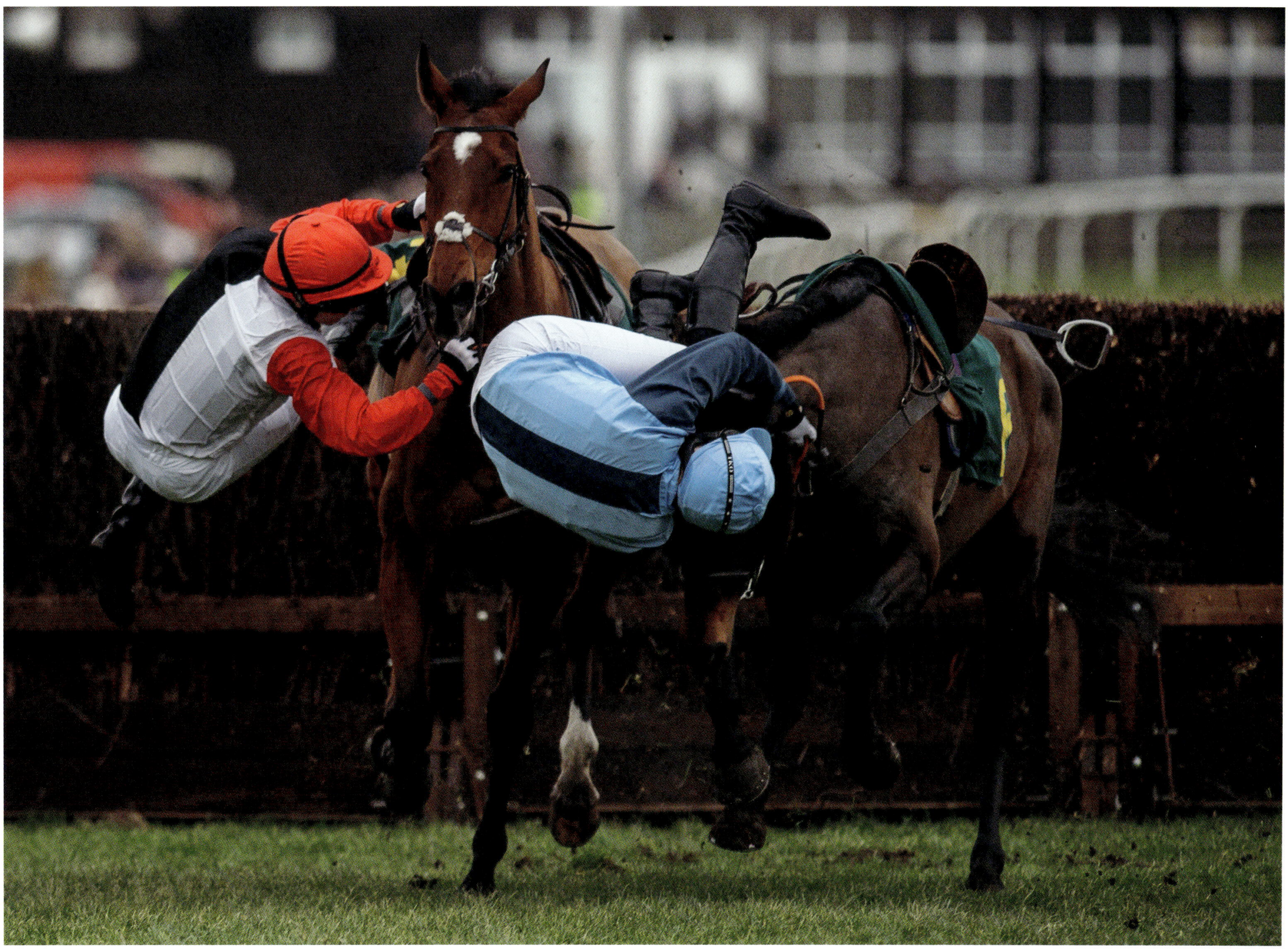

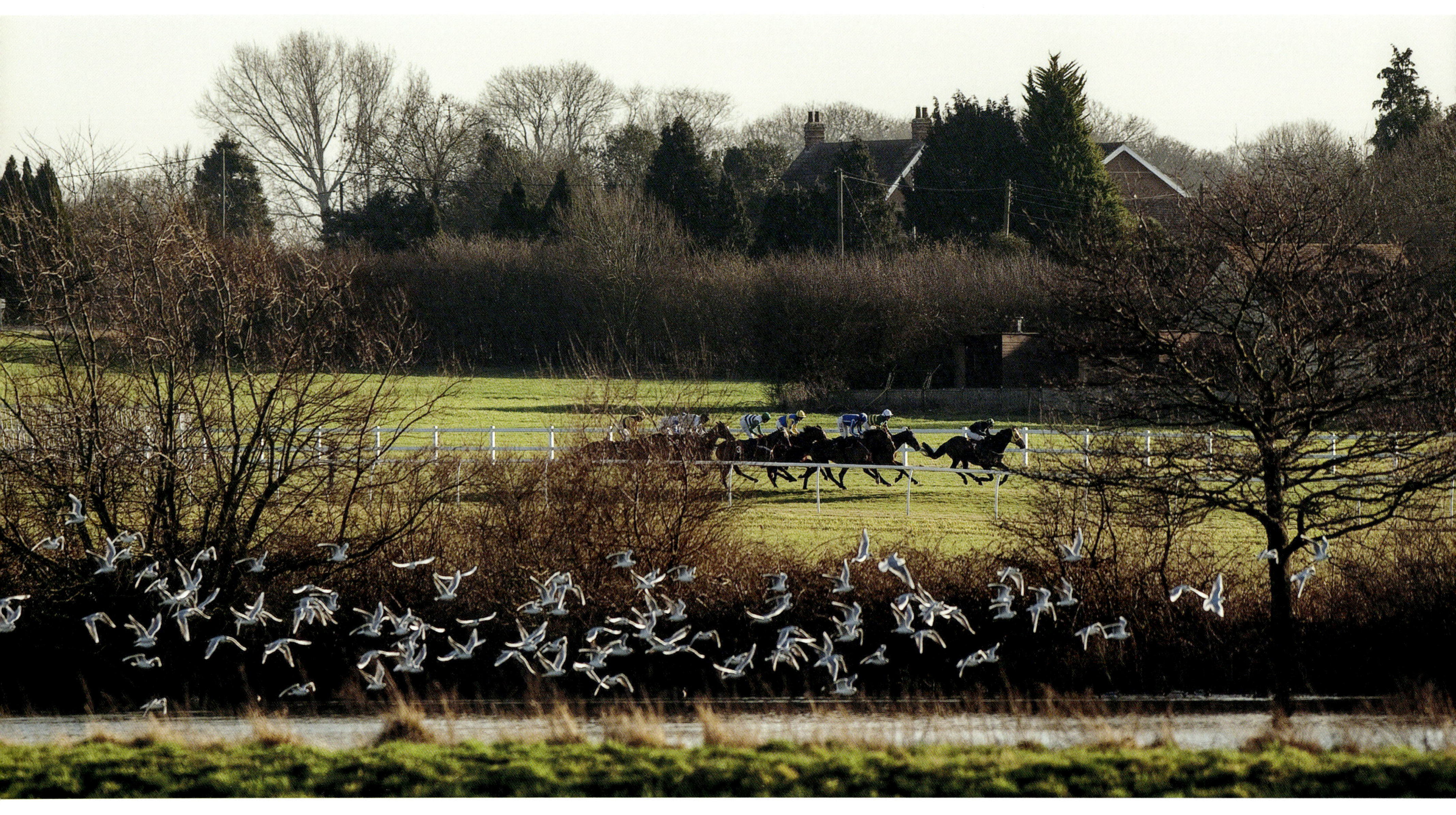

Water, water
When the rain gets heavy, natural
springs pop up in the paddocks
at Seven Barrows. Here Oscar
Whisky leads the string over
the watercourse.

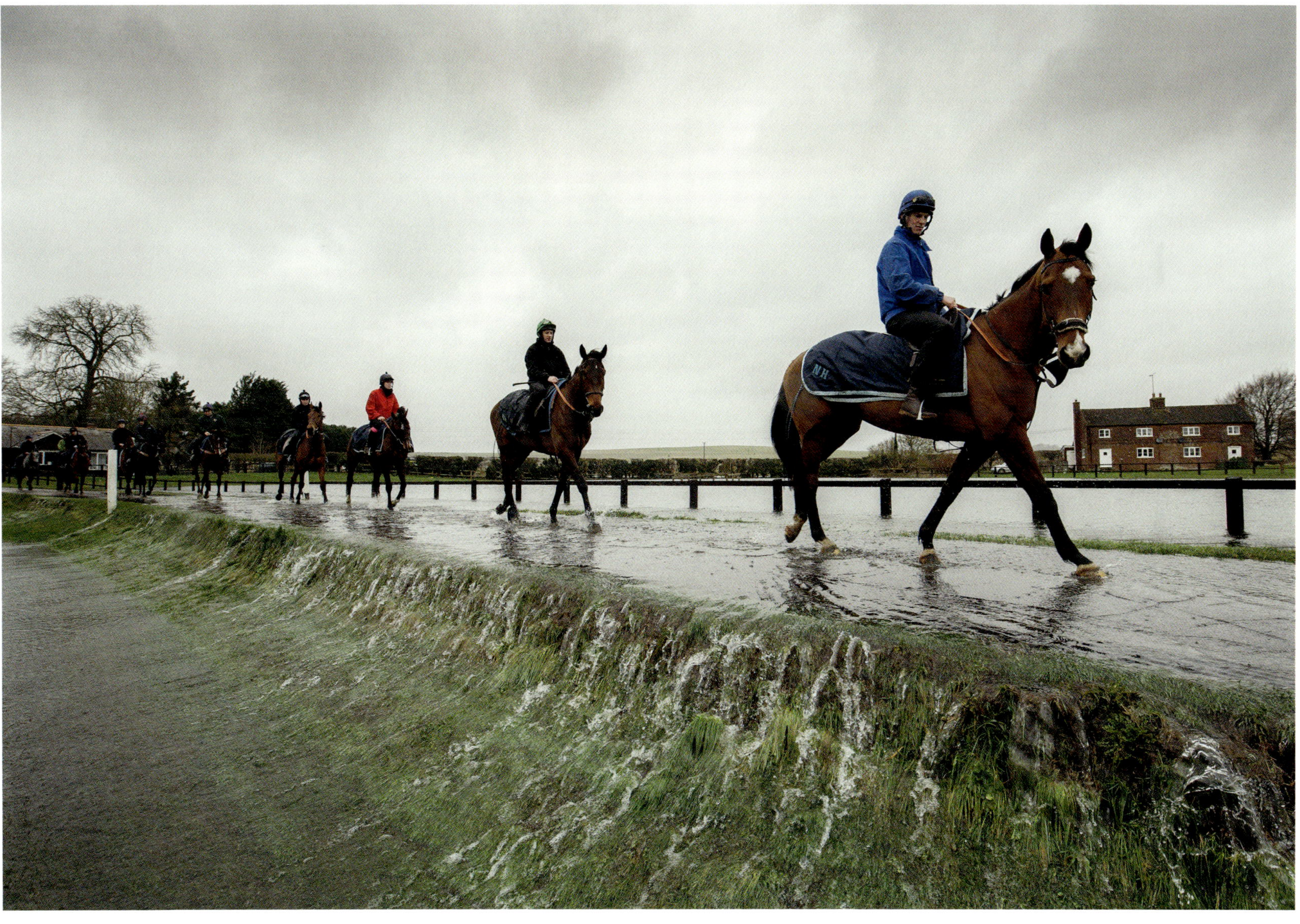

Seagull salute
Folkestone closed its gates in
December 2012 but not before this
aerial tribute from the local seagulls.

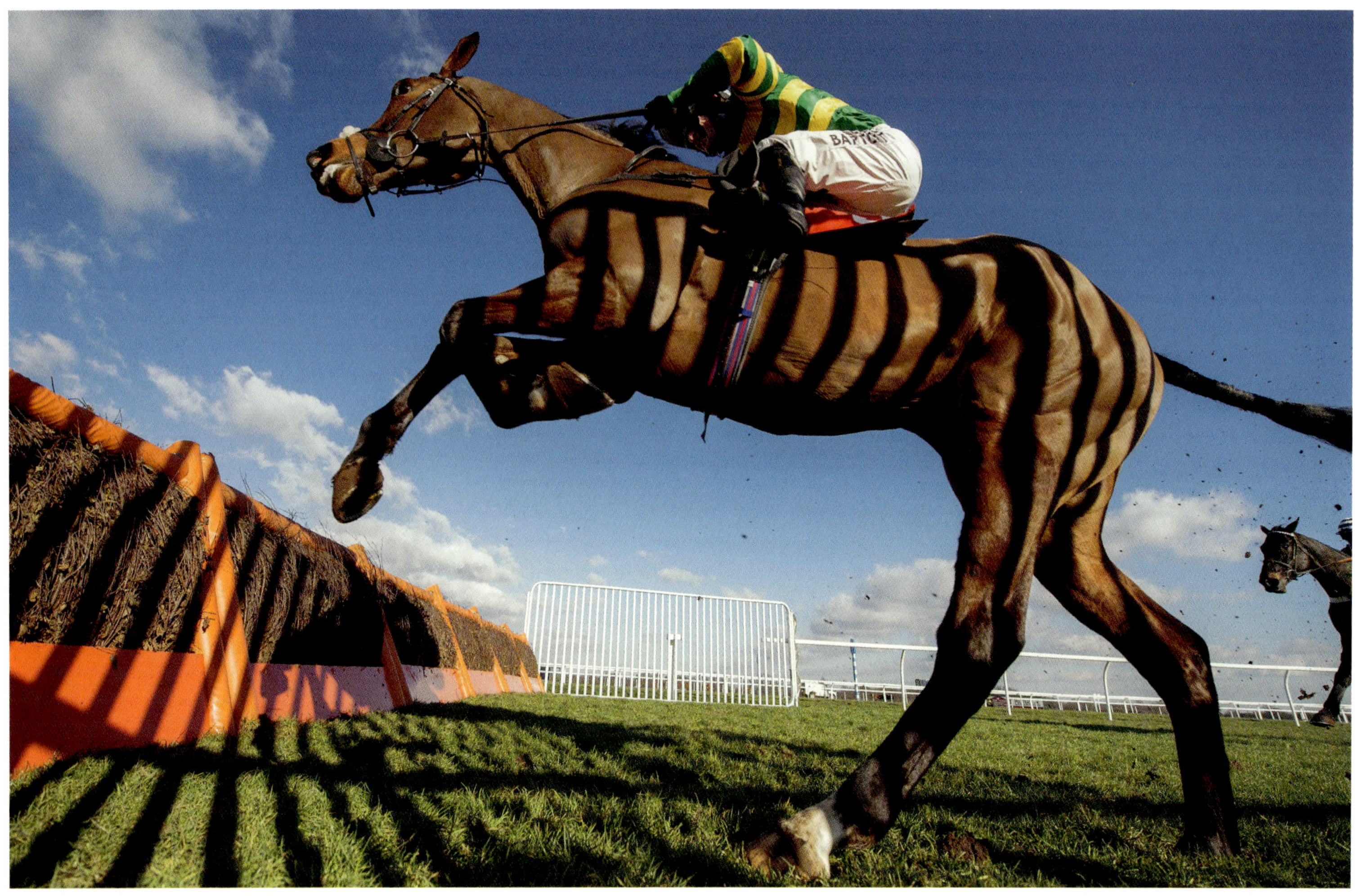

Zebra stripes
Shadow-striped Minella Rocco
is lifted over Kempton's final flight
by AP McCoy. No zebra ever did
it better.

White turf
A trotting race on the frozen lake at
St Moritz. I love the crowd's interest
at this unlikeliest of venues, but I
am a bit worried about the shivering
dogs in the foreground!

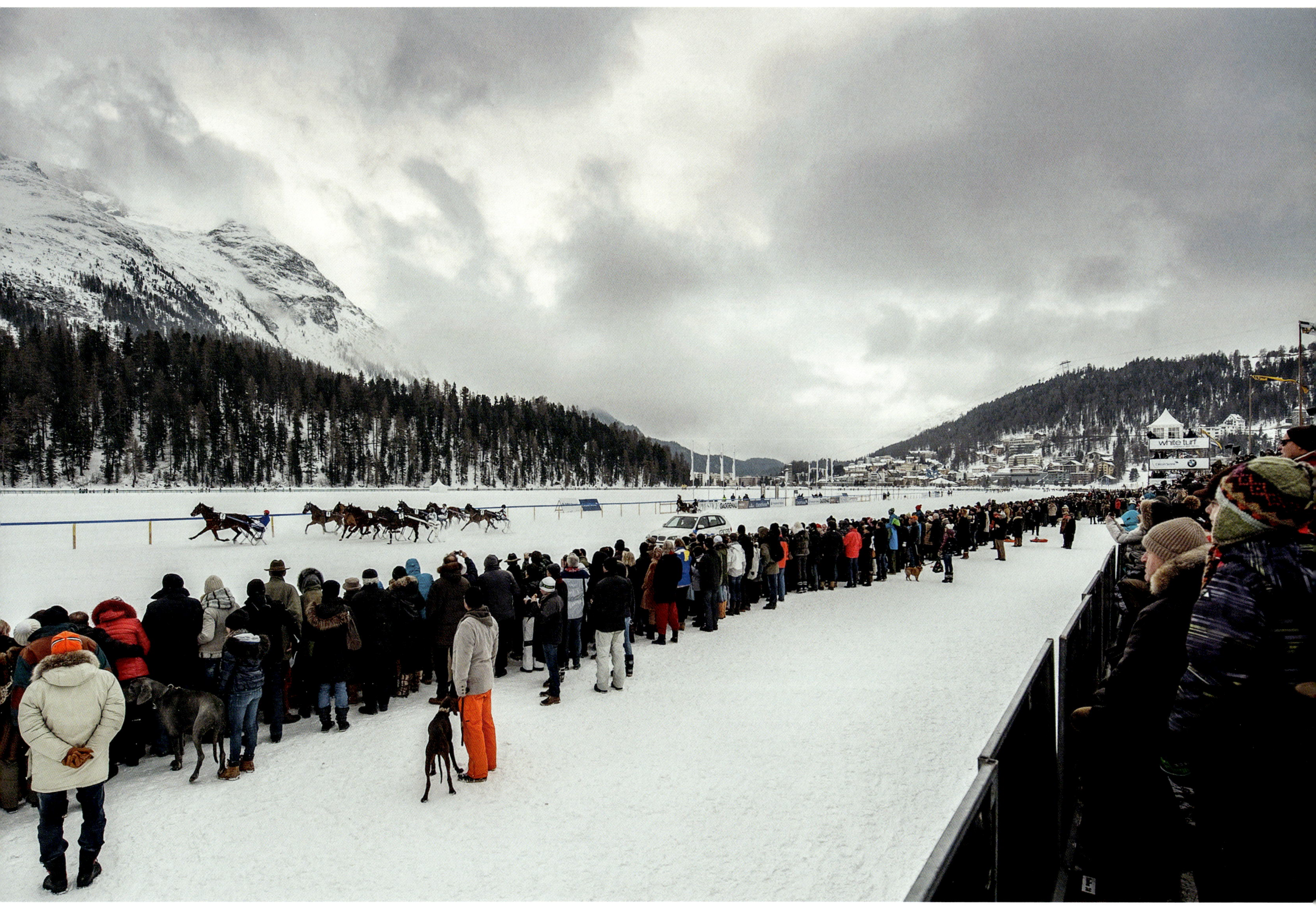

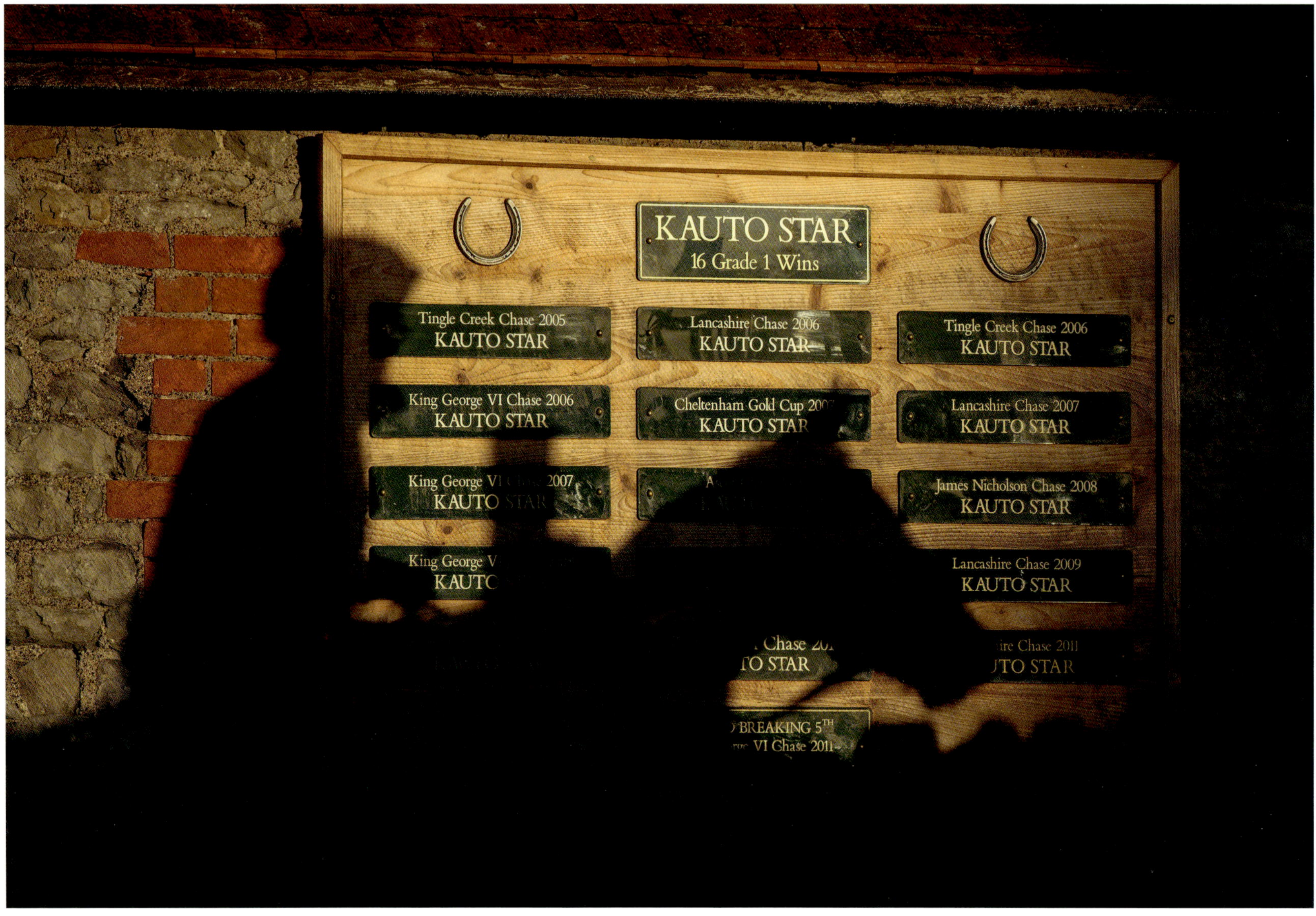

Shadow horse

The Kauto Star honours board at Paul Nicholls' yard at Ditcheat in Somerset is unique in racing. As was the horse this shadow pays homage to.

The ultimate warrior

Kauto Star in his box at Ditcheat, winner of £2.3 million and 23 of his 41 races, starting in Bordeaux Le Bouscat in March 2003 and ending nine full years later in his sixth consecutive Cheltenham Gold Cup.

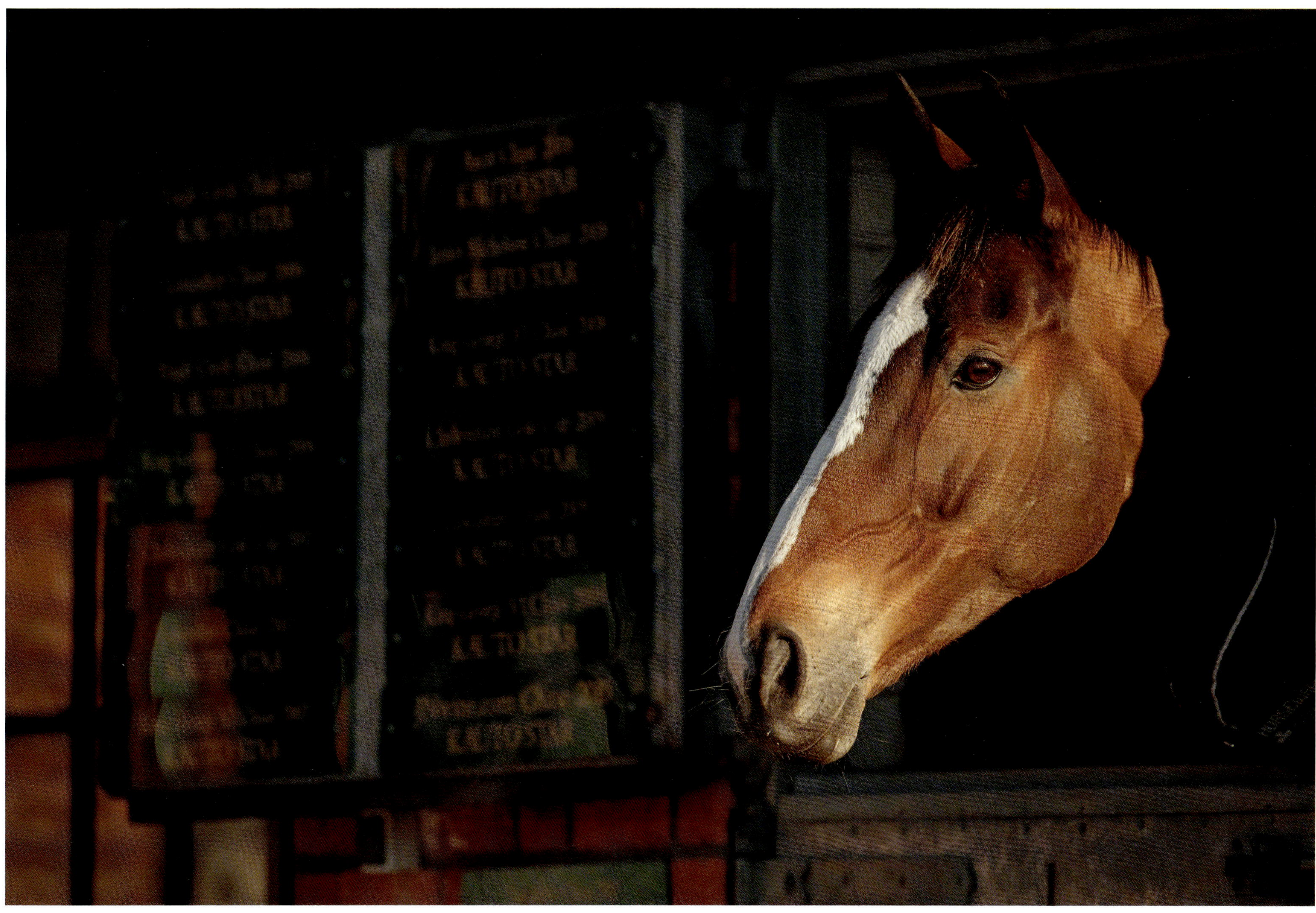

New fields to conquer
Former star hurdler Big Buck's,
one-time winner of 18 races in a row,
leads the Blackmore Vale Hunt under
Lucy Tucker.

Aidan Coleman at take-off
Reach for the stars. Aidan Coleman
and Shangani stretch out at the open
ditch at Kempton.

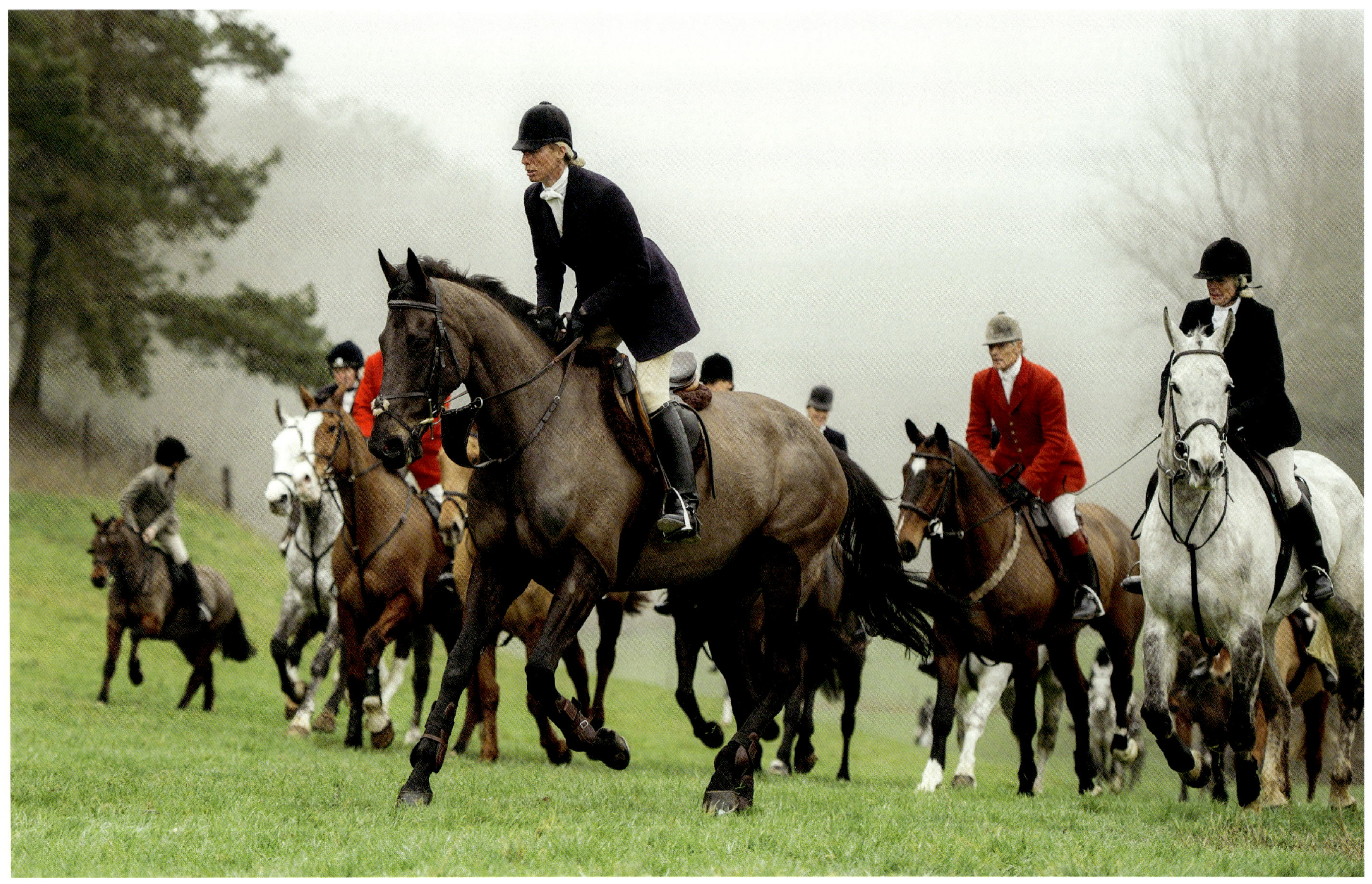

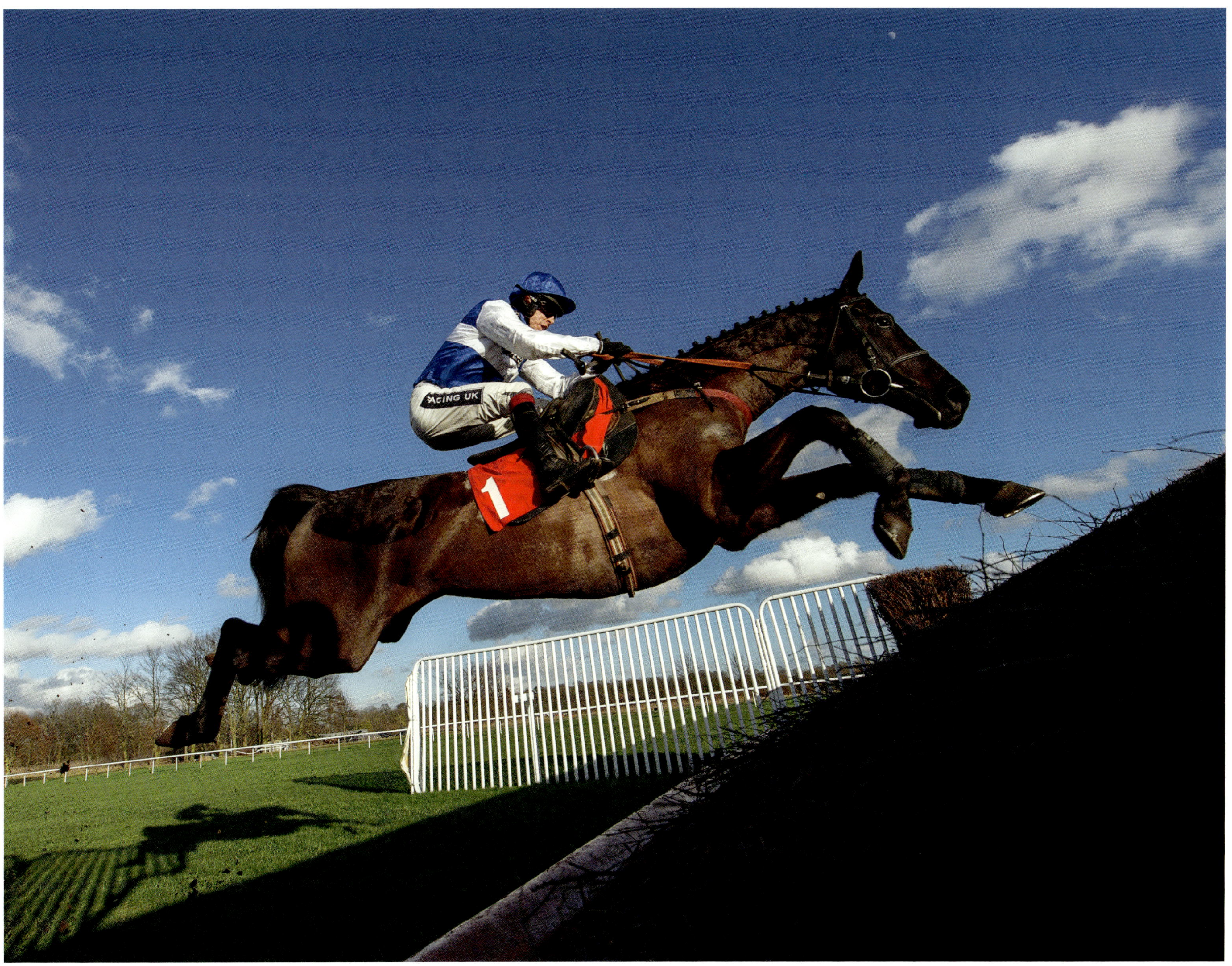

March

Serenity before consternation
Might Bite and Nico de Boinville
sail over the water jump a picture
of poise in the 2017 RSA Chase at
Cheltenham. Three minutes later
he almost threw the race away
when swerving on the run-in.

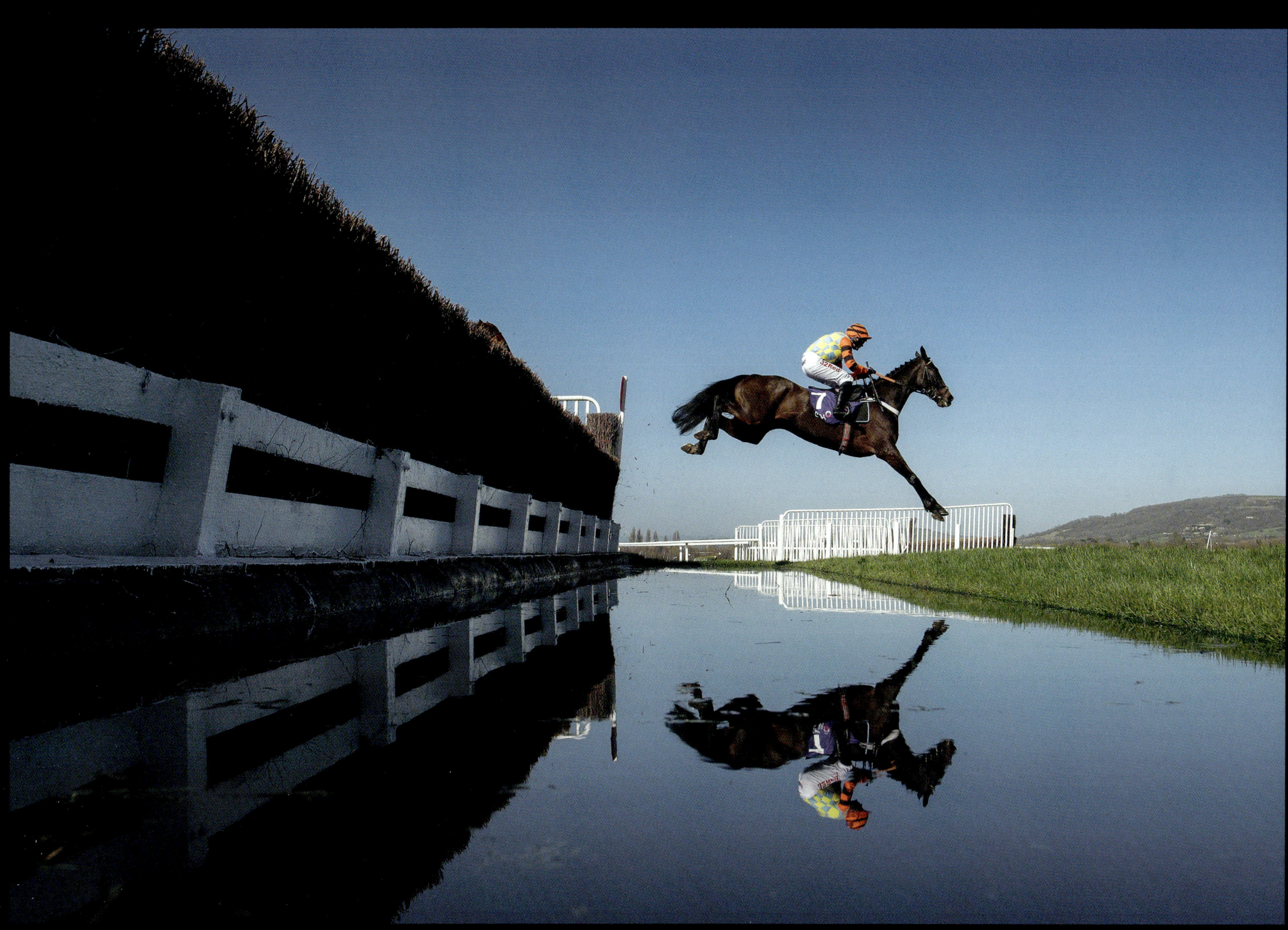

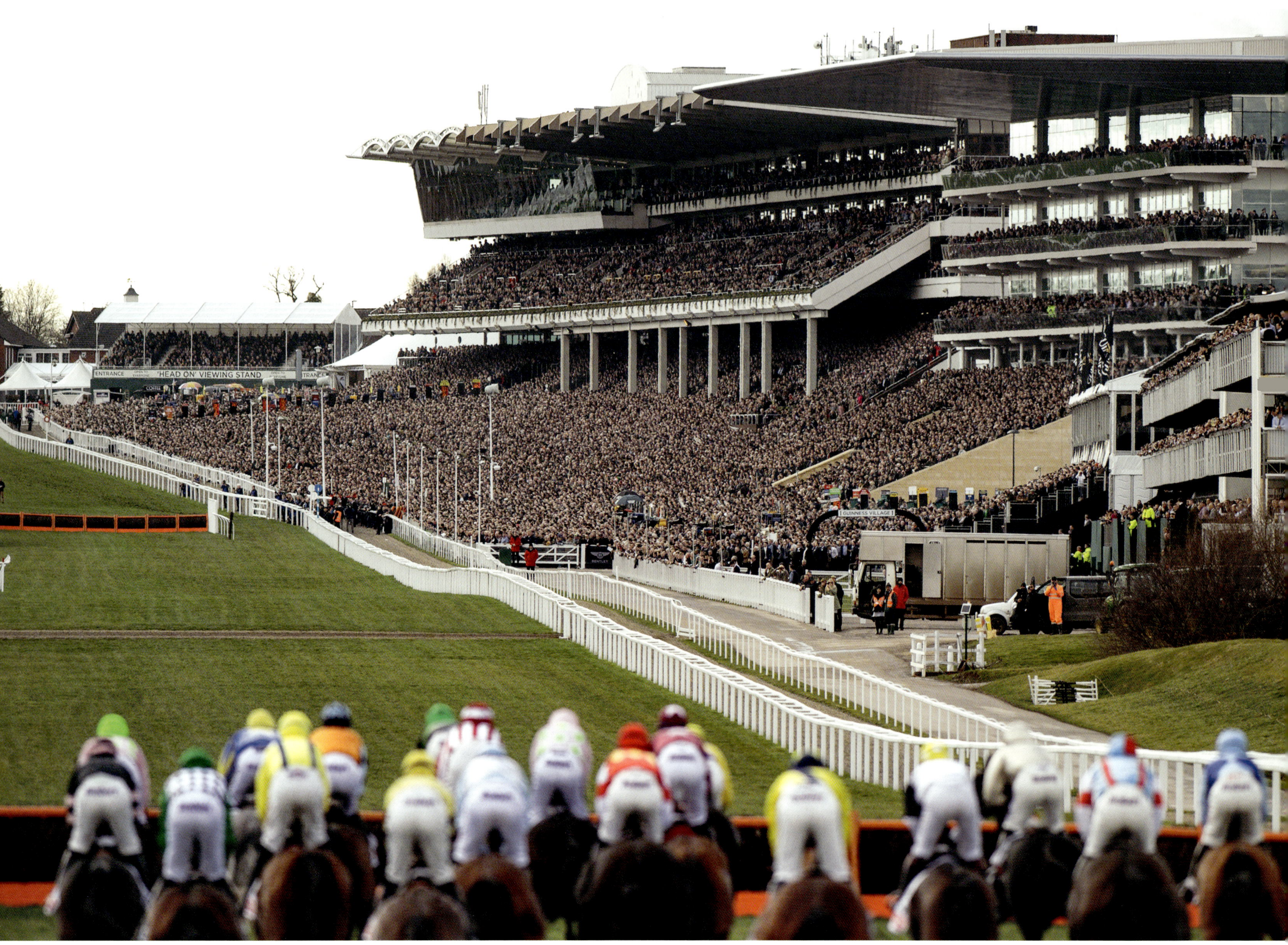

'HEAD ON' VIEWING STAND
ENTRANCE
GUINNESS VILLAGE

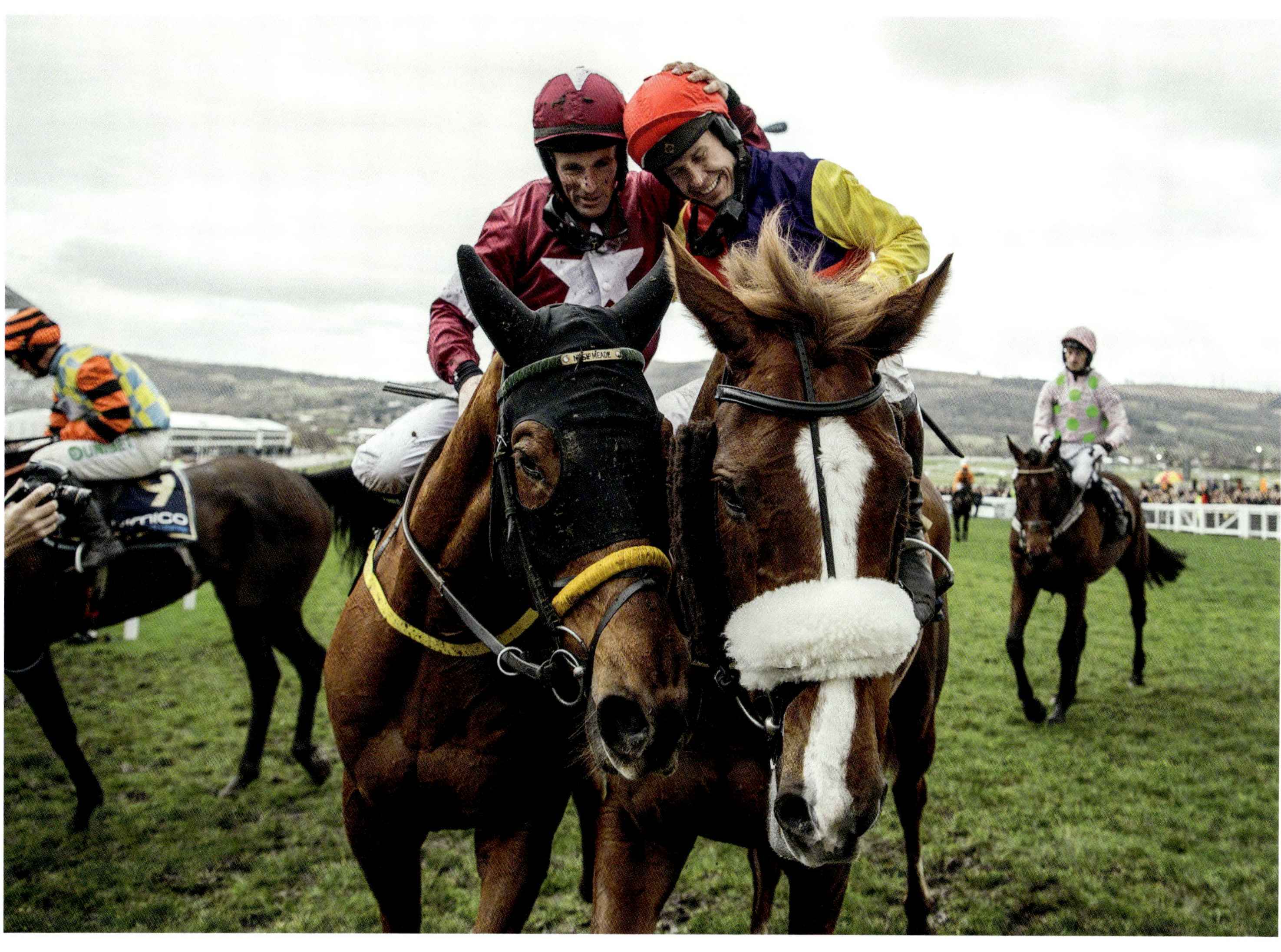

**Richard Johnson and
Native River congratulated**
Sean Flanagan (left) on Road
To Respect hugs Richard Johnson
after Native River's heroic Gold
Cup victory. I love the way Road To
Respect seems to be congratulating
Native River on his own behalf.

The opening thunder
The packed field run down to the
first hurdle on the first day of the
Cheltenham Festival 2018. Around
66,000 pairs of eyes and my camera
willed them forward.

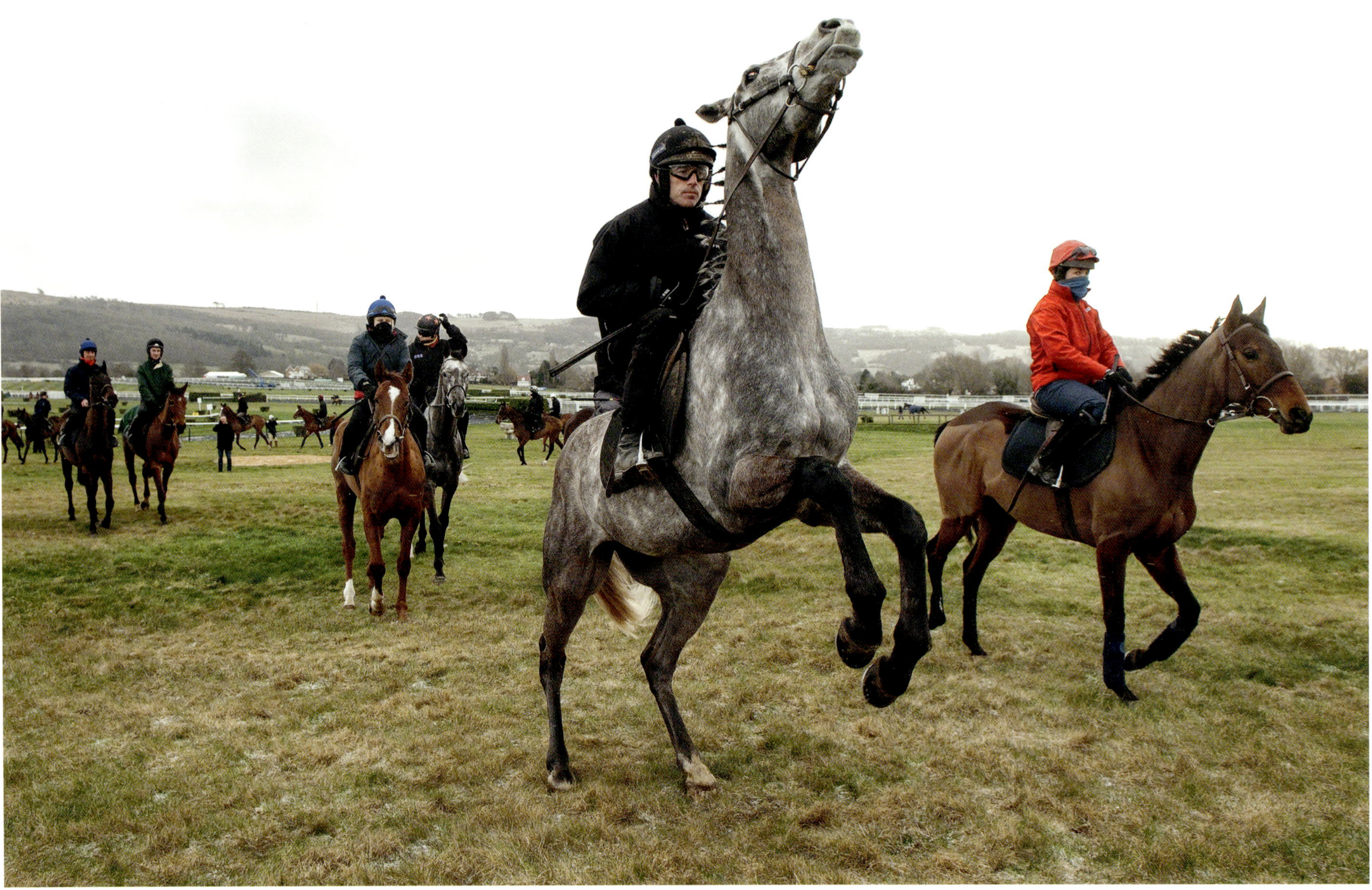

Easy rider
Ruby Walsh remains totally dialled in
as that afternoon's Supreme Novices'
winner Champagne Fever bubbles
with energy on big-race morning.

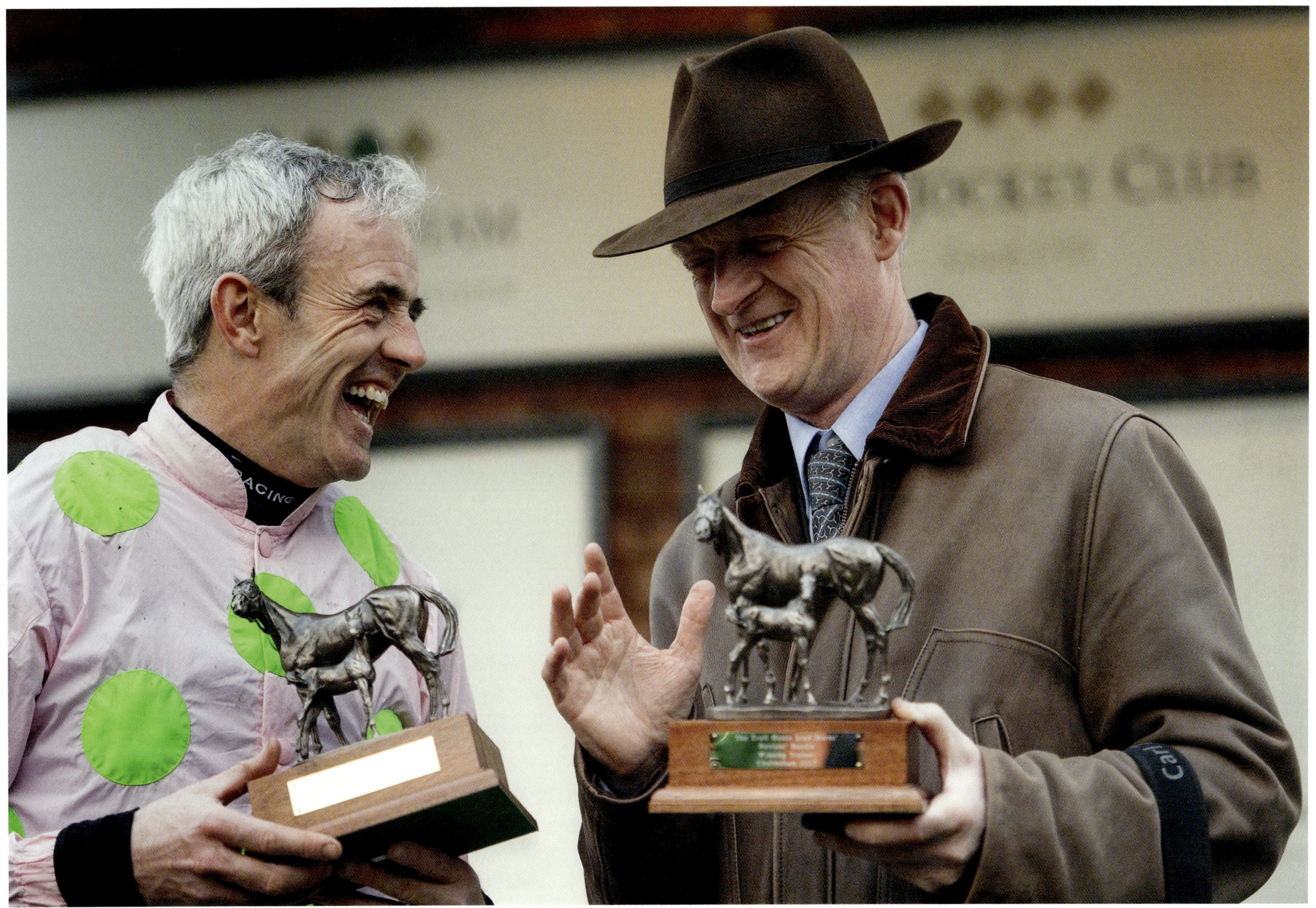

Not two handed but four handed
The mare Let's Dance had just landed
a Ruby Walsh/Willie Mullins four-
timer on the Thursday of the 2017
Cheltenham Festival. It doesn't come
any better than this.

On the attack
The runners for the Coral Cup drill away from stands which could only be those of the Cheltenham Festival. A circuit to go and everything to play for.

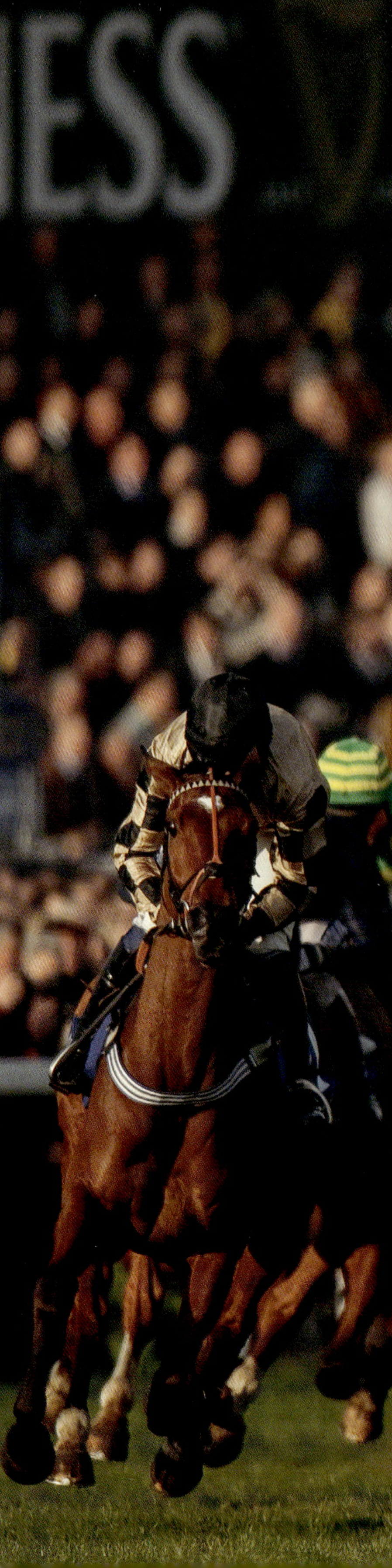

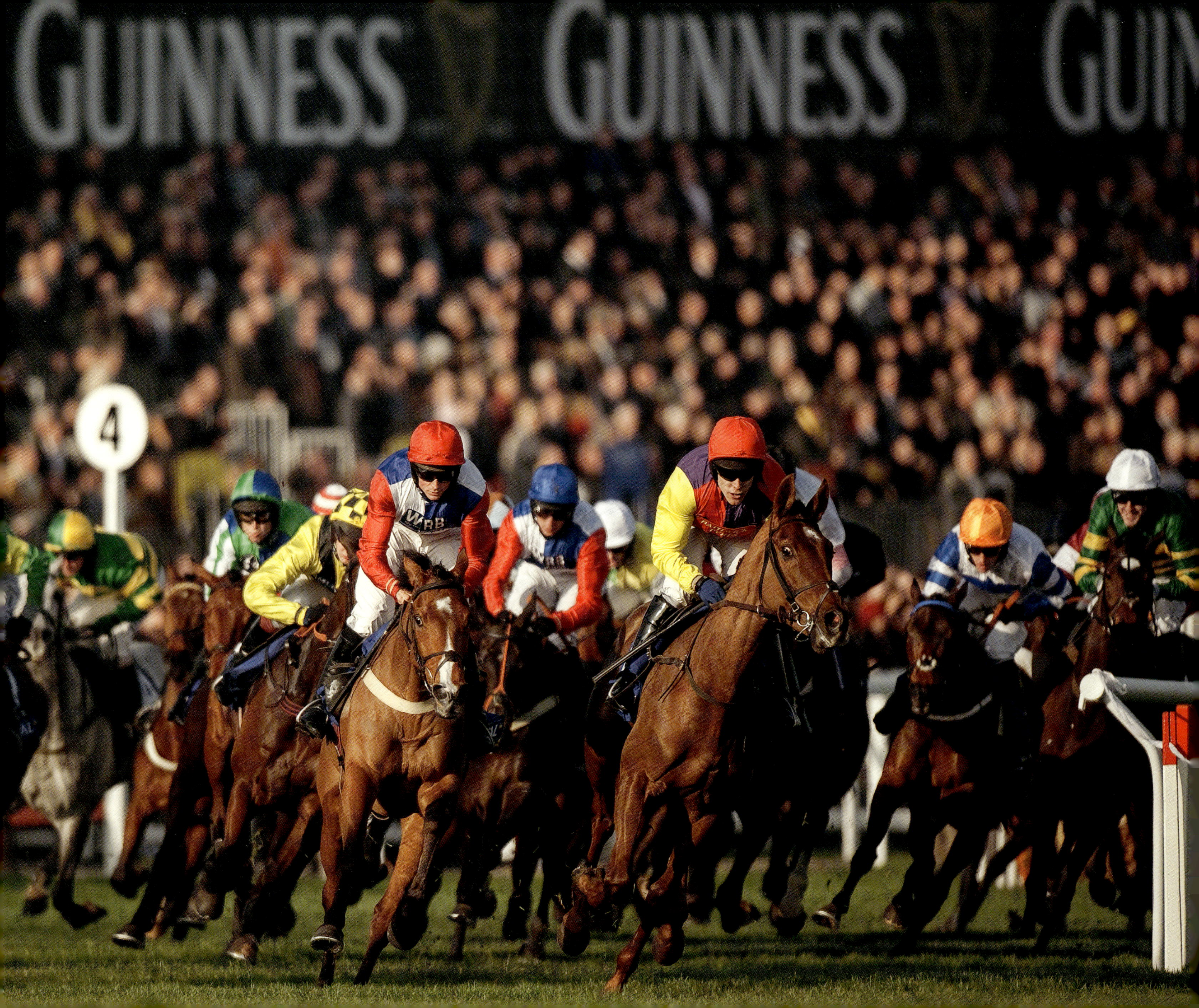
GUINNESS
GUINNESS
GUIN
4

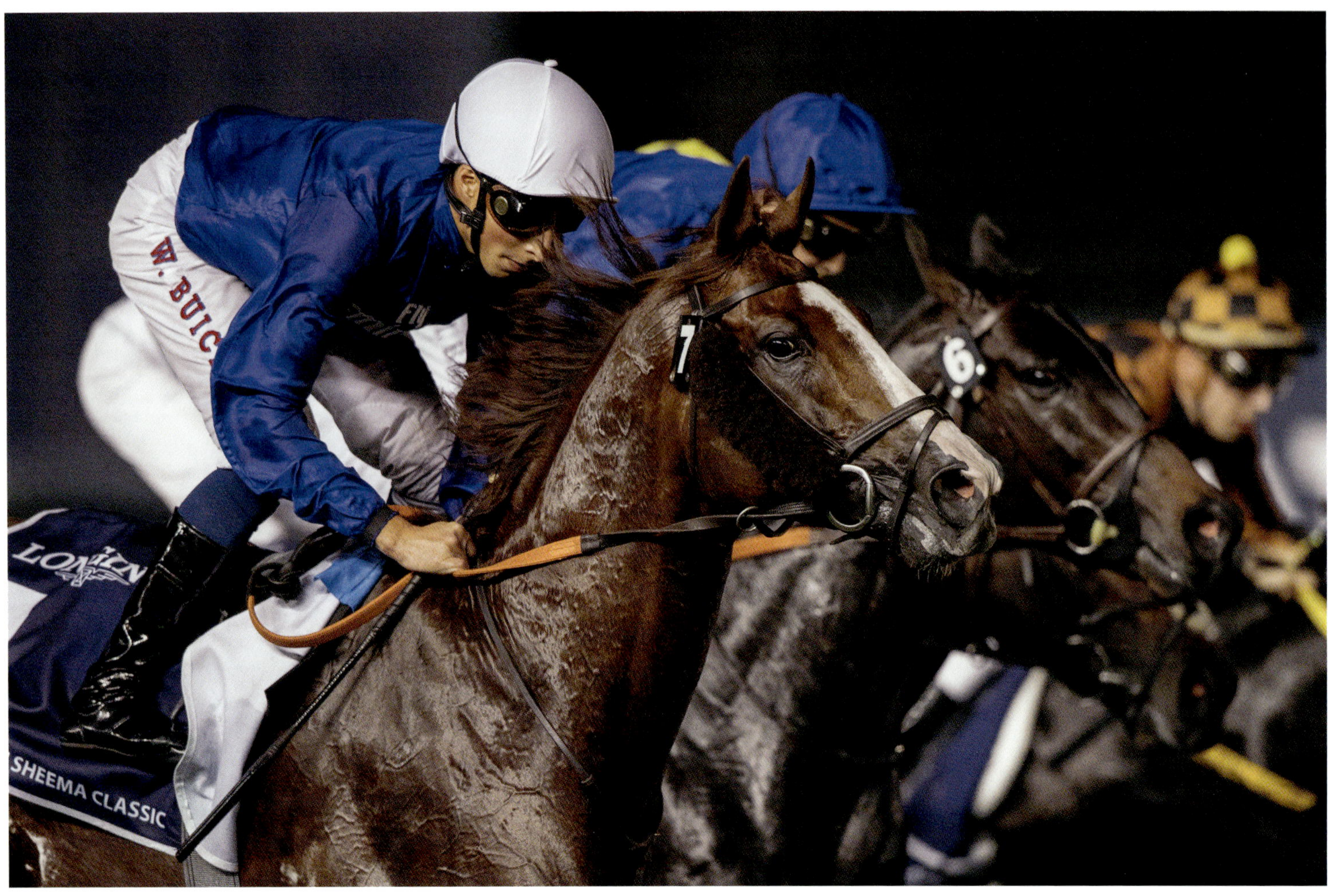

The winning gleam
Hawkbill looks in charge even as
William Buick rockets him from the
stalls at the start of the Sheema
Classic on Dubai World Cup night
at Meydan.

The ecstasy of victory
Mickael Barzalona wins the Dubai
World Cup on Monterosso with a
wave of triumph as much to do with
toe-in-the-iron acrobatics as with
horsemanship.

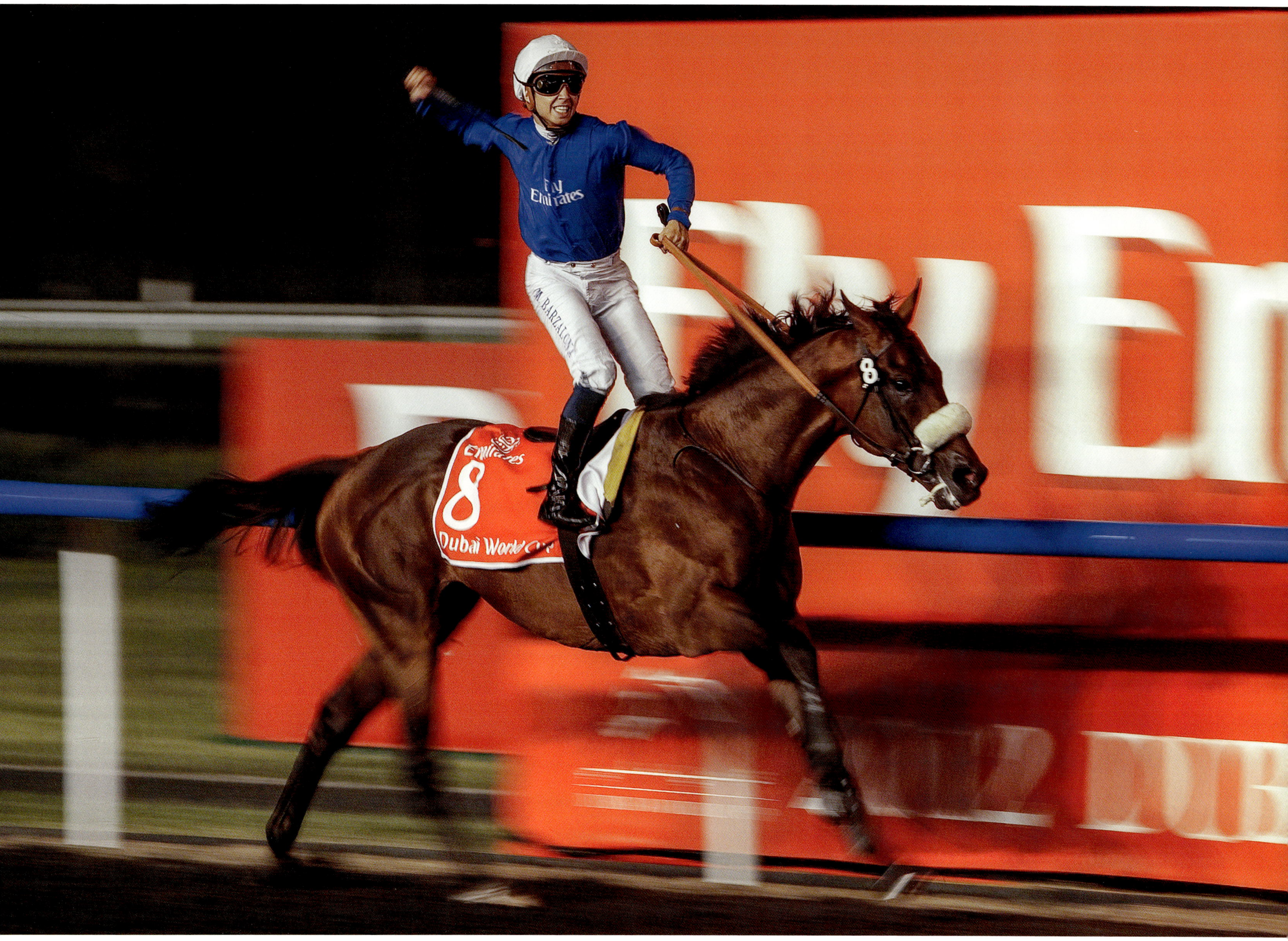

Fly Emirates
8
Emirates
Dubai World Cup
M. BARZALONA

Super smart, super dude
Ace Canadian rider Chantal
Sutherland canters Game On Dude
at Meydan in the morning. Chantal
was the first woman to ride in the
Dubai World Cup. This picture shows
she was a fashion winner too.

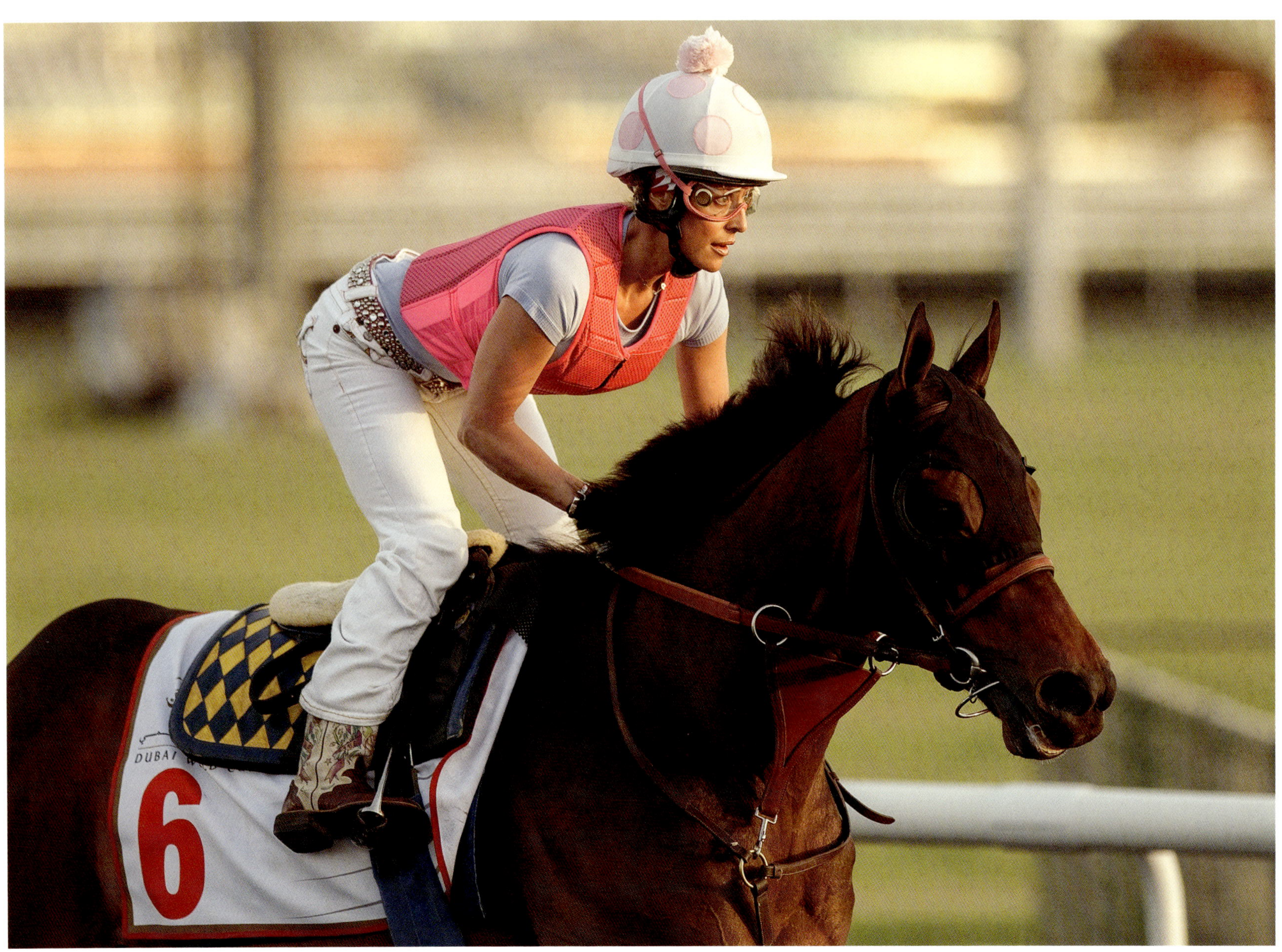

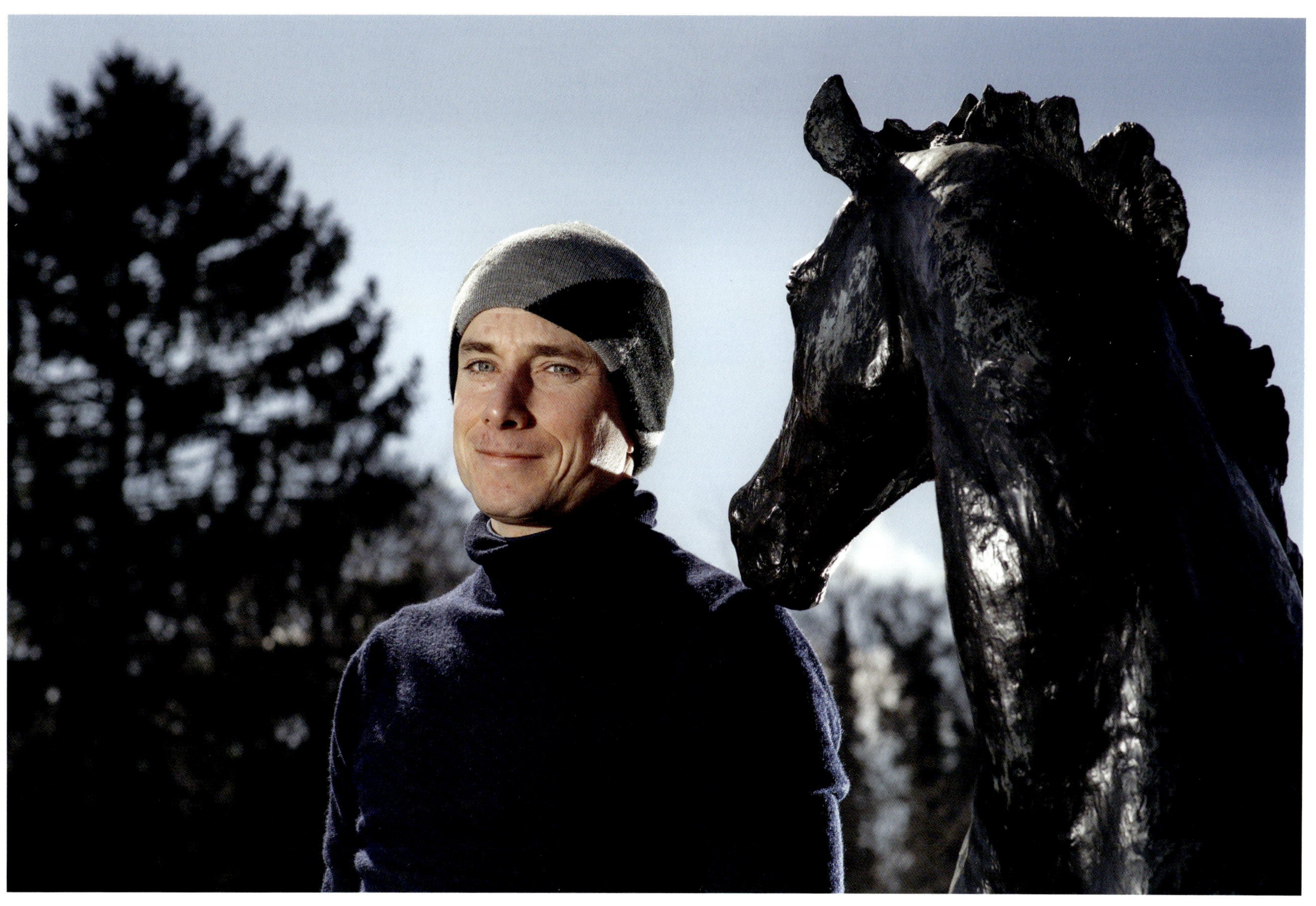

Beanie boy
Ryan Moore in pre-season mode at Newmarket in 2018. The beanie hat was to cover a savage haircut whilst riding in Hong Kong.

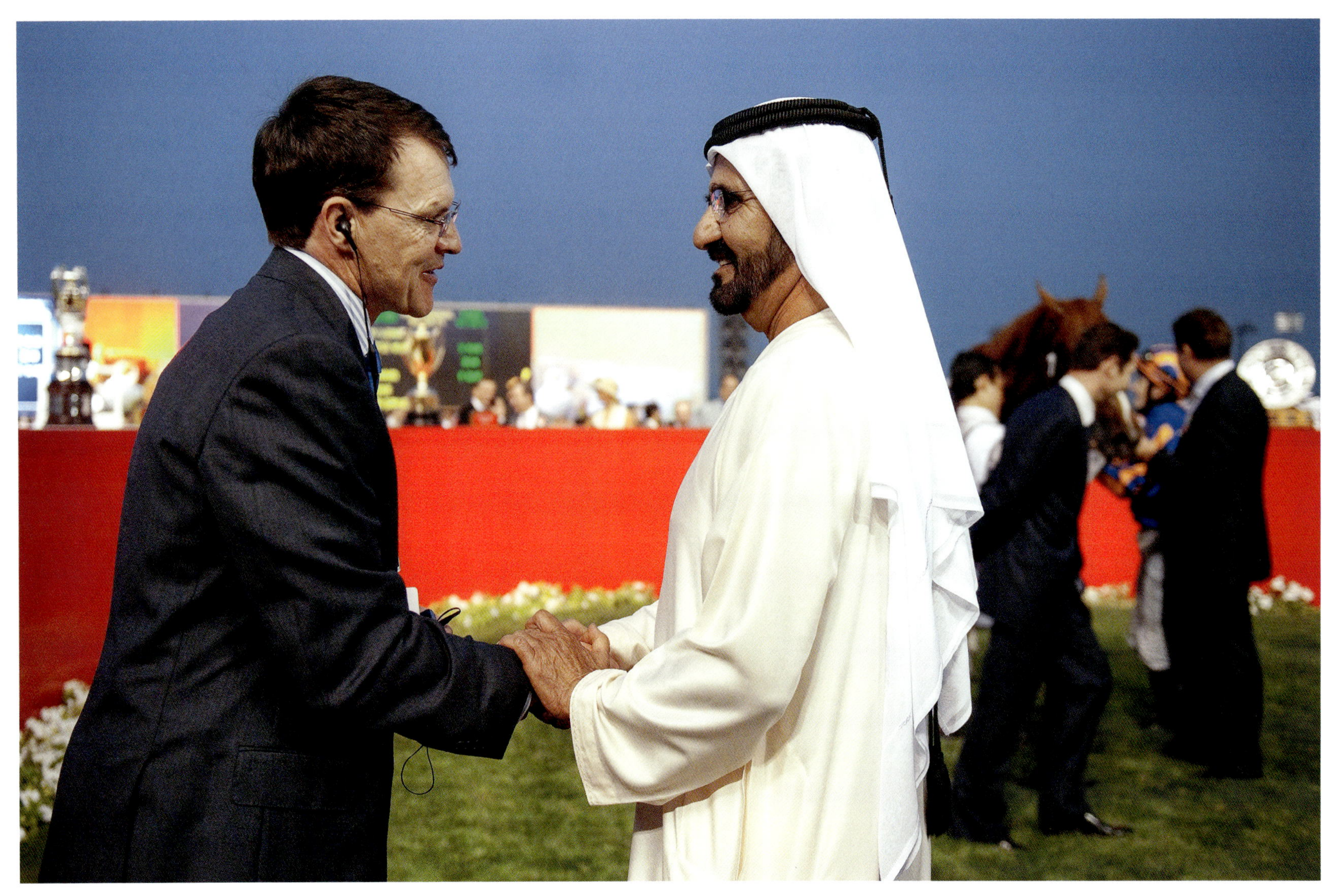

The host meets the invader
Sheikh Mohammed gives the
warmest of handshakes to Aidan
O'Brien after the Irish trainer had
won the 2012 UAE Derby with
Daddy Long Legs.

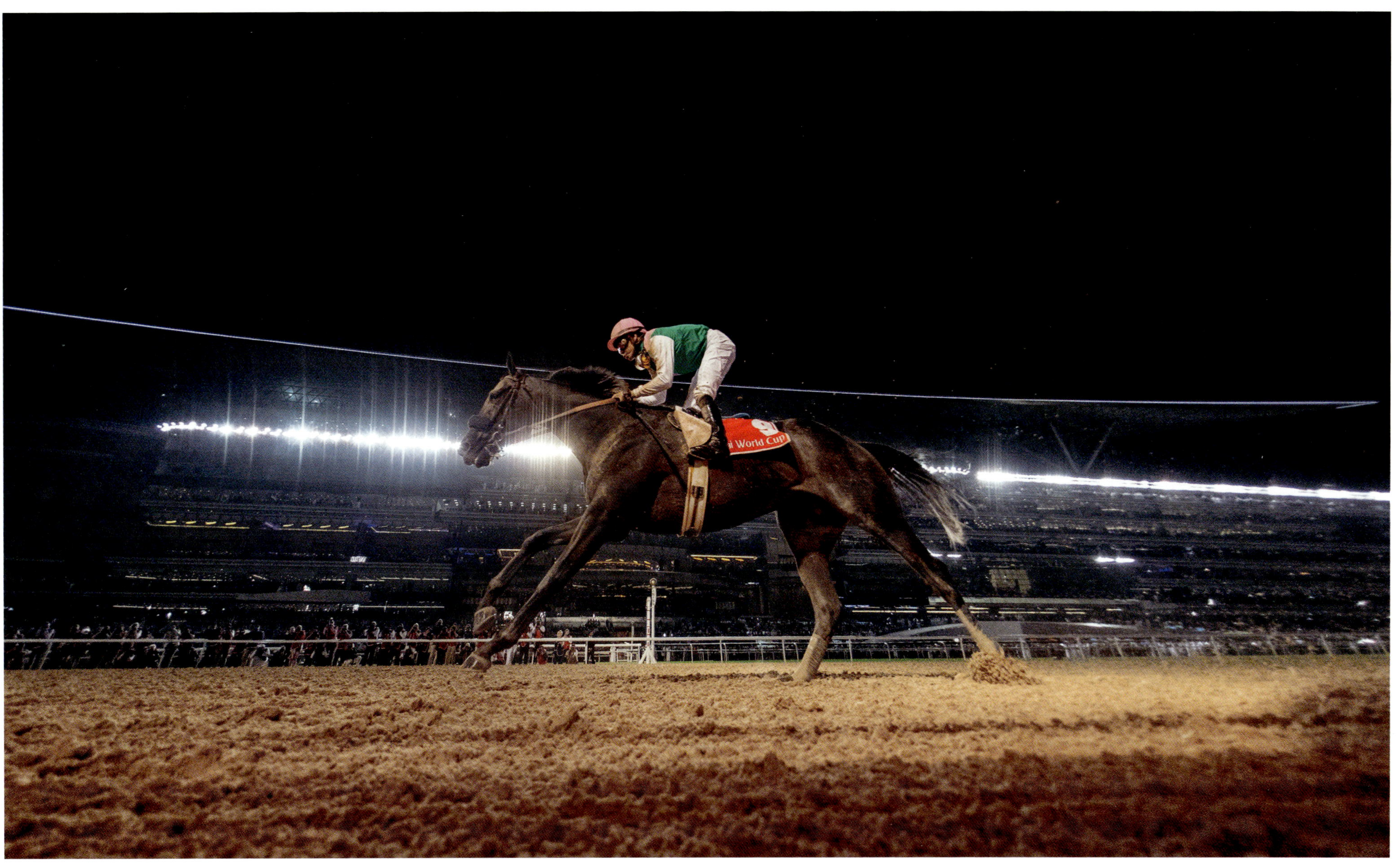

Image of greatness
Arrogate's backstretch surge to take the Dubai World Cup apart four months after winning the Breeders' Cup Classic had him hailed as one of the best we had ever seen. He never won again. This must have taken its toll.

April

Joe's Water Splash
Punchestown has many different attractions. On the track, nothing used to hit the eye as strongly as the runners galloping through 'Joe's Water Splash'. It has now been discontinued but this memory stays with me still.

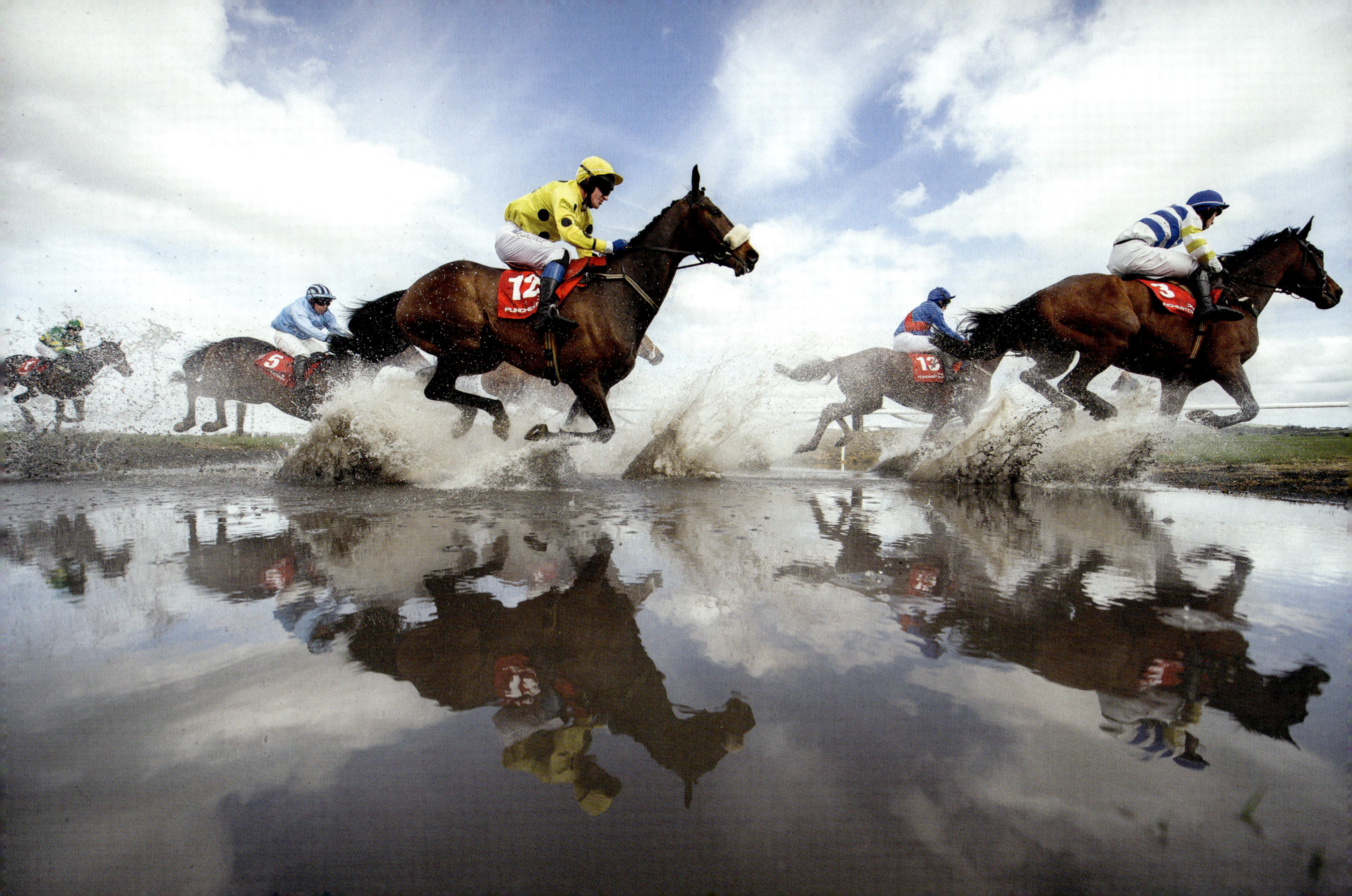

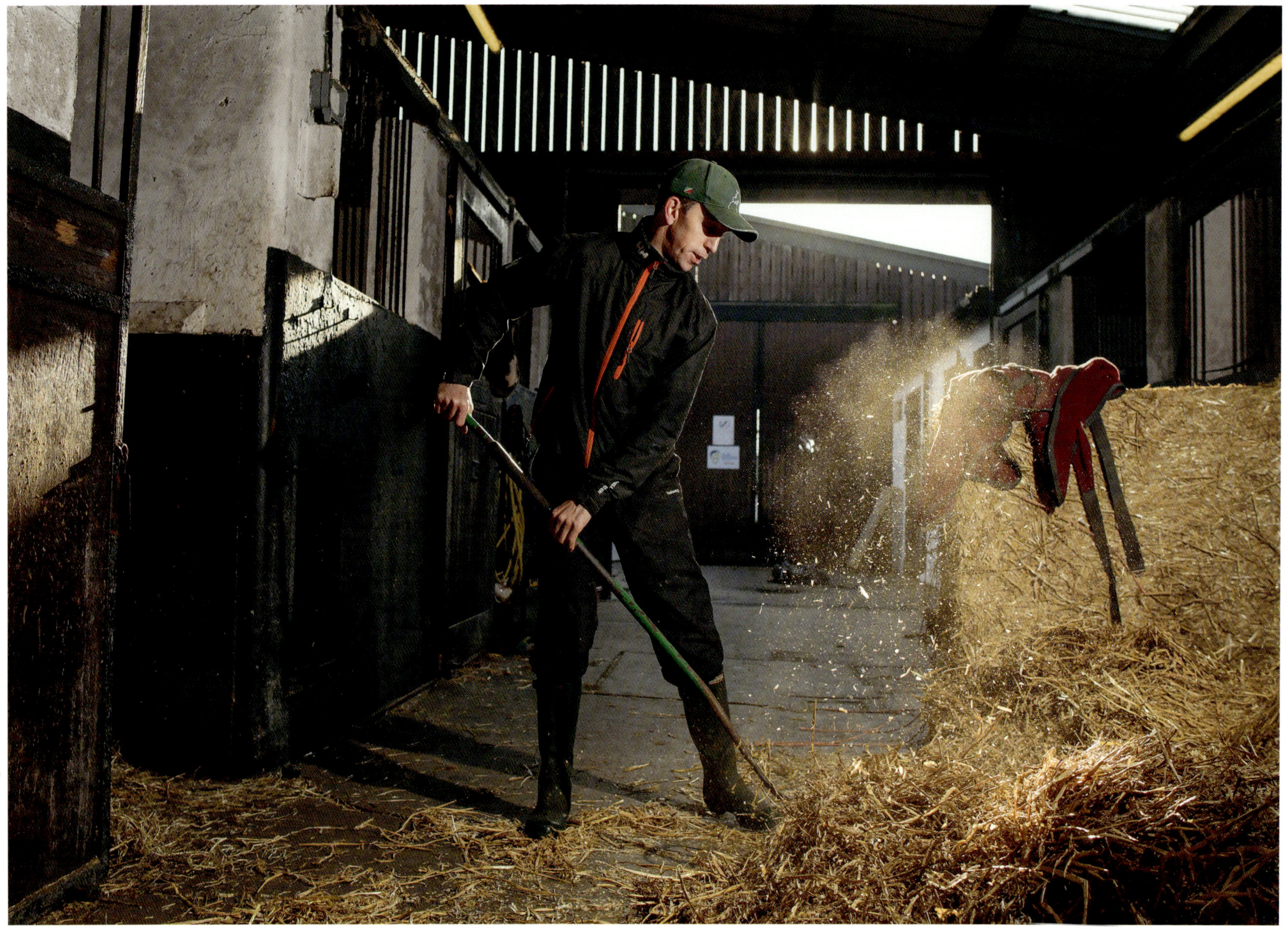

Keeping stable
Leighton Aspell had won the Grand
National on Pineau De Re in 2014
and Many Clouds in 2015 and his
preparations to ride that horse again
in 2016 involved working away at his
pre-training yard at Coombelands
in Sussex.

Homecoming
The whole of Lambourn comes
out to greet Many Clouds after his
Grand National heroics in 2015. It
was the village's first National victory
in 20 years and this picture in the
church square has local pride written
all over it.

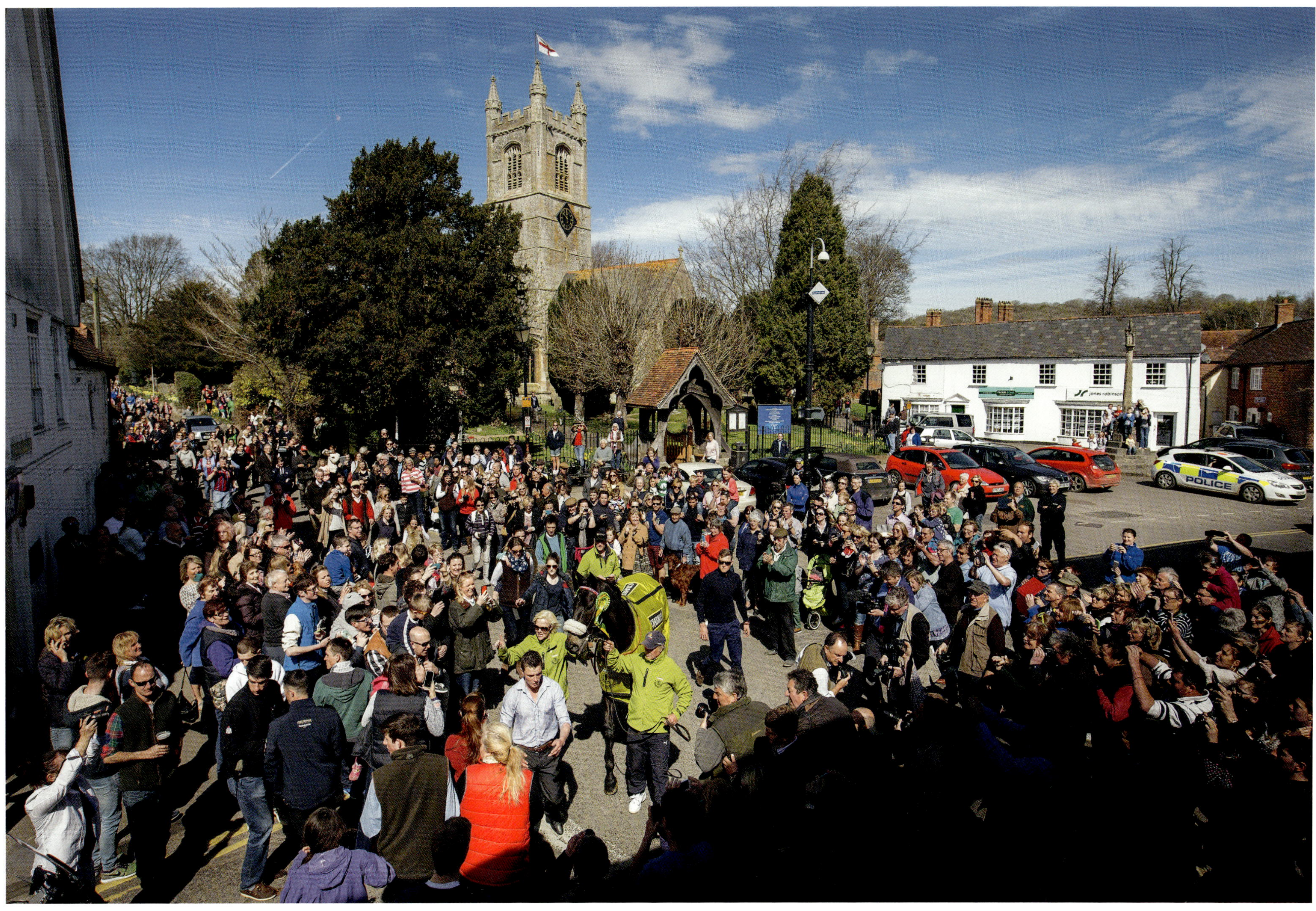

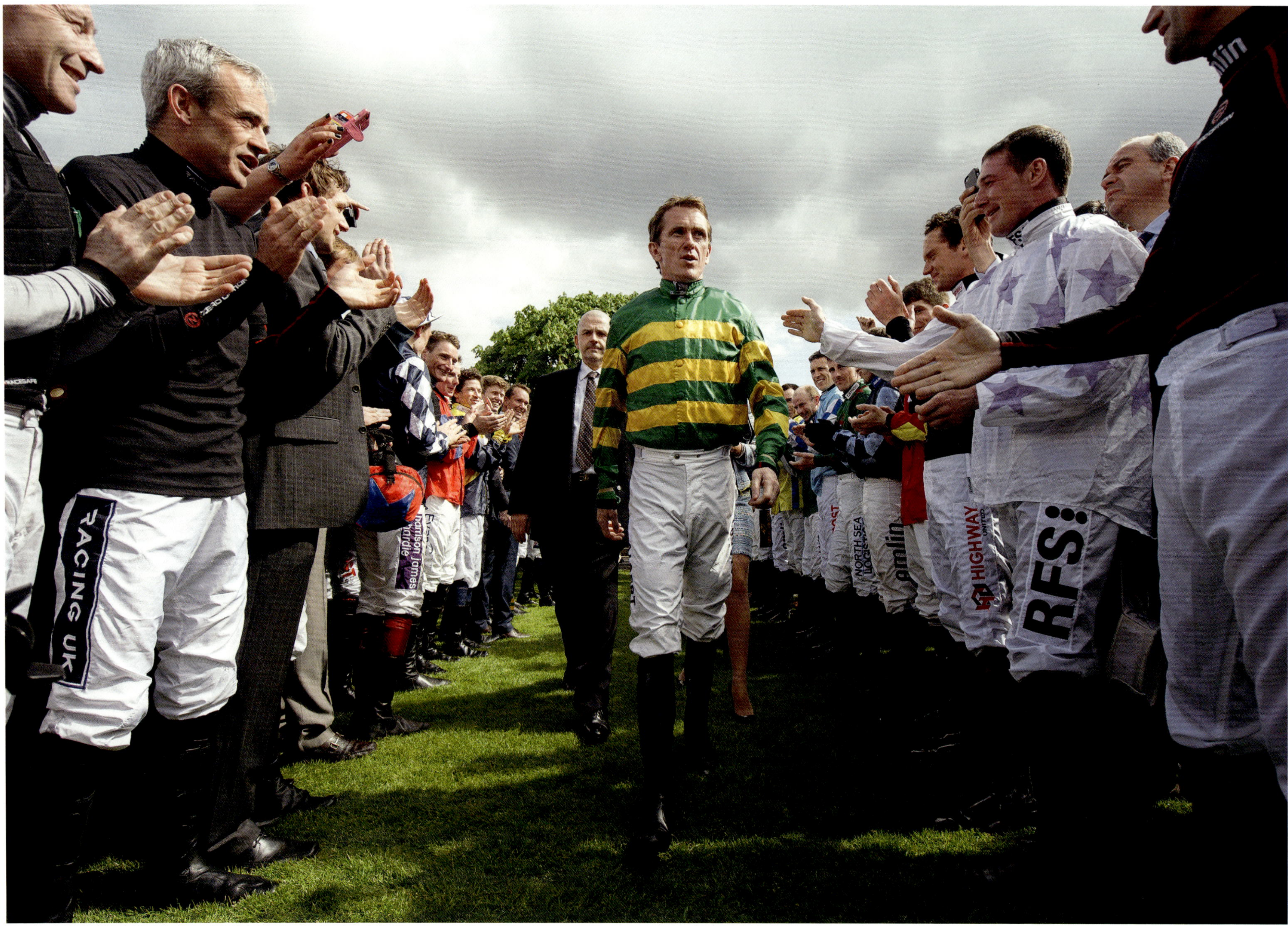

Line of honour
Fellow jockeys salute 20-times champion AP McCoy on his retirement day at Sandown in April 2015. McCoy's long-serving agent Dave Roberts follows him at the jockey's special request.

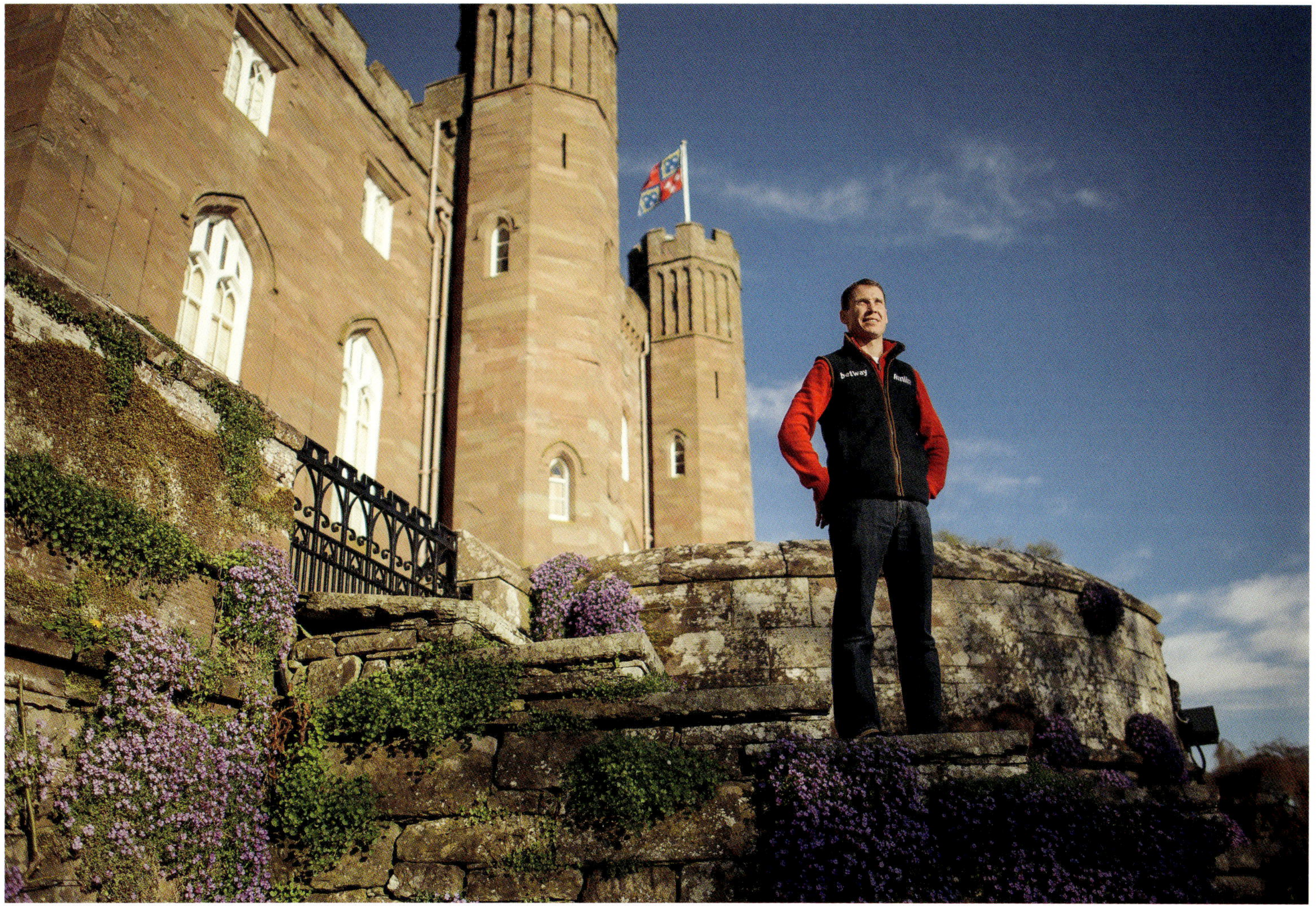

Champion at last
Richard Johnson stands in the grounds of Scone Palace in Perthshire, secure in the knowledge that he was finally champion in his own right. Sixteen times he had been runner-up to AP McCoy. No more.

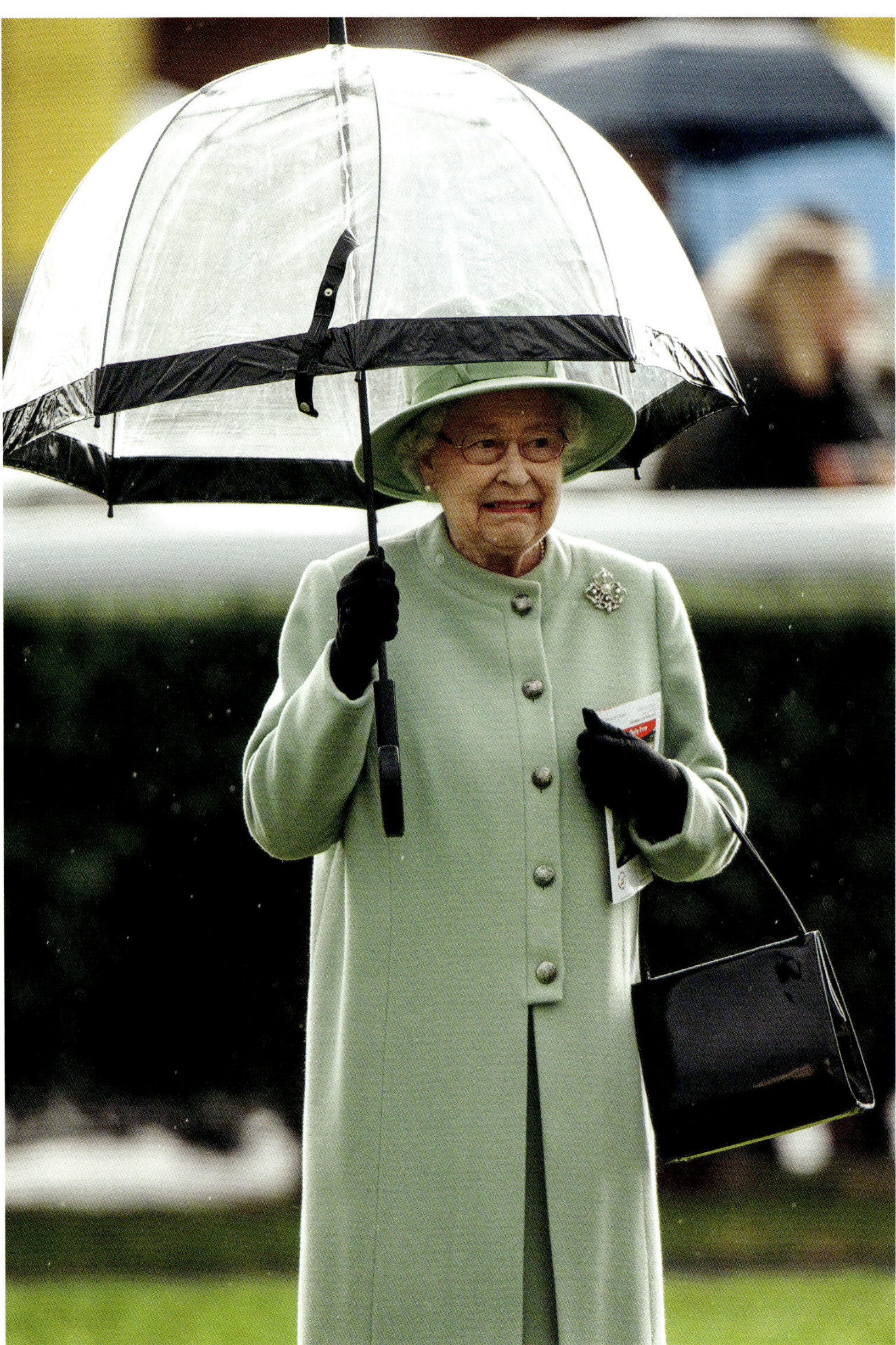

We are quite amused
The Queen pulls a face on her annual spring visit to the Greenham meeting at Newbury. It always amazes me how relaxed she is at the races.

It's good on the grass
Two foals relax in the paddock of the National Stud at Newmarket. It's the way the right-hand one looks over his shoulder that makes the picture.

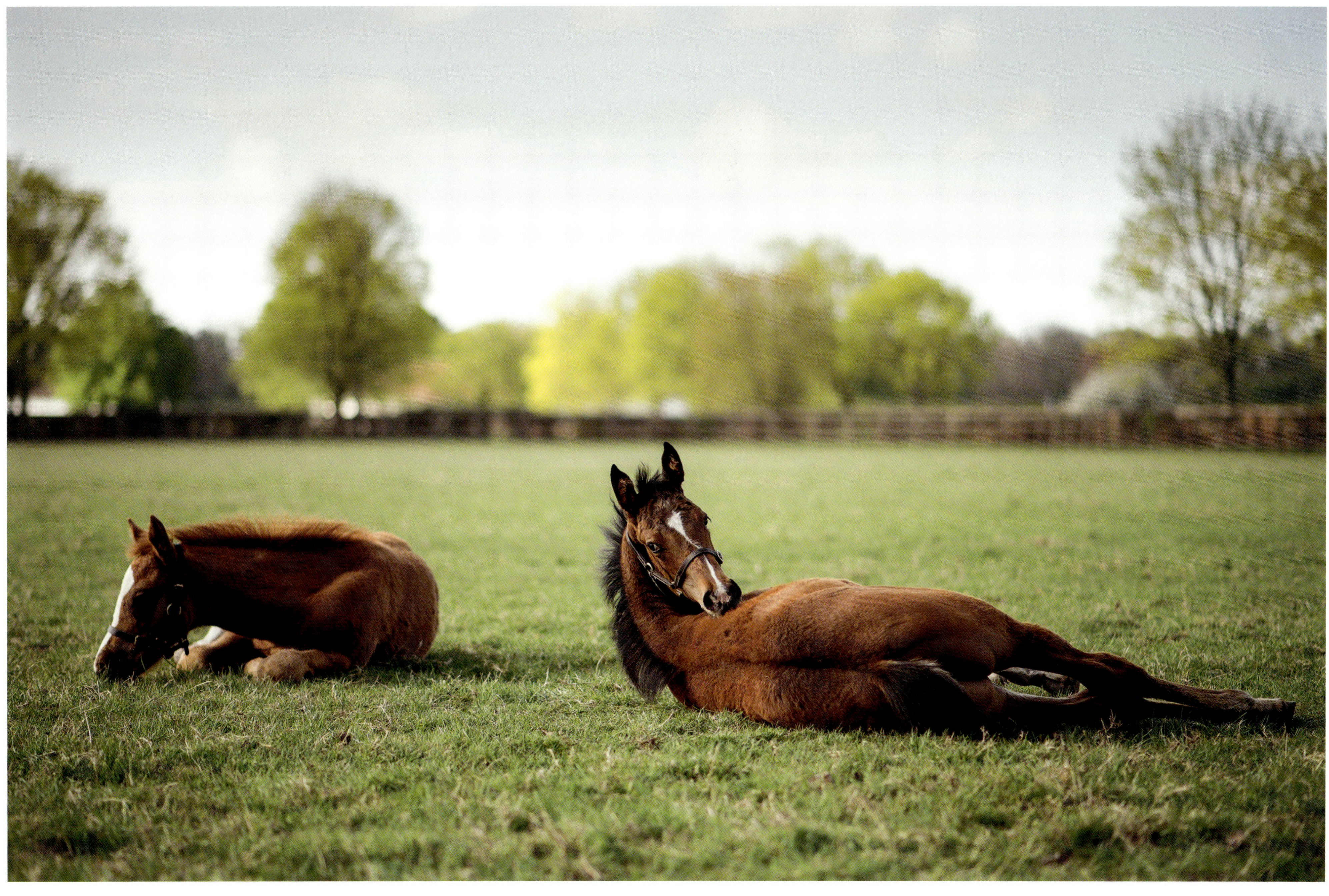

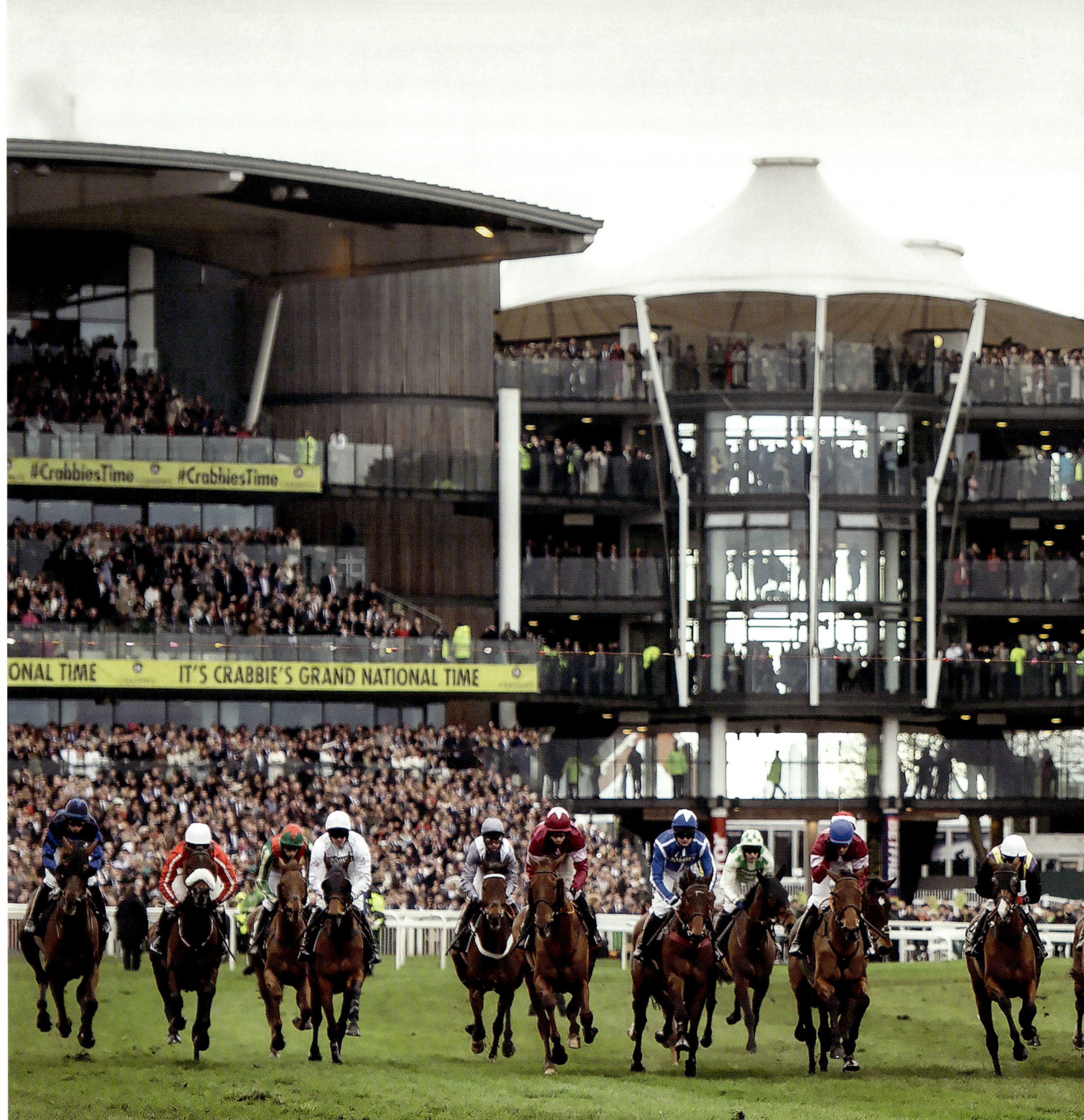

Aintree charge, 2016
No other race has 40 runners let alone 30 jumps and over four and a quarter miles to travel. It's a whole panorama of horses at the gallop.

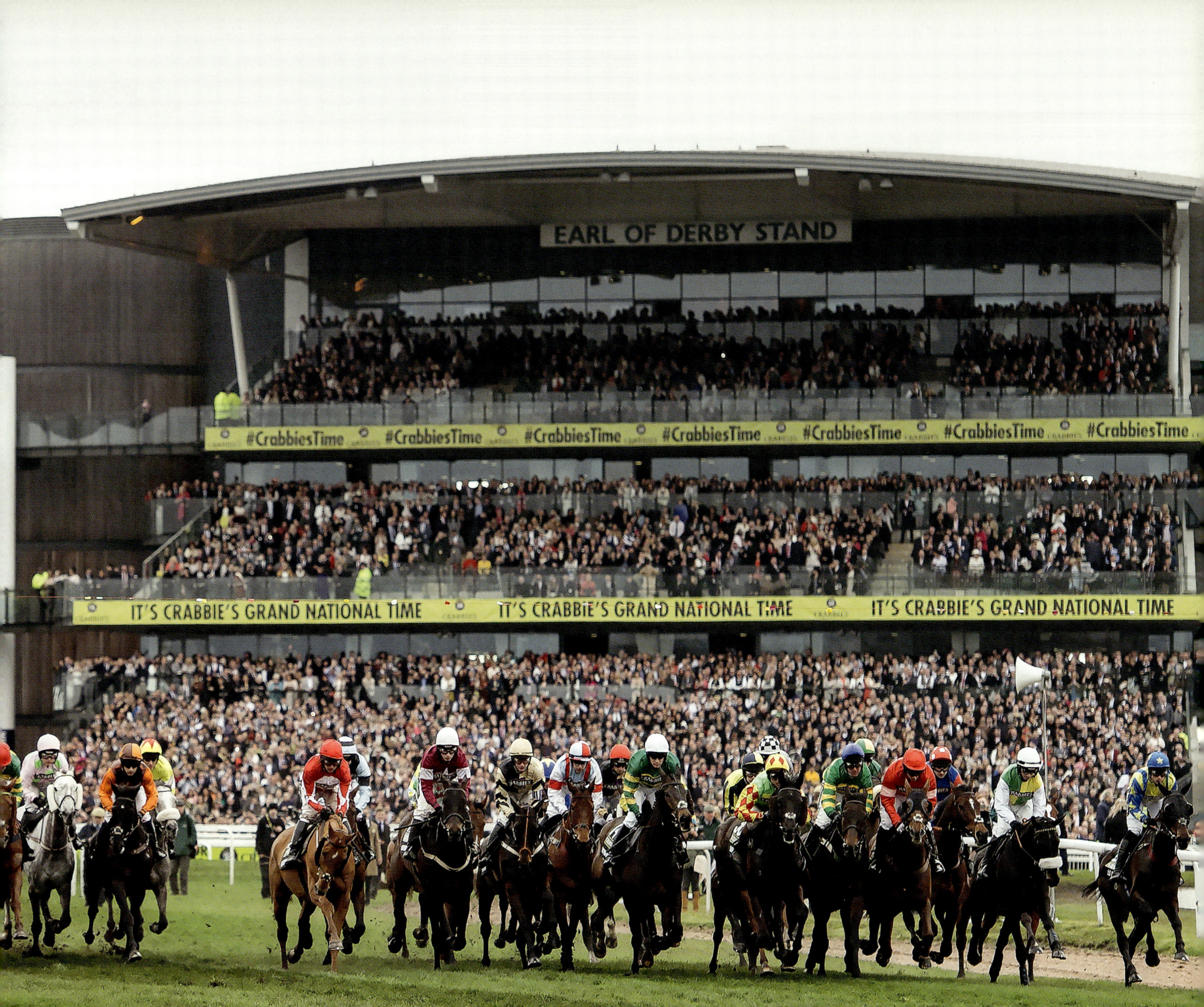

EARL OF DERBY STAND
#CrabbiesTime #CrabbiesTime #CrabbiesTime #CrabbiesTime #CrabbiesTime #CrabbiesTime #CrabbiesTime
IT'S CRABBIE'S GRAND NATIONAL TIME IT'S CRABBIE'S GRAND NATIONAL TIME IT'S CRABBIE'S GRAND NATIONAL TIME

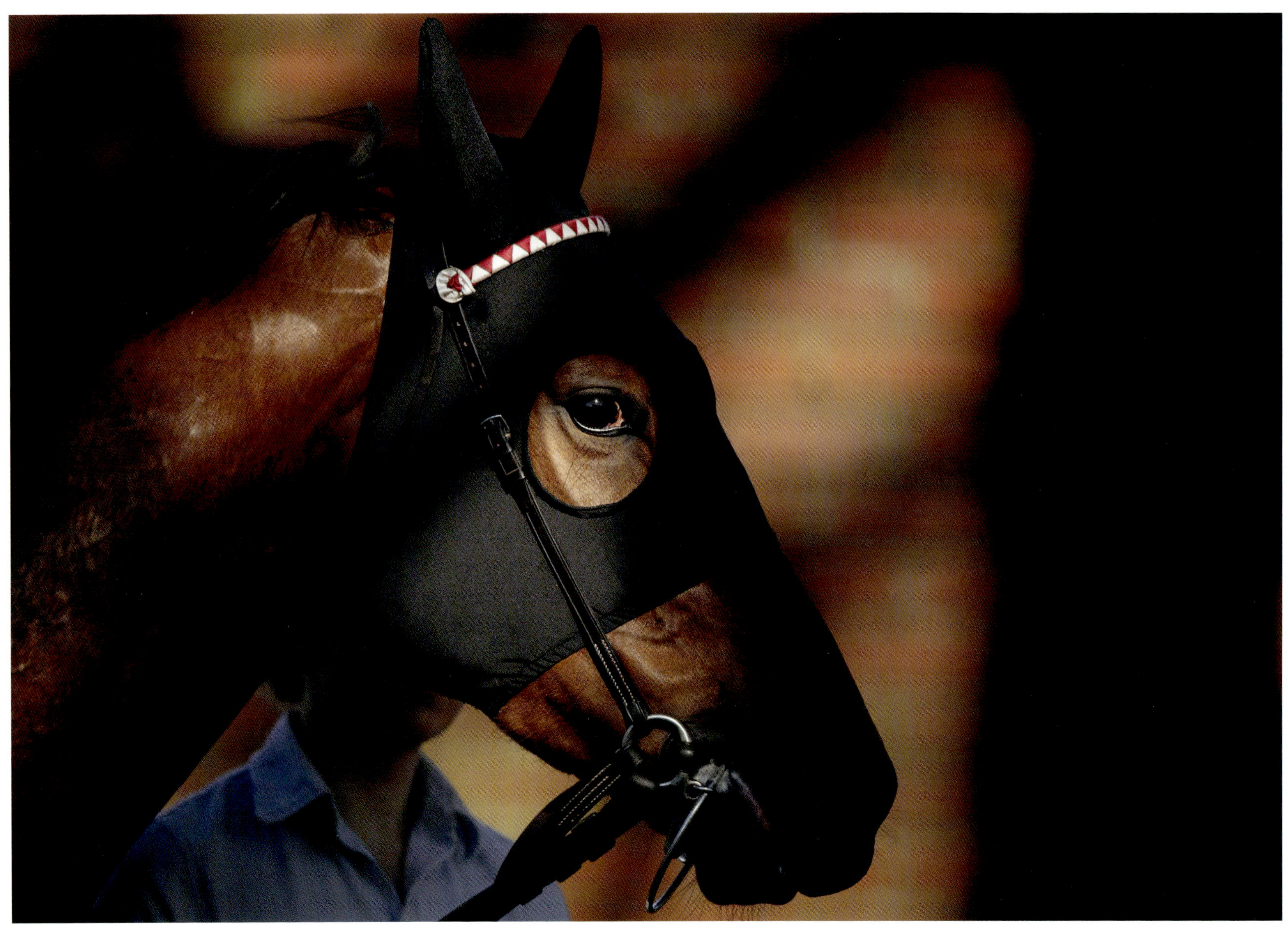

Giving the eye
The hooded Ripley didn't win this
day at Newmarket in April 2018, but
she gave me a splendidly sinister
look in the afternoon light.

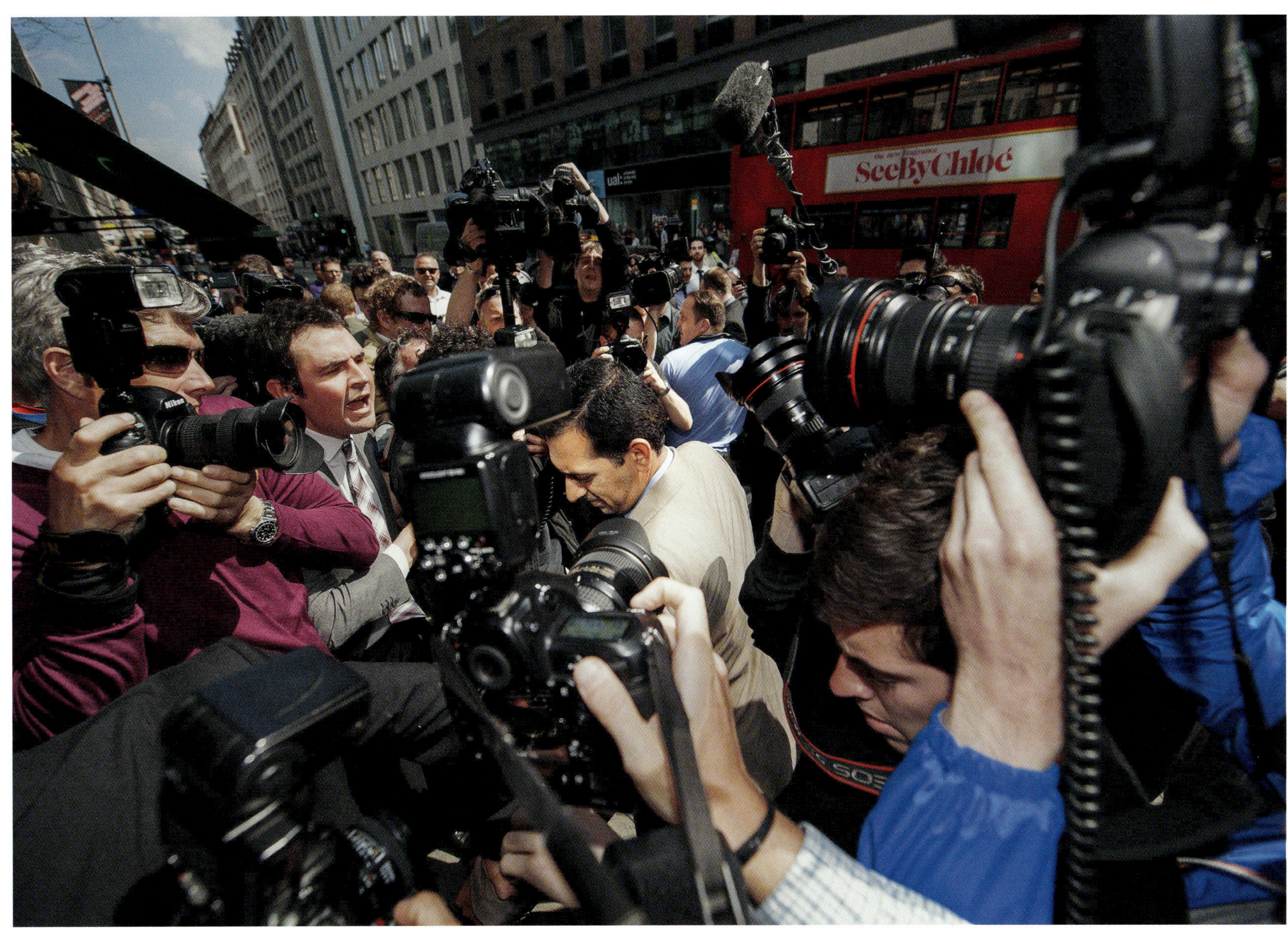

The storm of scandal
Dubai trainer Mahmood Al Zarooni
pushes through the media scrum
to receive an eight-year worldwide
sentence for the doping of the
Godolphin horses in his care at
Newmarket.

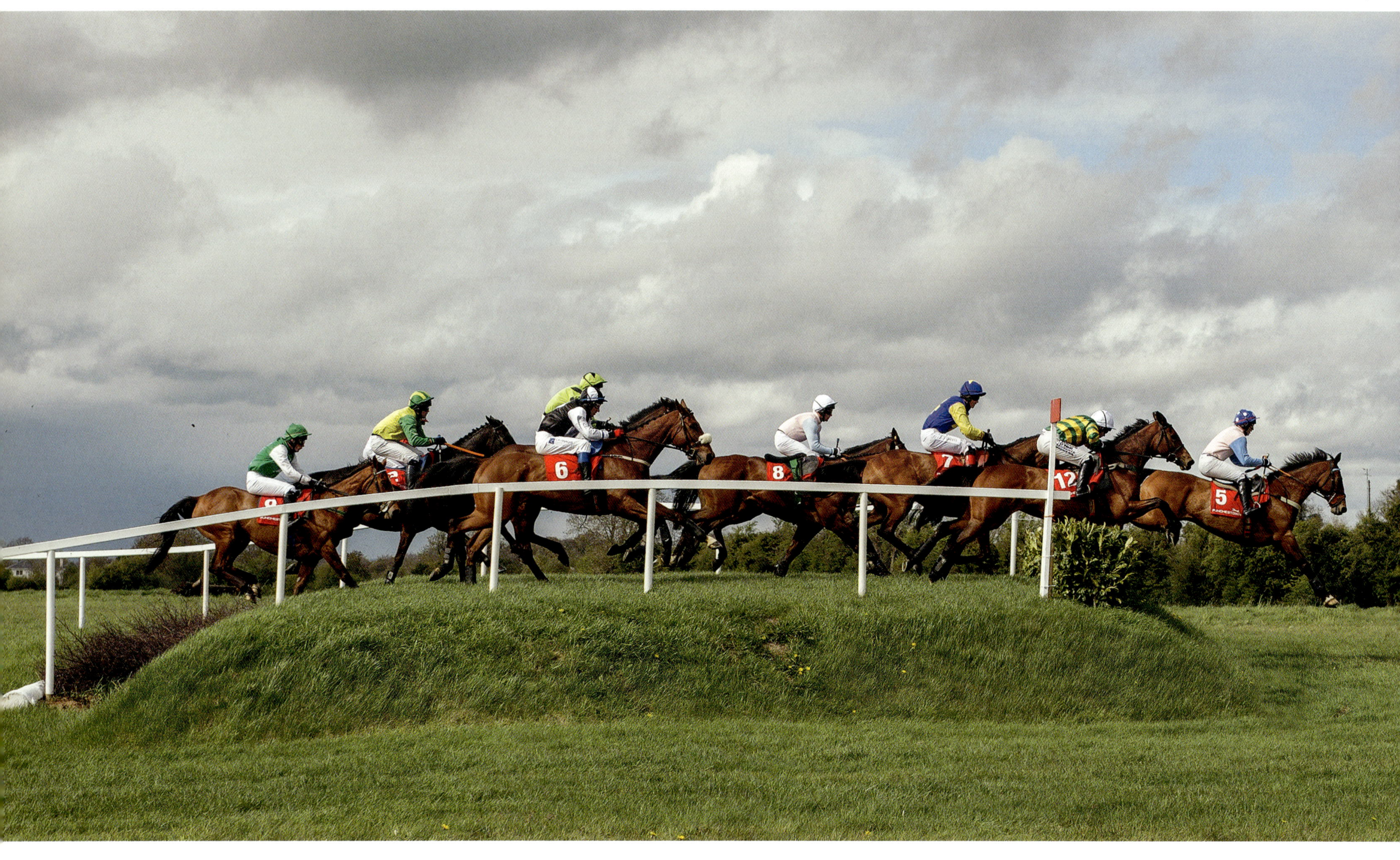

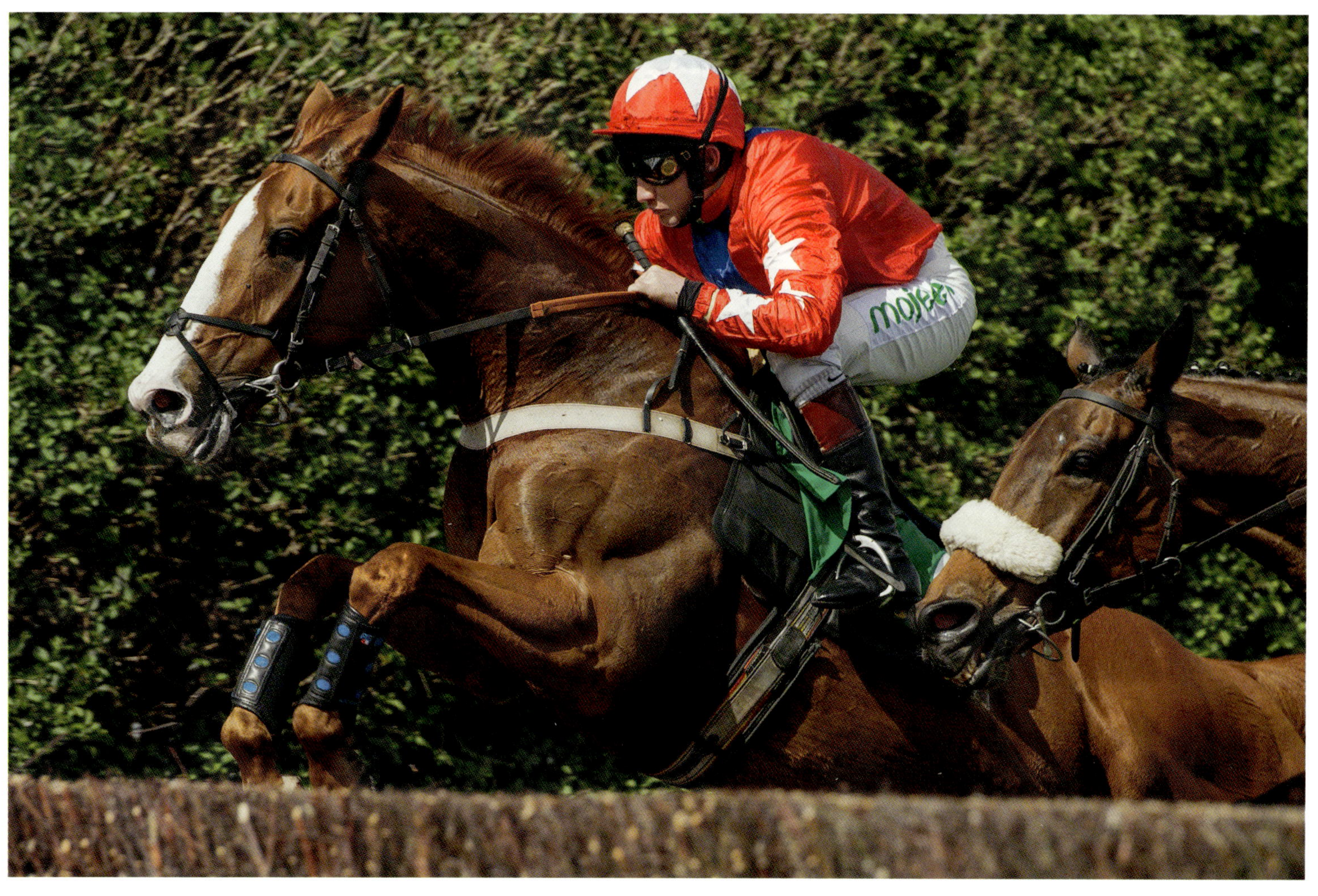

The Bank at Punchestown
The Cheltenham Bank is not the most taxing of the obstacles at Punchestown but this image makes it one of the most aesthetically pleasing. How many times would we have to rehearse such symmetry?

Scarlet soarer
Sire De Grugy and Jamie Moore clear the open ditch at Sandown en route to victory in the Celebration Chase. A month earlier he had won the Champion Chase at Cheltenham. This was his year.

May

The flint wall at Goodwood
Storm clouds above the flint wall
at Goodwood. People talk about all
the fashions, panama hats and the
gorgeous downland at the track,
but the Sussex flint is just as much
a part of it.

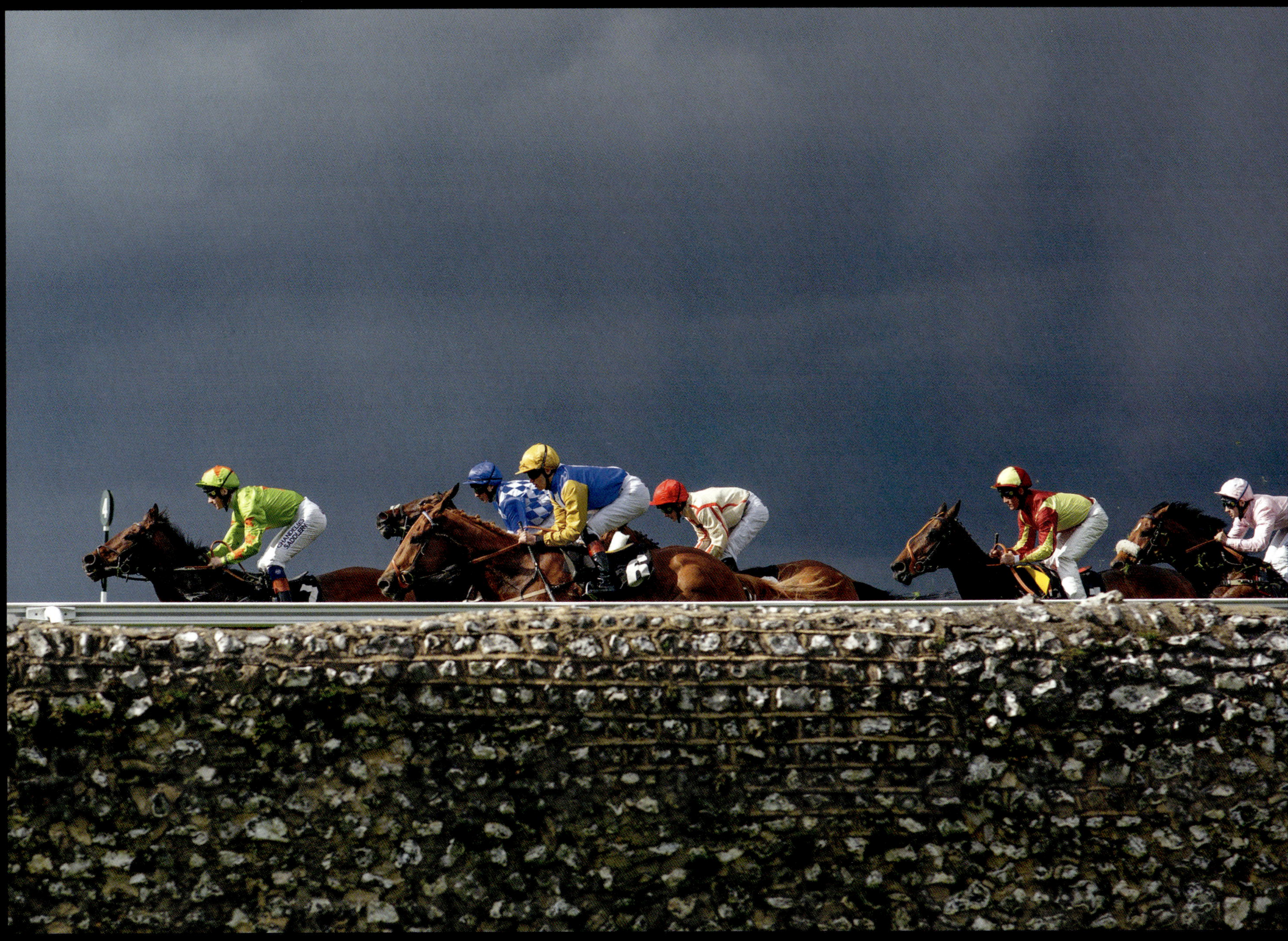

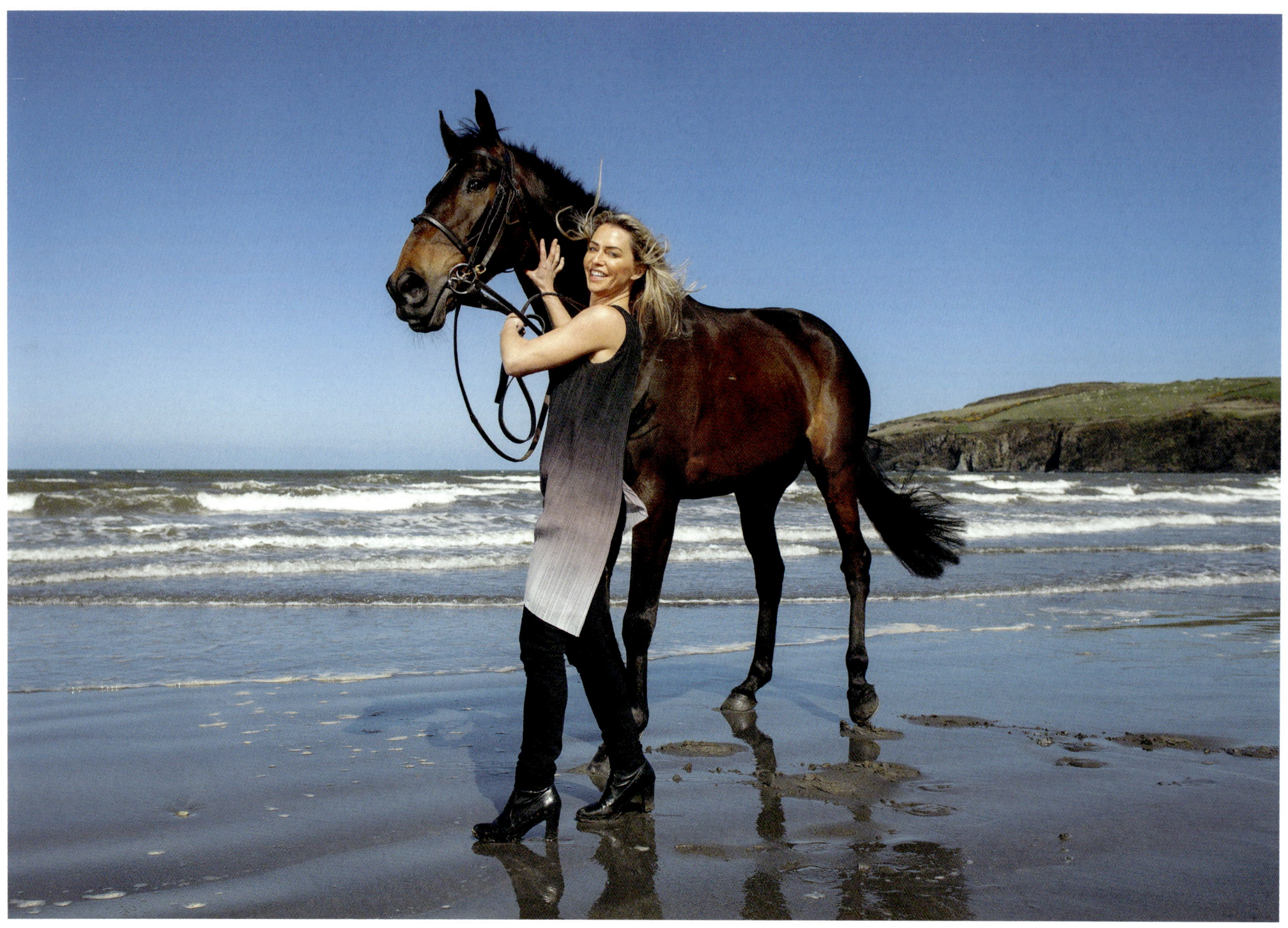

Waves of pleasure
Rebecca Curtis and her Scottish
Grand National winner Joe Farrell
greet the sunshine on the beach
in Pembrokeshire.

Kicking up the dirt
A pair of white fetlocks kick up
the fibre at Mick Channon's indoor
school at West Ilsley. It's all about
the light and shade.

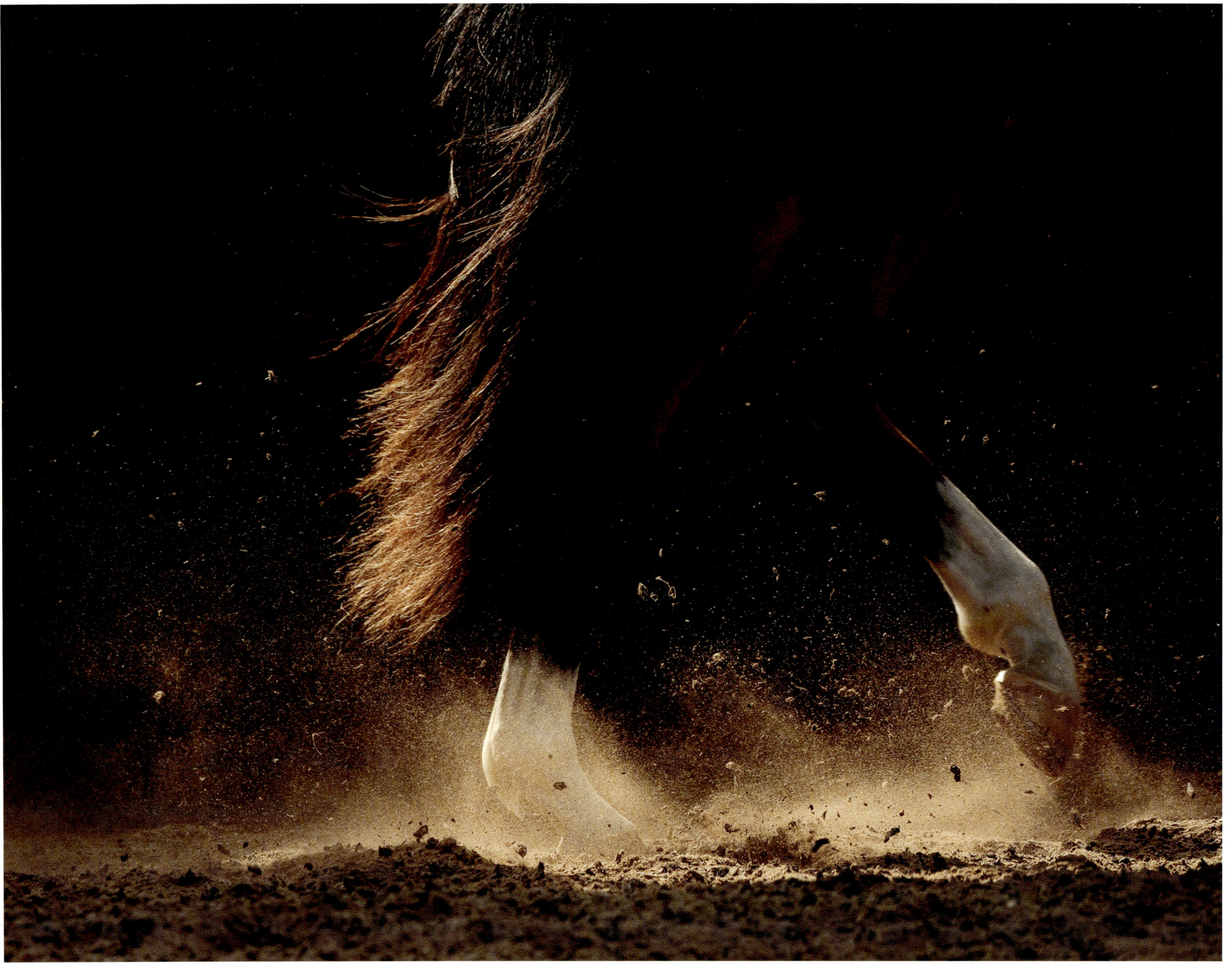

Stage fright
The two-year-old colt Cunco was
the first son of Frankel to appear on
the racetrack. He duly won but not
before these alarms in the saddling
box at Newbury.

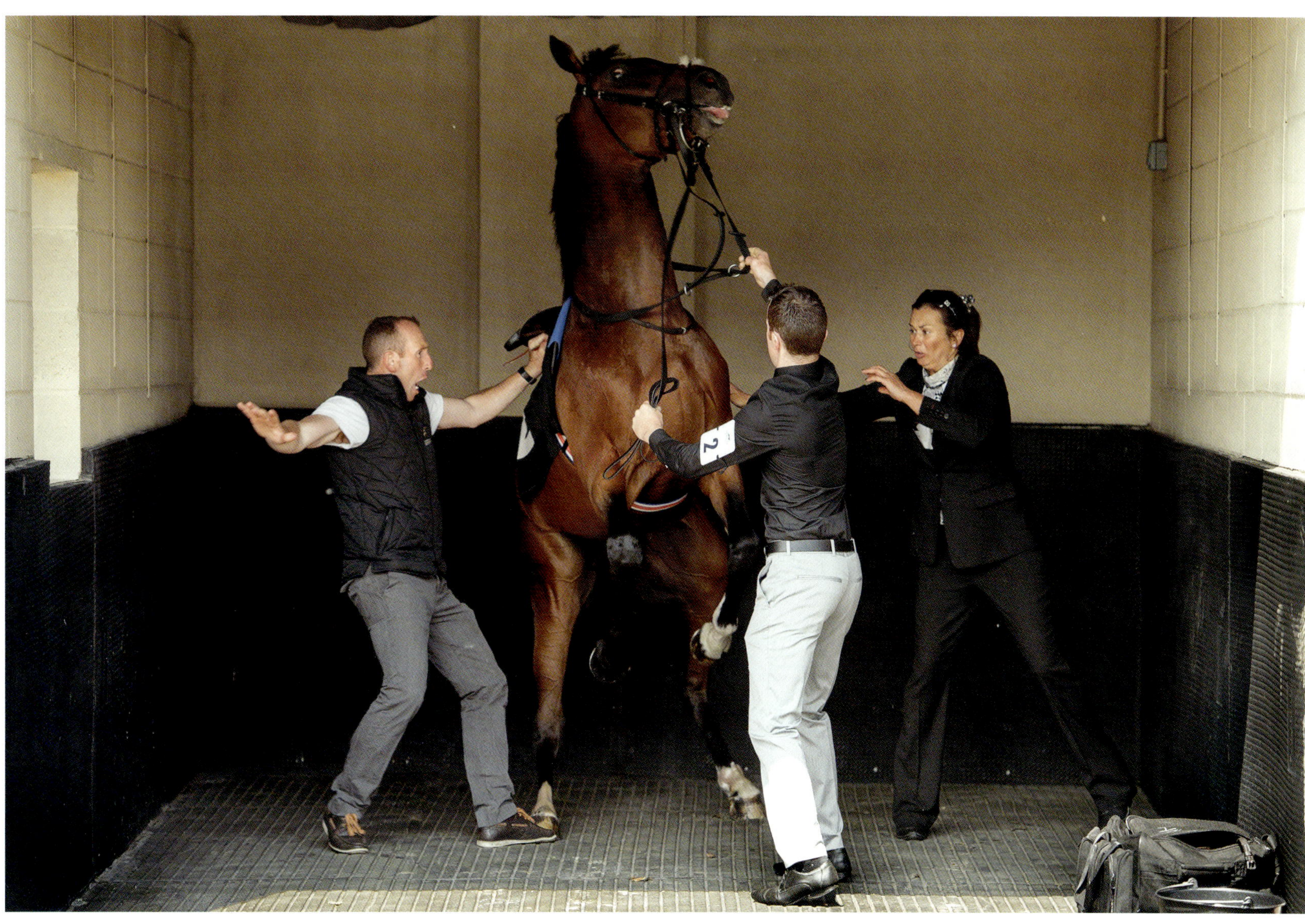

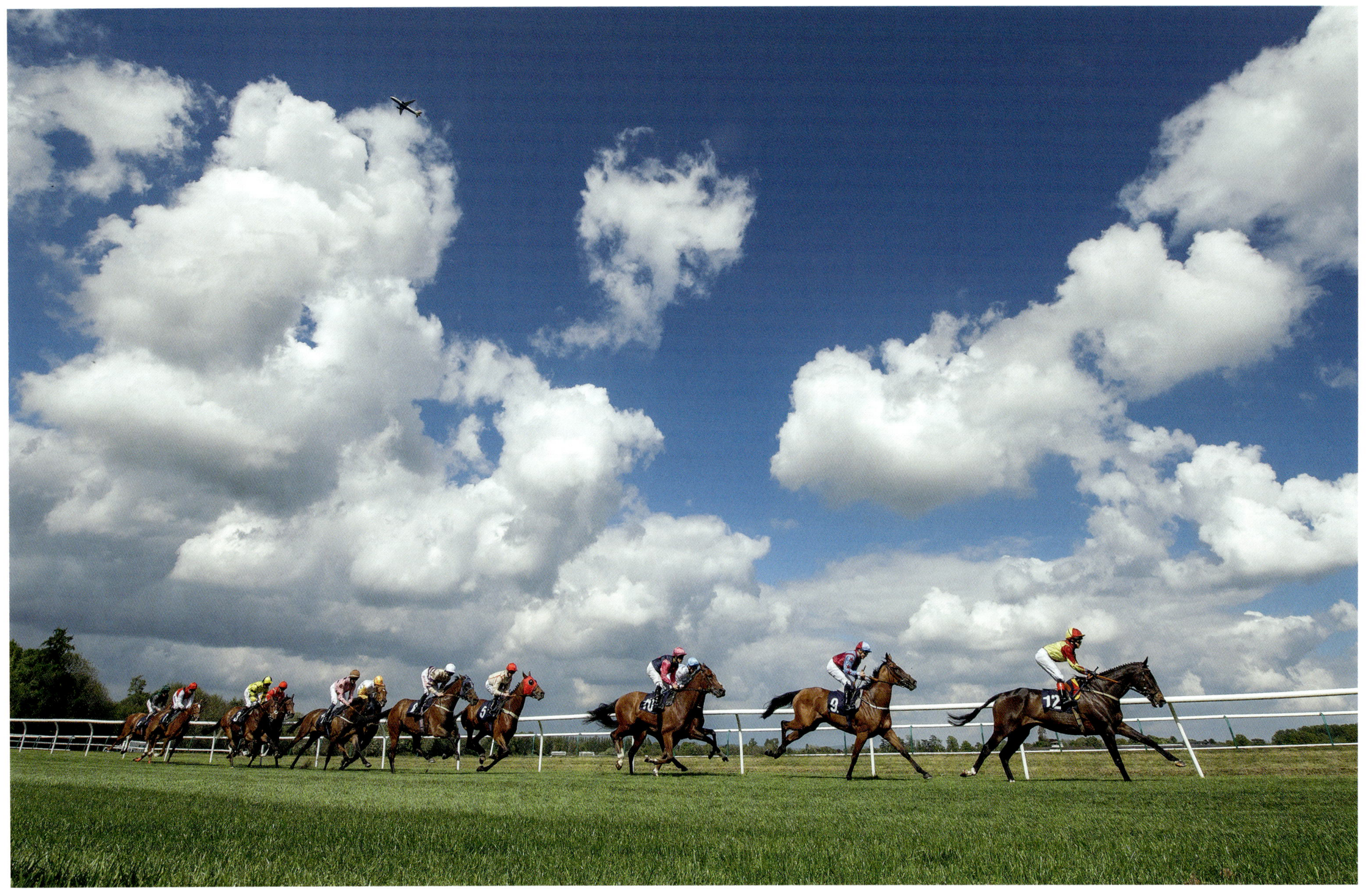

Cloudscape at Lingfield
With photographs the sky can be really important, especially when you have a set of cumulus clouds as we had this day at Lingfield.

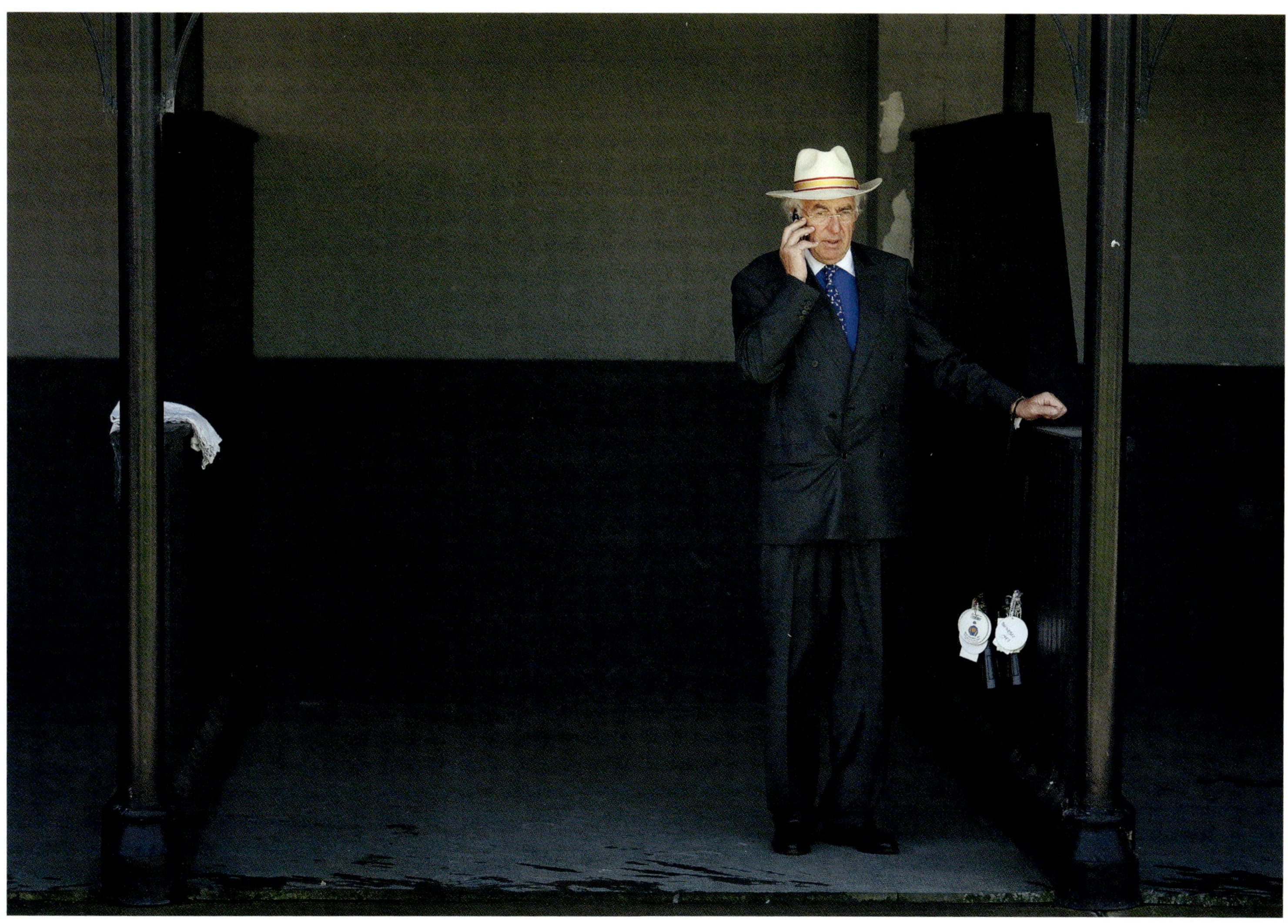

The chief
John Magnier has a presence
to match his importance as the
founding head of the Coolmore
empire. These days we see
little of him on the track but this
sighting at the Curragh in 2012
tells of his influence.

Gleneagles wins the 2015
2,000 Guineas
Gleneagles was Aidan O'Brien's
seventh 2,000 Guineas winner and
one of his most straightforward.
Ryan Moore was always in command
and I just wished I had backed him.
At 4-1 he was a bargain.

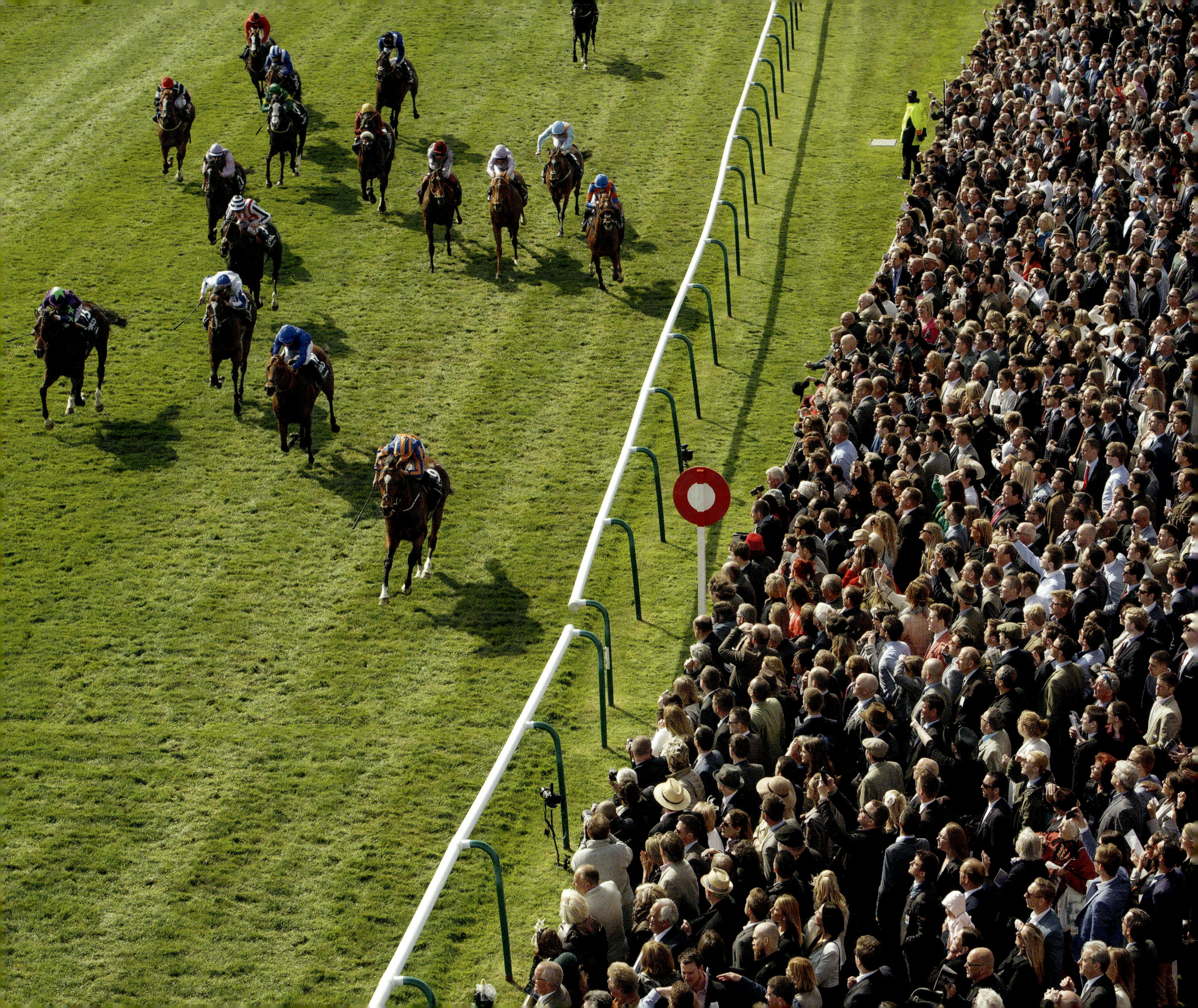

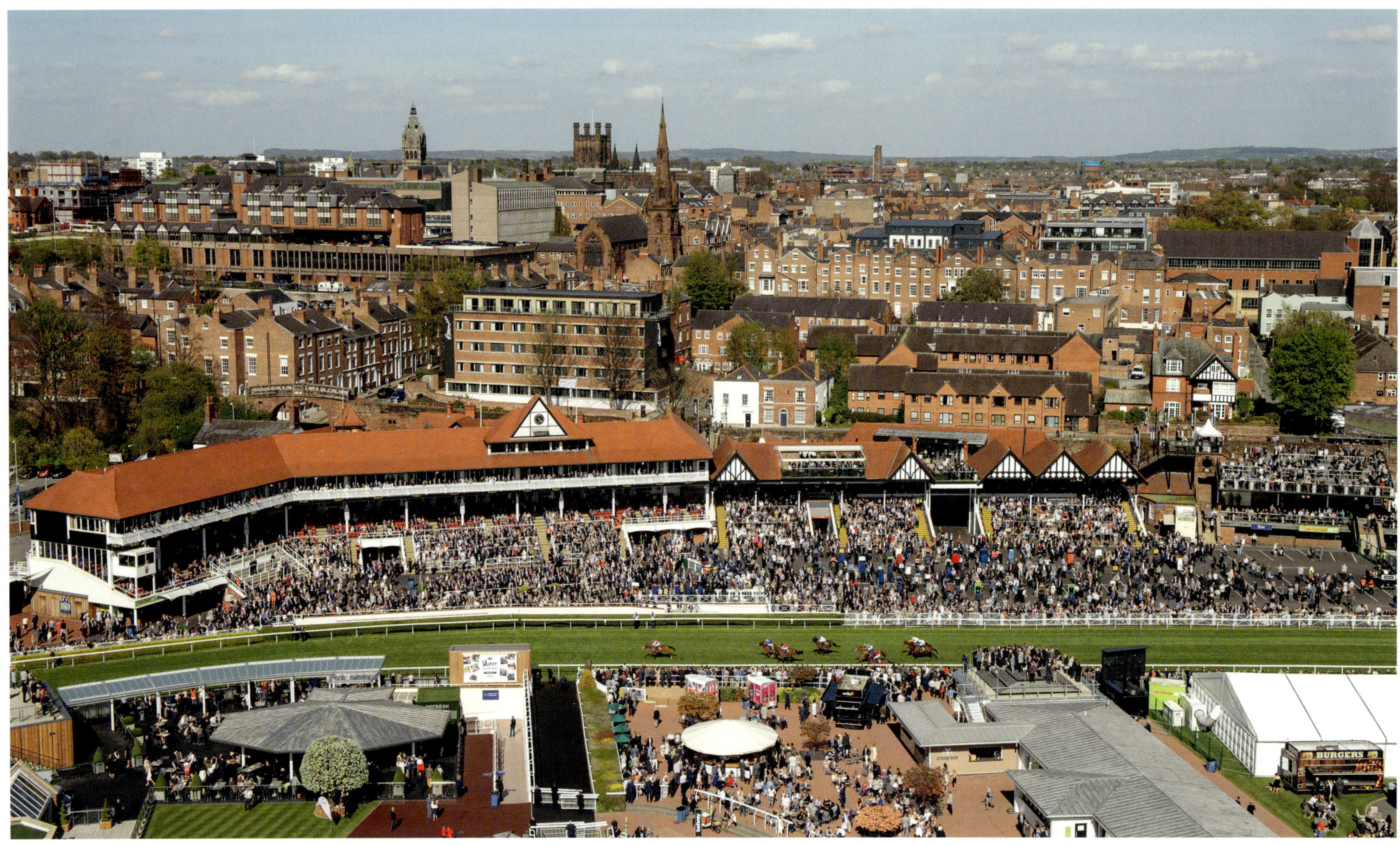

Chester bird's-eye view
From on high you can see just how
Chester racecourse is integrated
within the city. This is taken from the
top of the 70-metre cherry picker
used for the Channel 4 coverage –
and I suffer from vertigo.

Skyline at Longchamp
The modern buildings of La Défense
make a contrasting backdrop to the
timeless harlequinade of the jockeys'
silks. It's a long time since Degas was
captivated by the same scene but
without the skyscrapers.

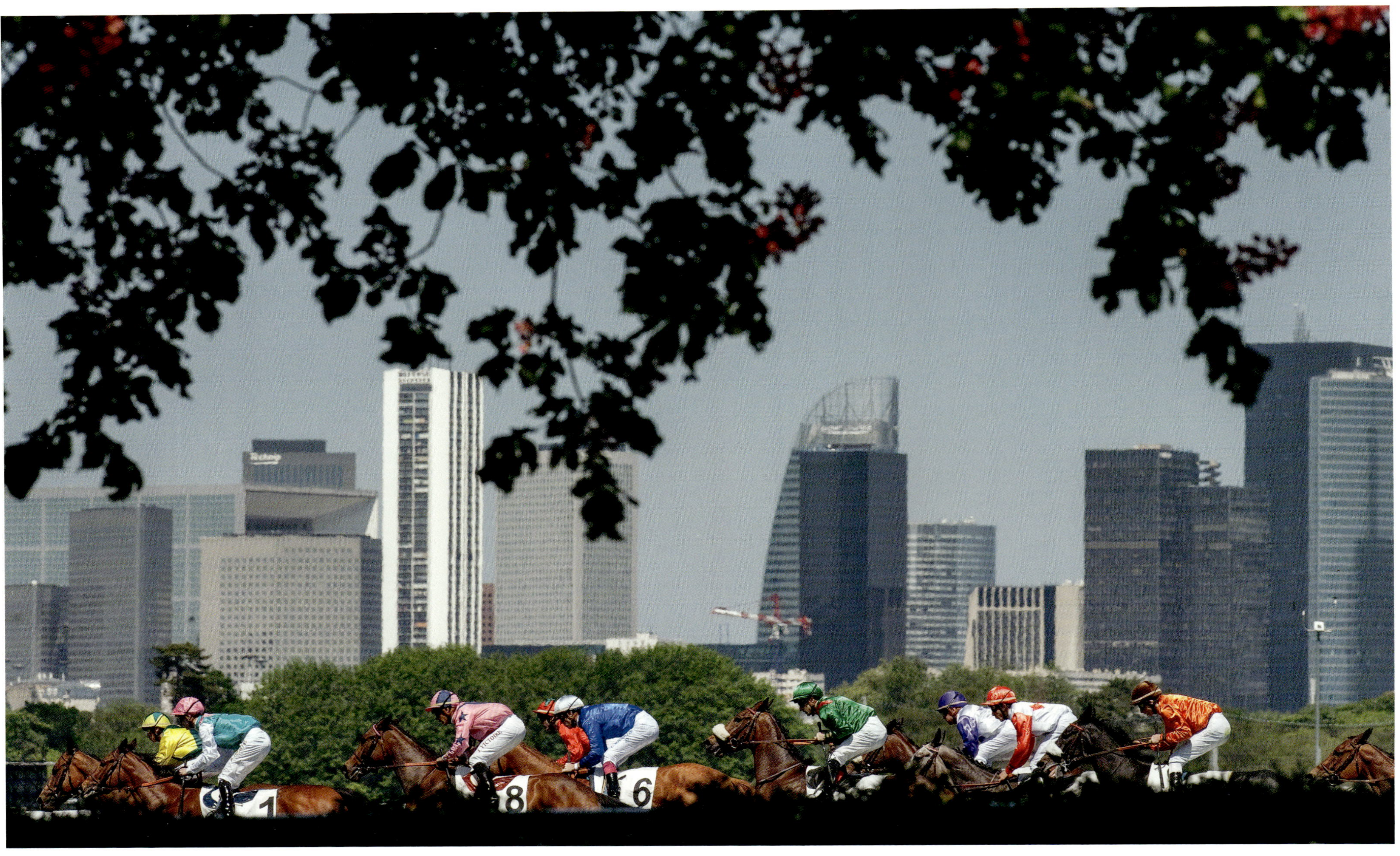

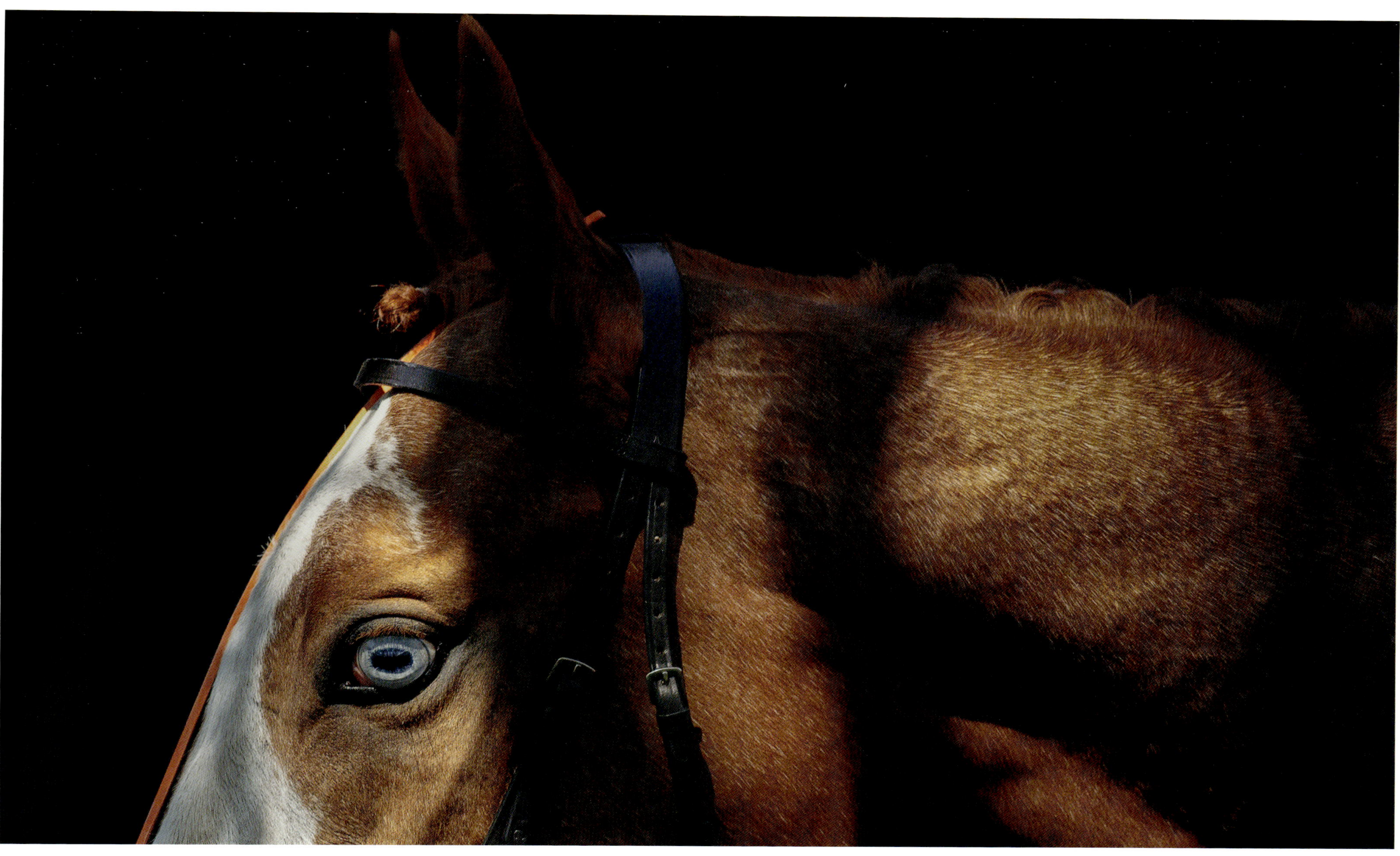

Eyeline
Almost all horses have brown eyes
so the blue pigmentation of what
they call a 'wall eye' is a special
image. No doubt Cote D'Azur got
his name from his eye colouring.

I ****ing backed it!
Ladies Day at the Chester May
Meeting is never understated. There
are usually enough professional
footballers around to call this 'Wags'
Week' and these racegoers are going
to enjoy every minute.

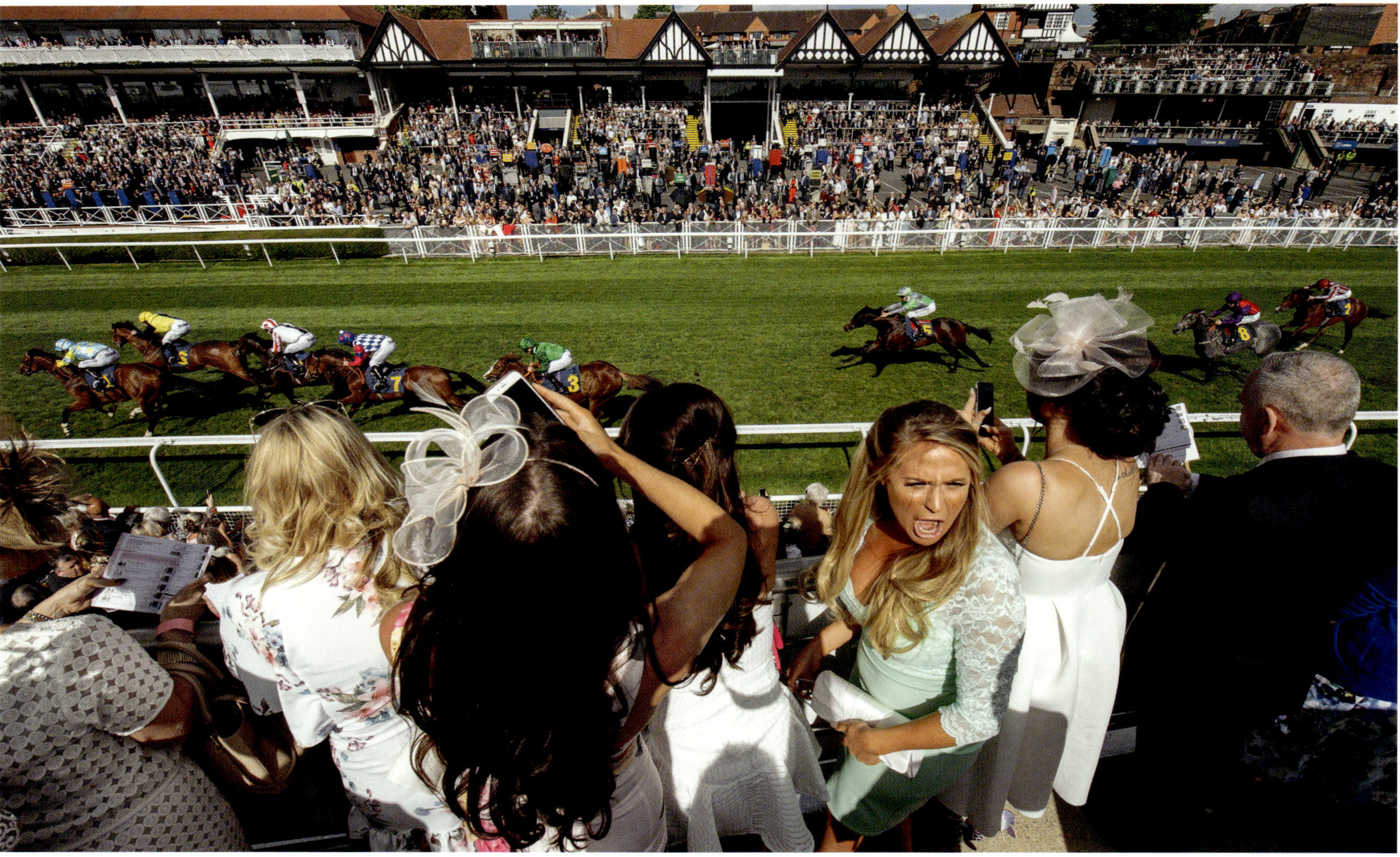

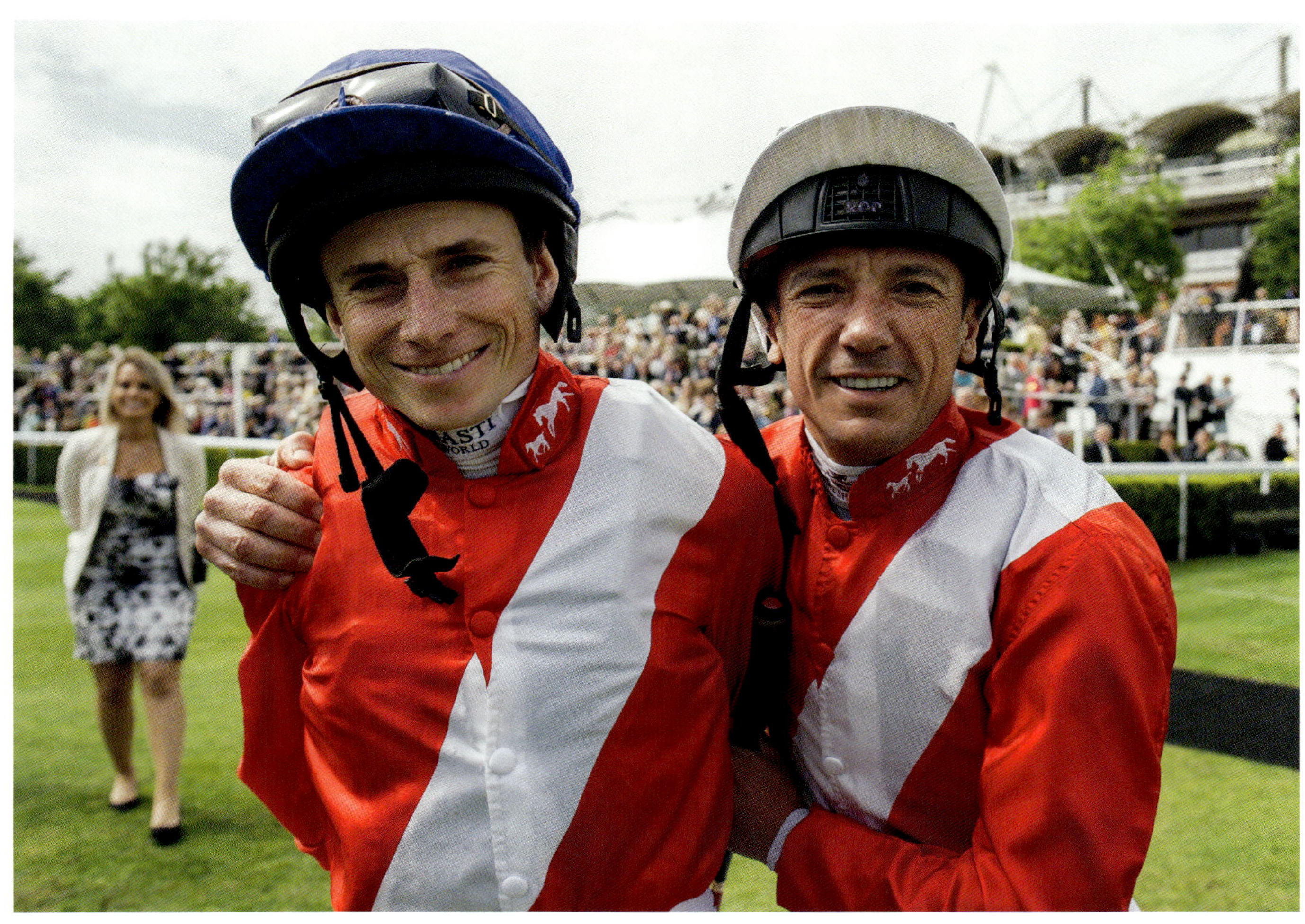

Horsing around
Ryan Moore and Frankie Dettori
happy before both riding in the
Cheveley Park colours at Goodwood.
Frankie was the happiest as he and
Persuasive went on to beat Ryan on
Aristocratic in the race – opposite.

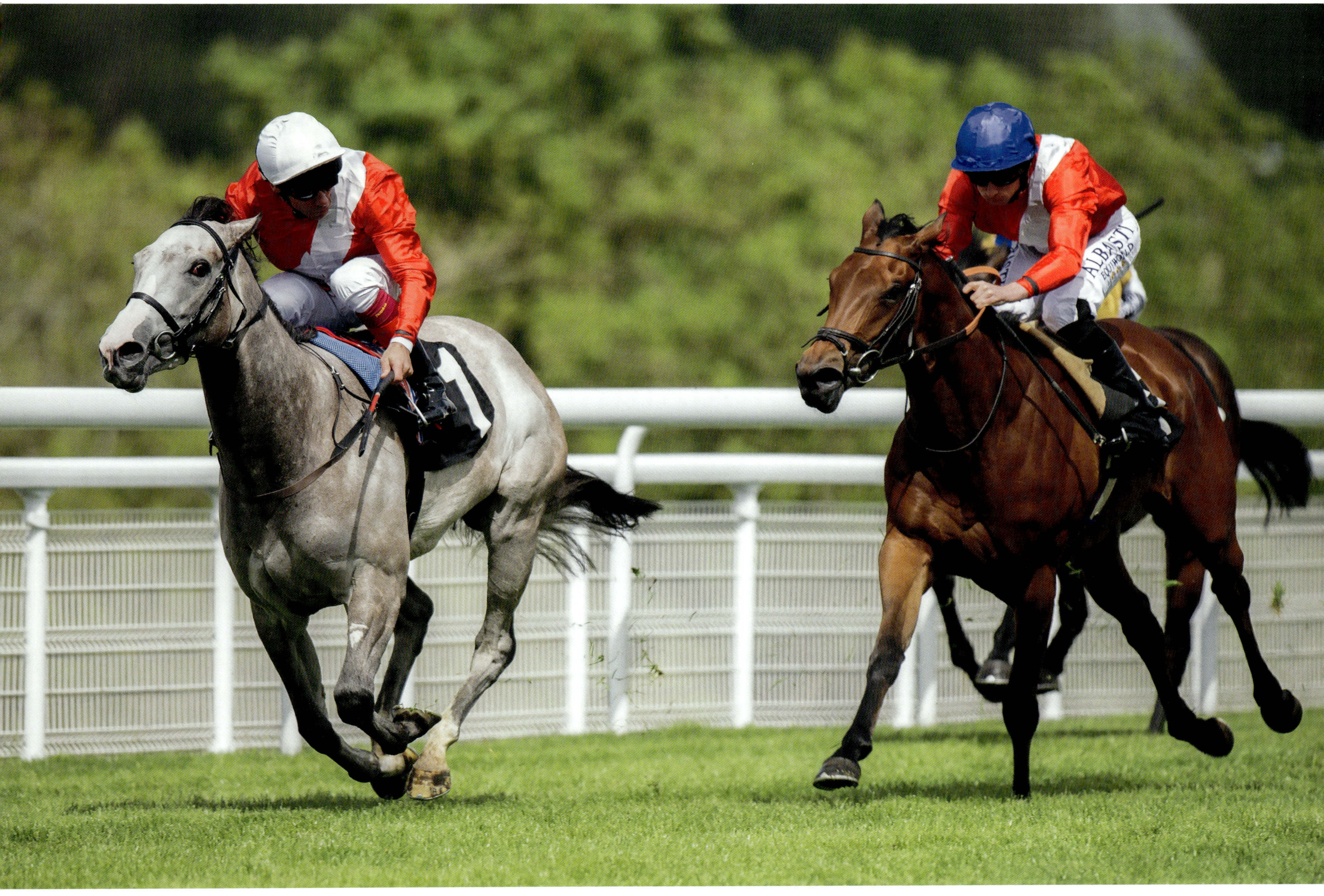

June

The Royal Procession
This remains the most historically
colourful image in the whole racing
firmament. That the Queen still
heads an 18-horse, four-coach
parade on each of the five days
of Royal Ascot never ceases to
amaze me.

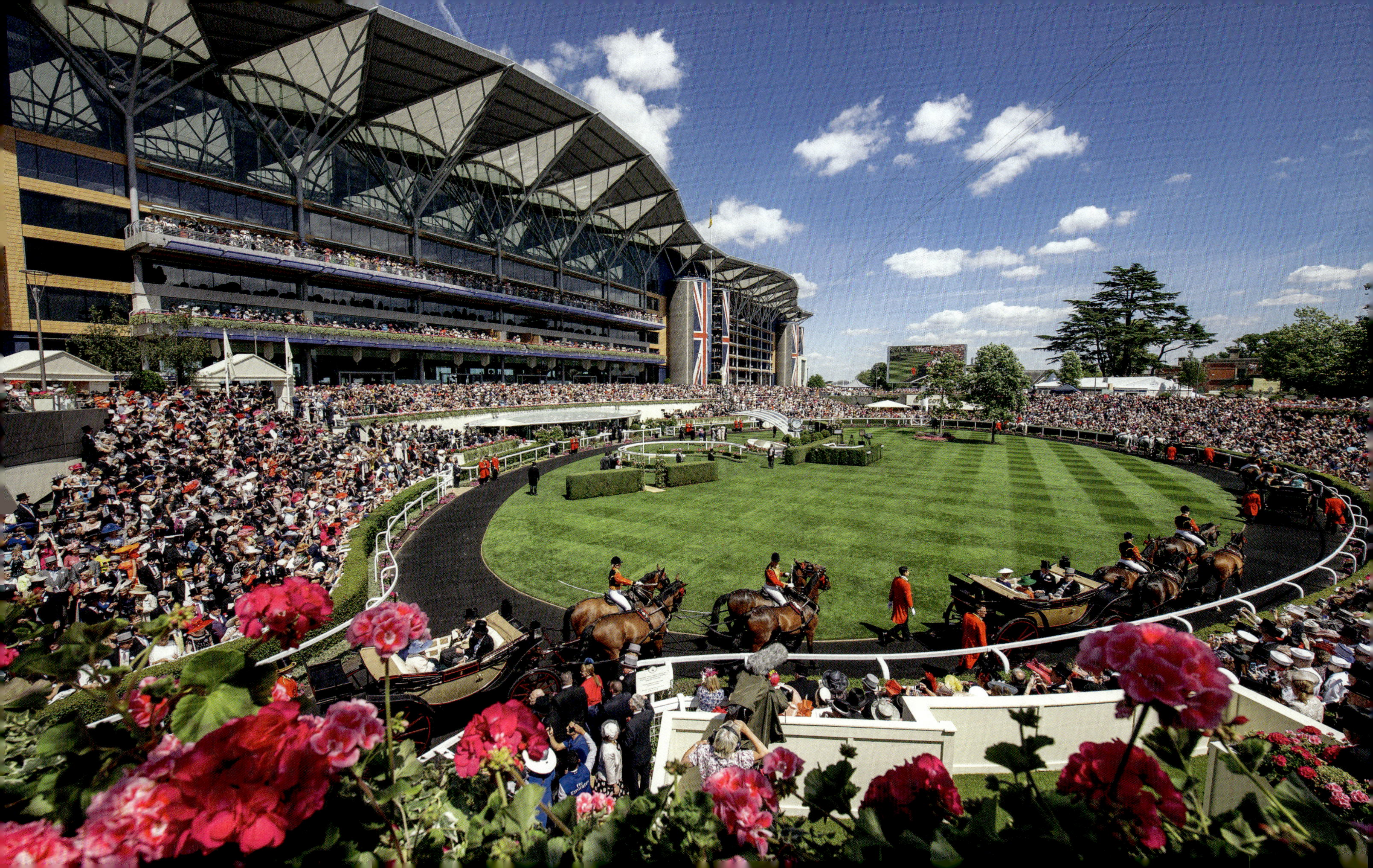

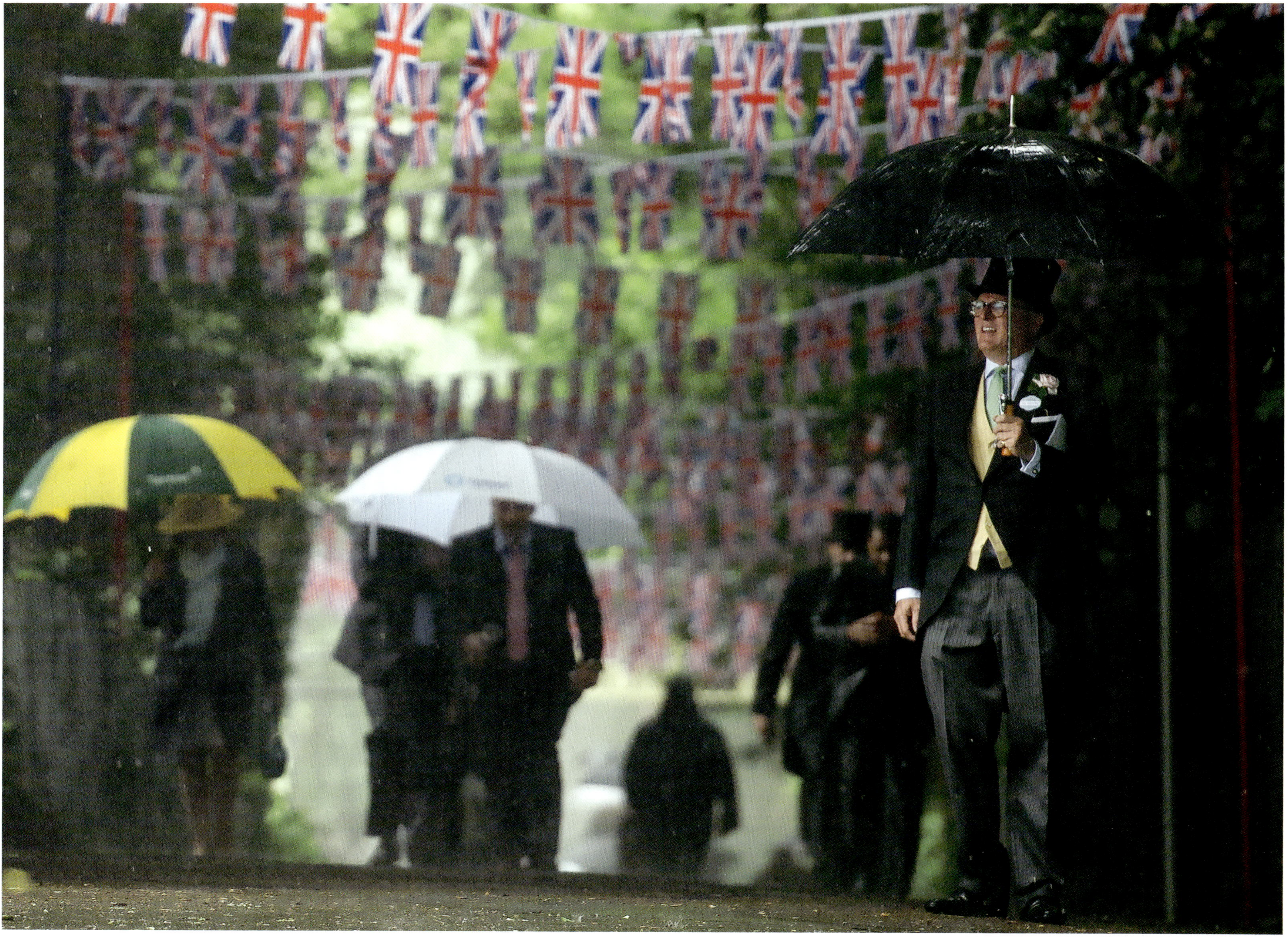

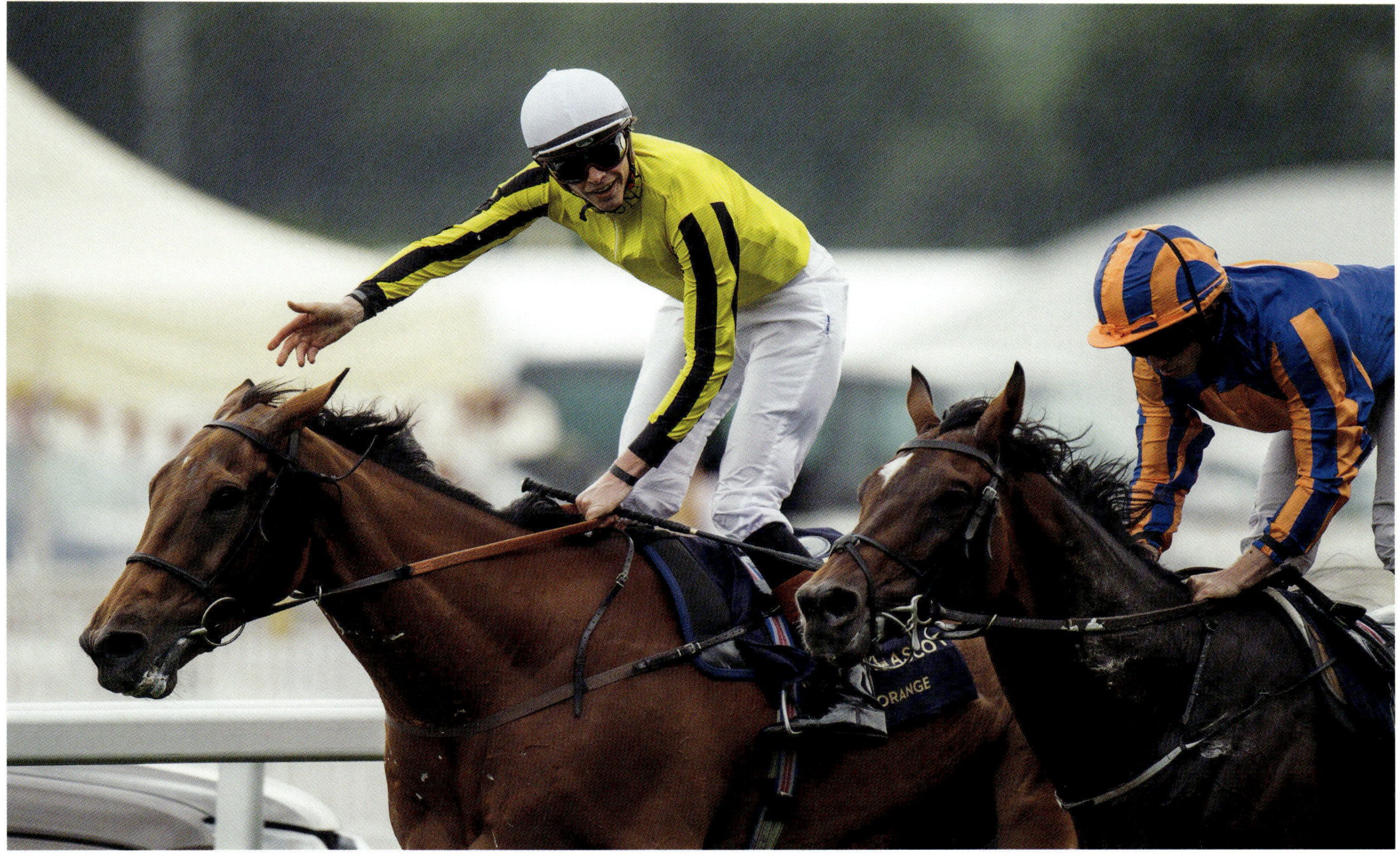

Rain at Ascot
It is England in June so we shouldn't
be surprised. The Union Jacks are
always there but in 2016 having an
umbrella was the key.

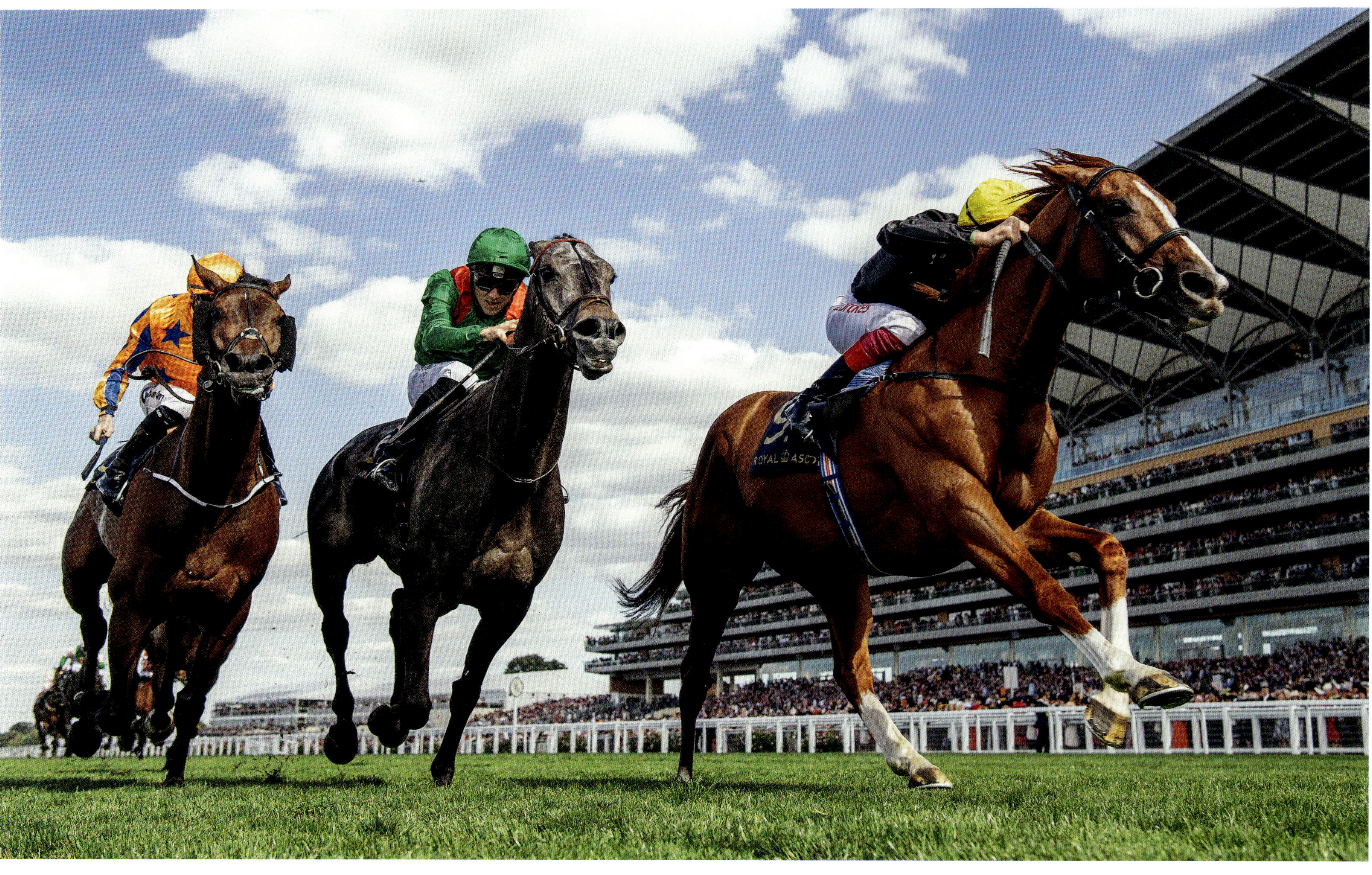

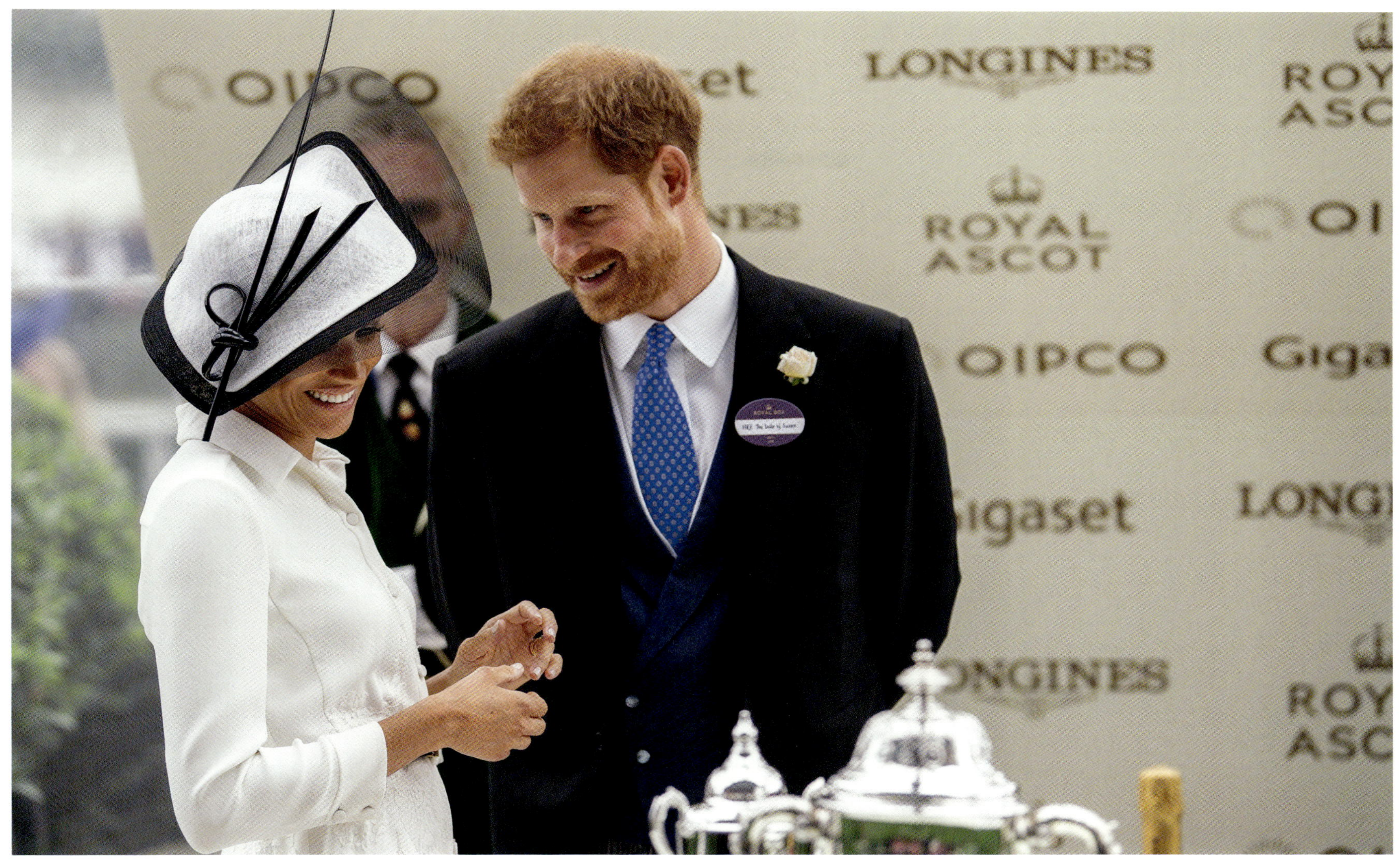

Stradivarius in perfect tune
Frankie Dettori clamps down
on Stradivarius to hold off French
challenger Vazirabad to win the 2018
Gold Cup at Ascot. The chestnut colt
must now be worth seven figures but
still some way short of the record
Stradivarius violin price. That's
£9.8 million.

The eyes have it
The Duke and Duchess of Sussex,
aka Prince Harry and Meghan
Markle, on the winning podium
before presenting the trophy for
the 2018 St James Palace Stakes.

Hat tricks at Ascot
A kaleidoscope of colours and
design beyond anything else
on the turf or off it.

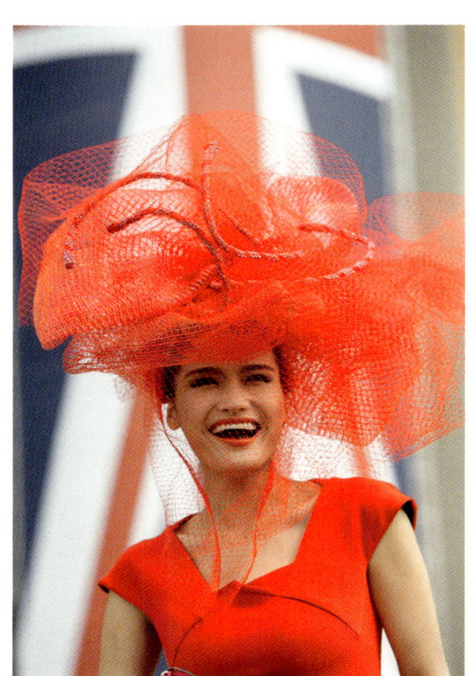

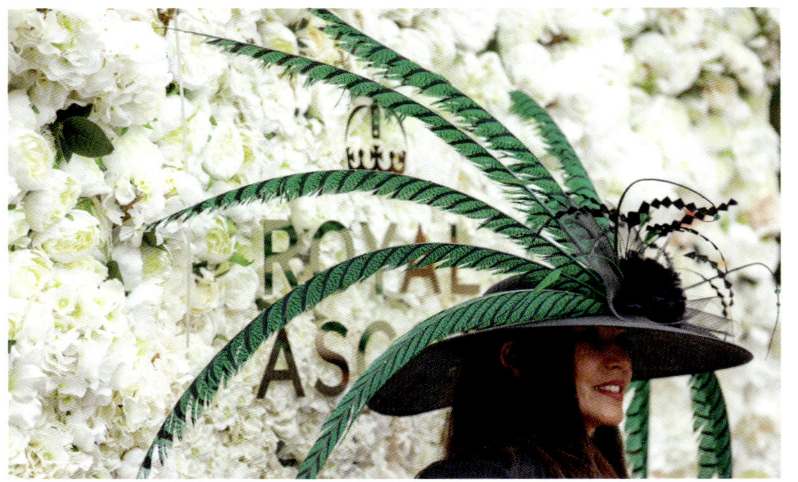

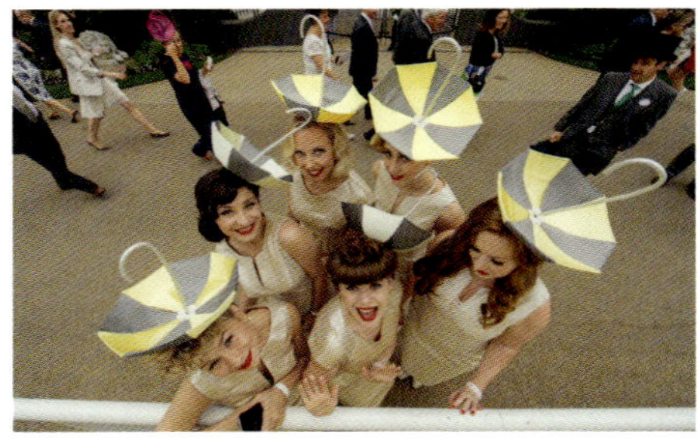

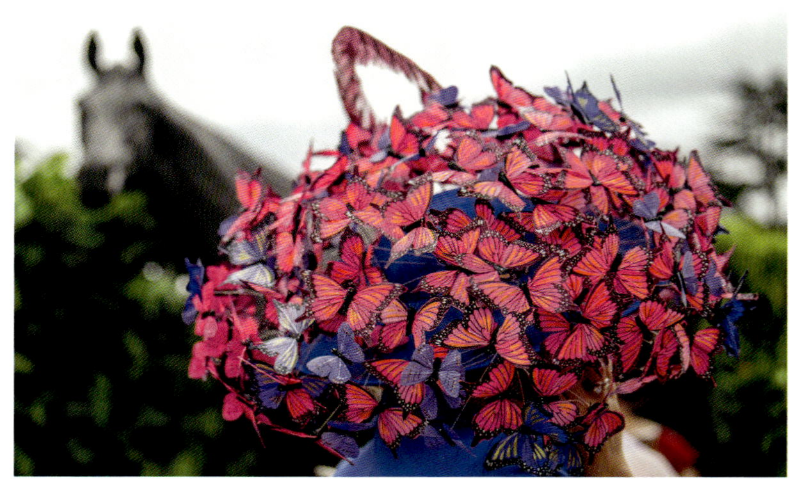

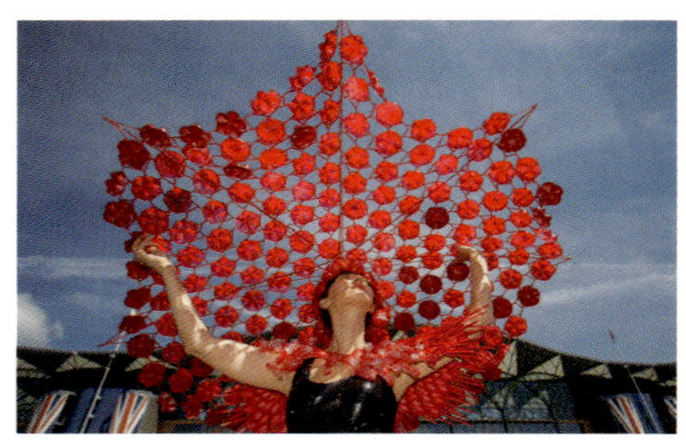

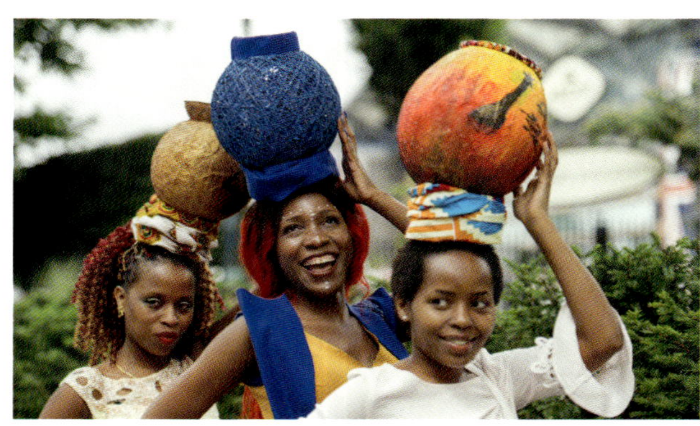

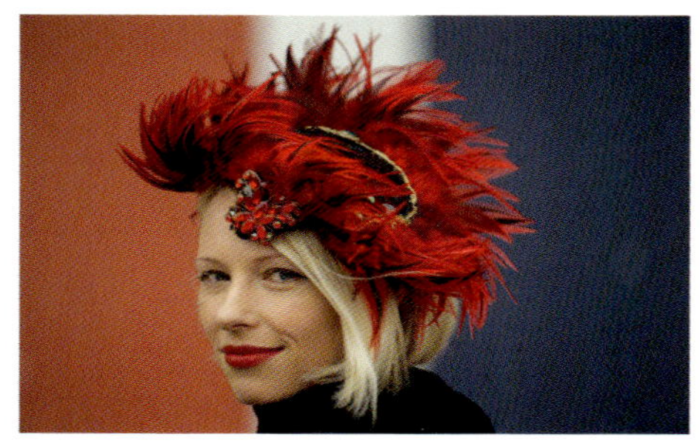

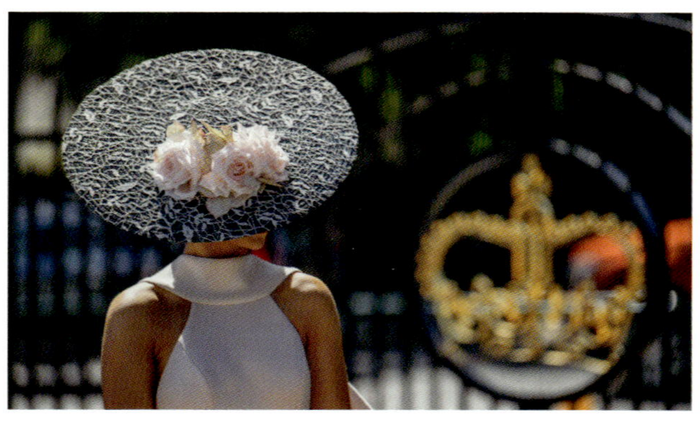

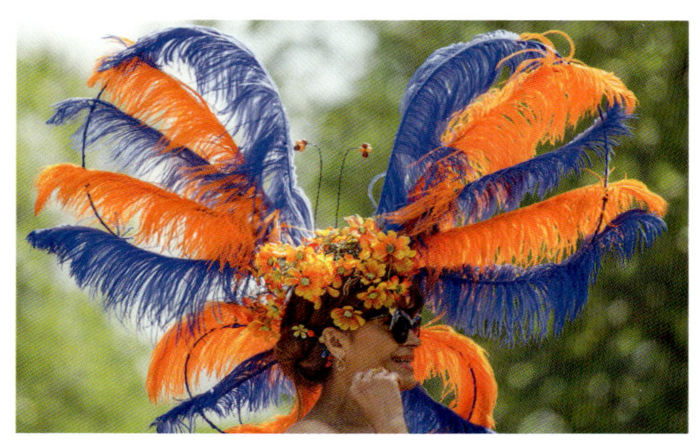
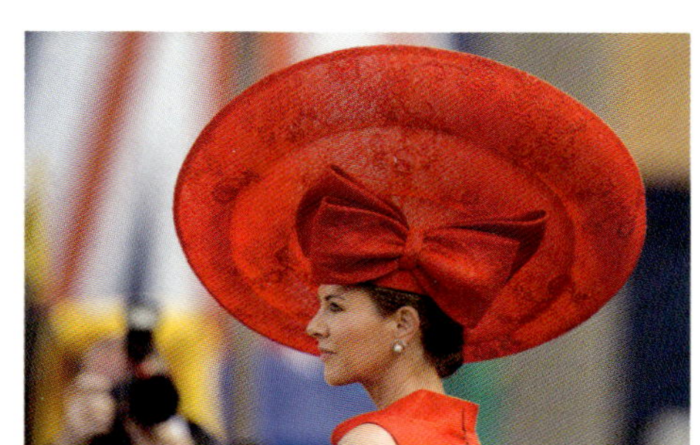
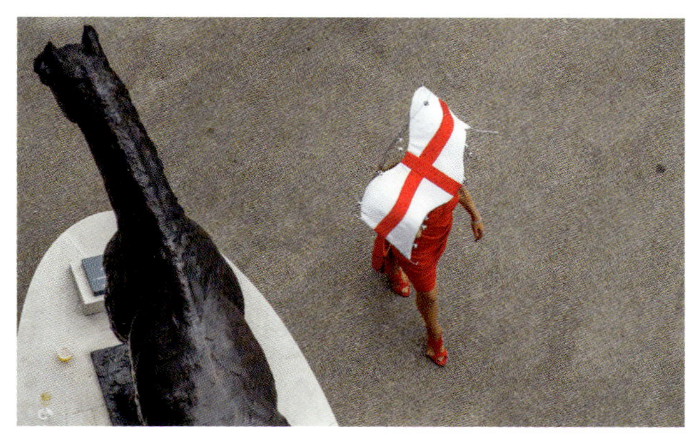
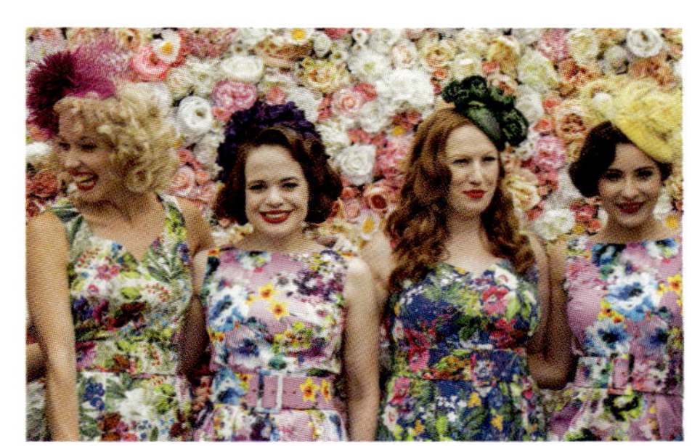
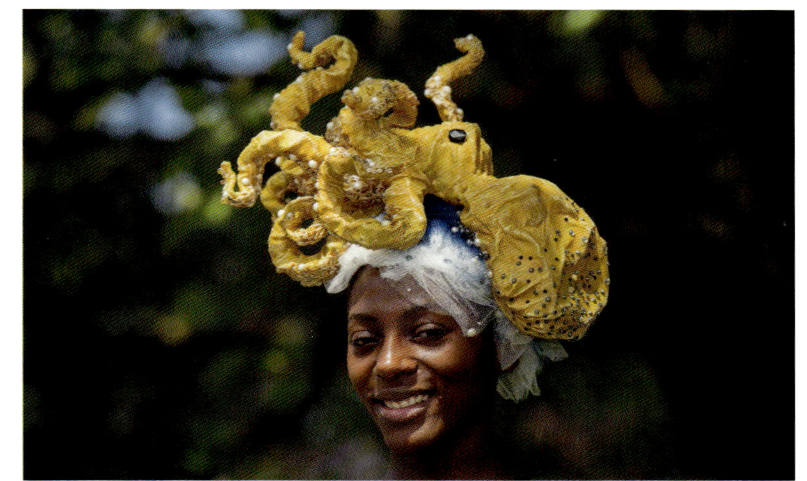
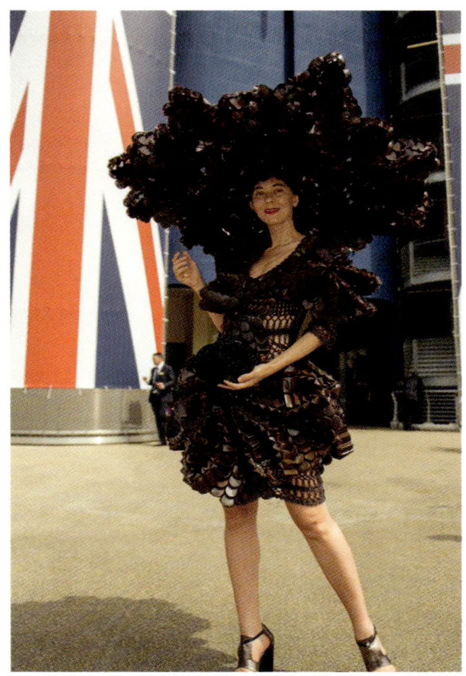
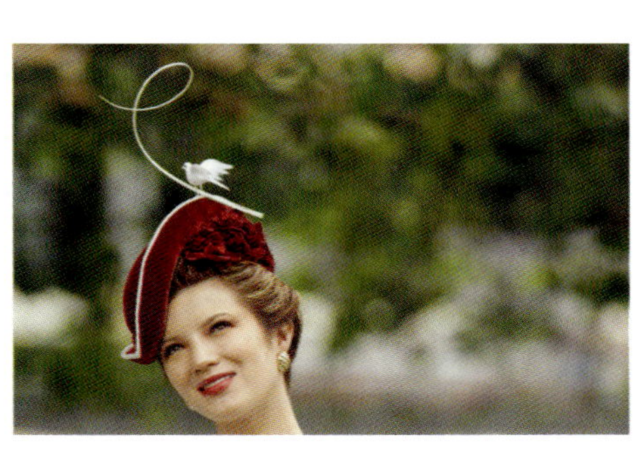
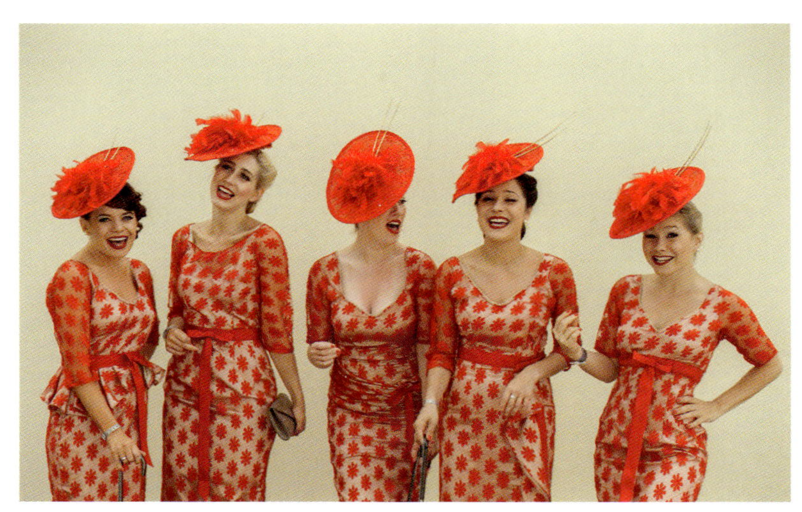

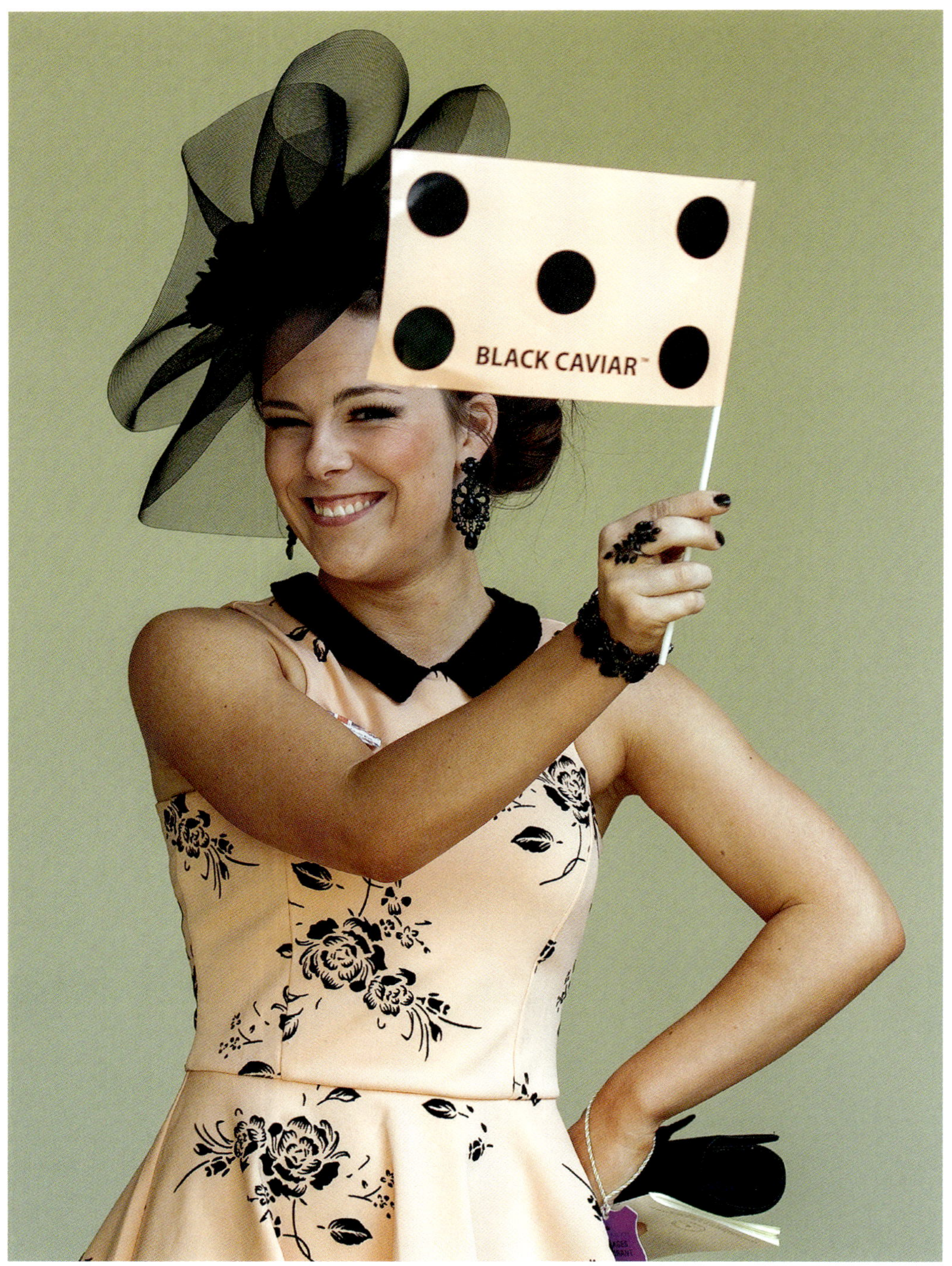

No fan like an Aussie fan
Australian sprint superstar
Black Caviar brought the biggest
international following ever seen
at Ascot. Supporters like this didn't
think they had travelled this far to see
her lose her 21-race winning streak.

Black Caviar wins – just
Luke Nolen's brain fade. Jockey
Luke Nolen swept 1/6 shot Black
Caviar through to head the Diamond
Jubilee field, only, at the moment
pictured, to ease down prematurely.
The wait for the photo-finish verdict
must have been the tensest moment
of his life.

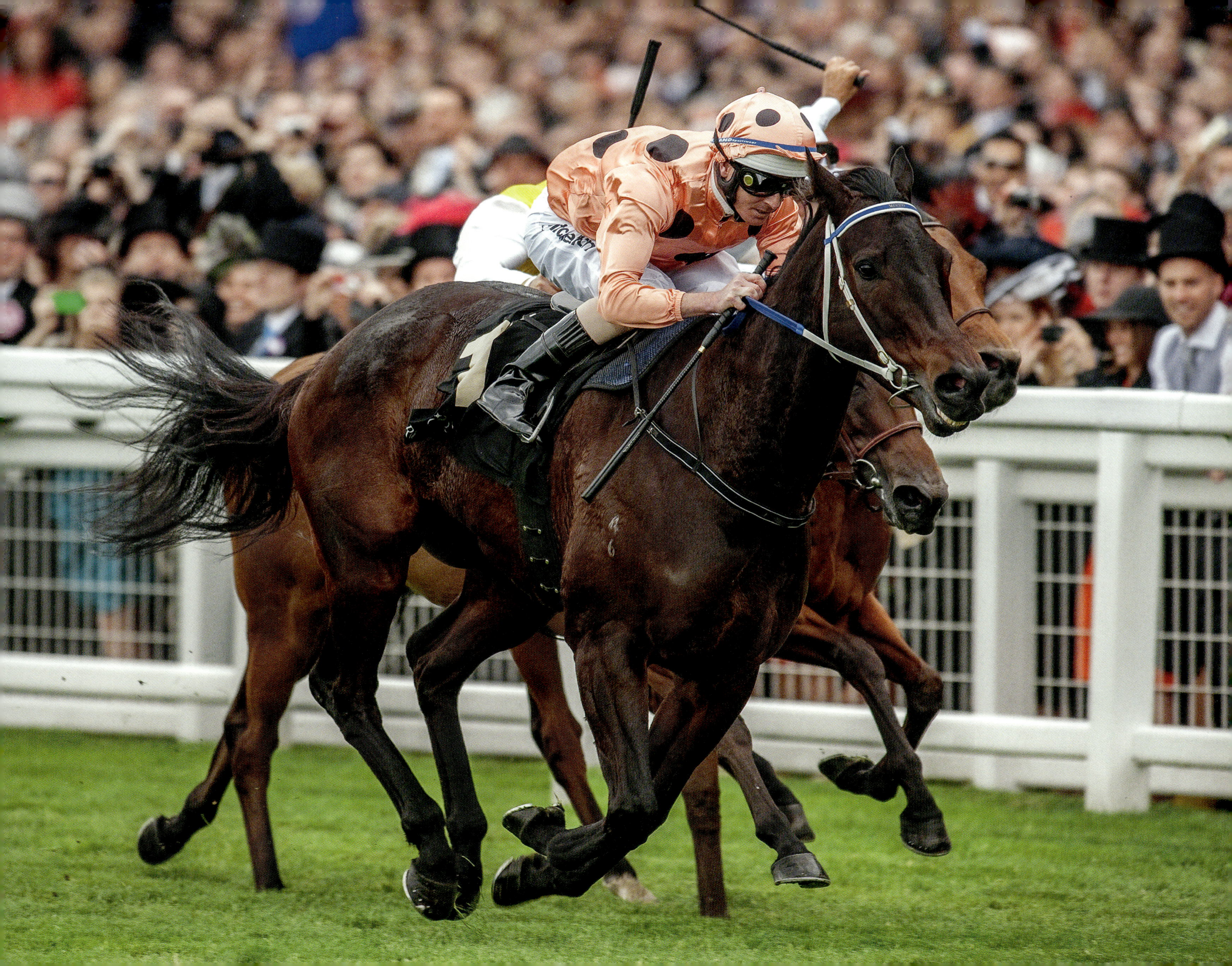

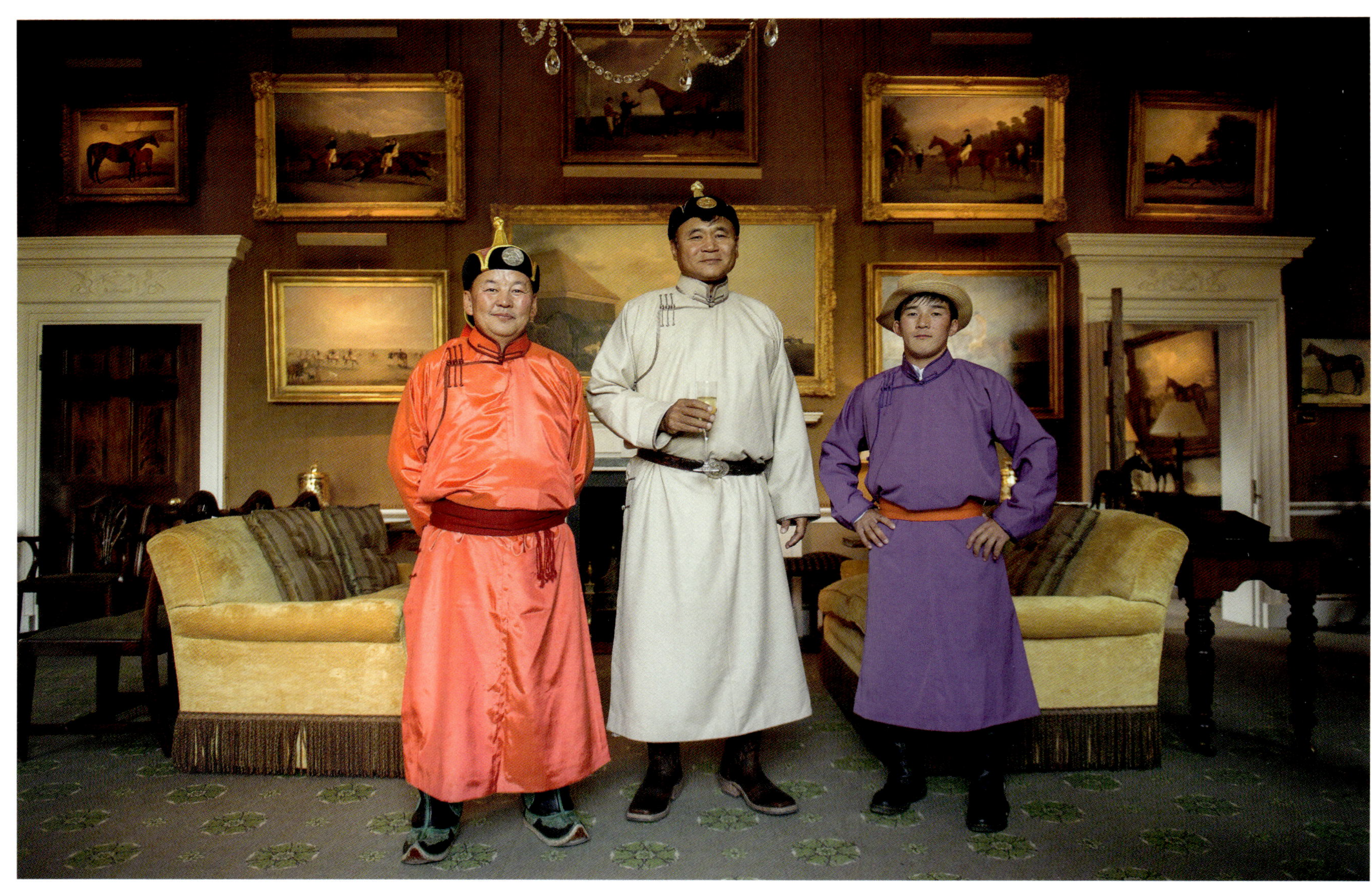

National costume at Newmarket
In 2016, Mongolian Saturday was
a first-ever Royal Ascot runner
from Mongolian connections. They
cut quite a figure at the pre-Ascot
reception held in the historic Jockey
Club Rooms at Newmarket.

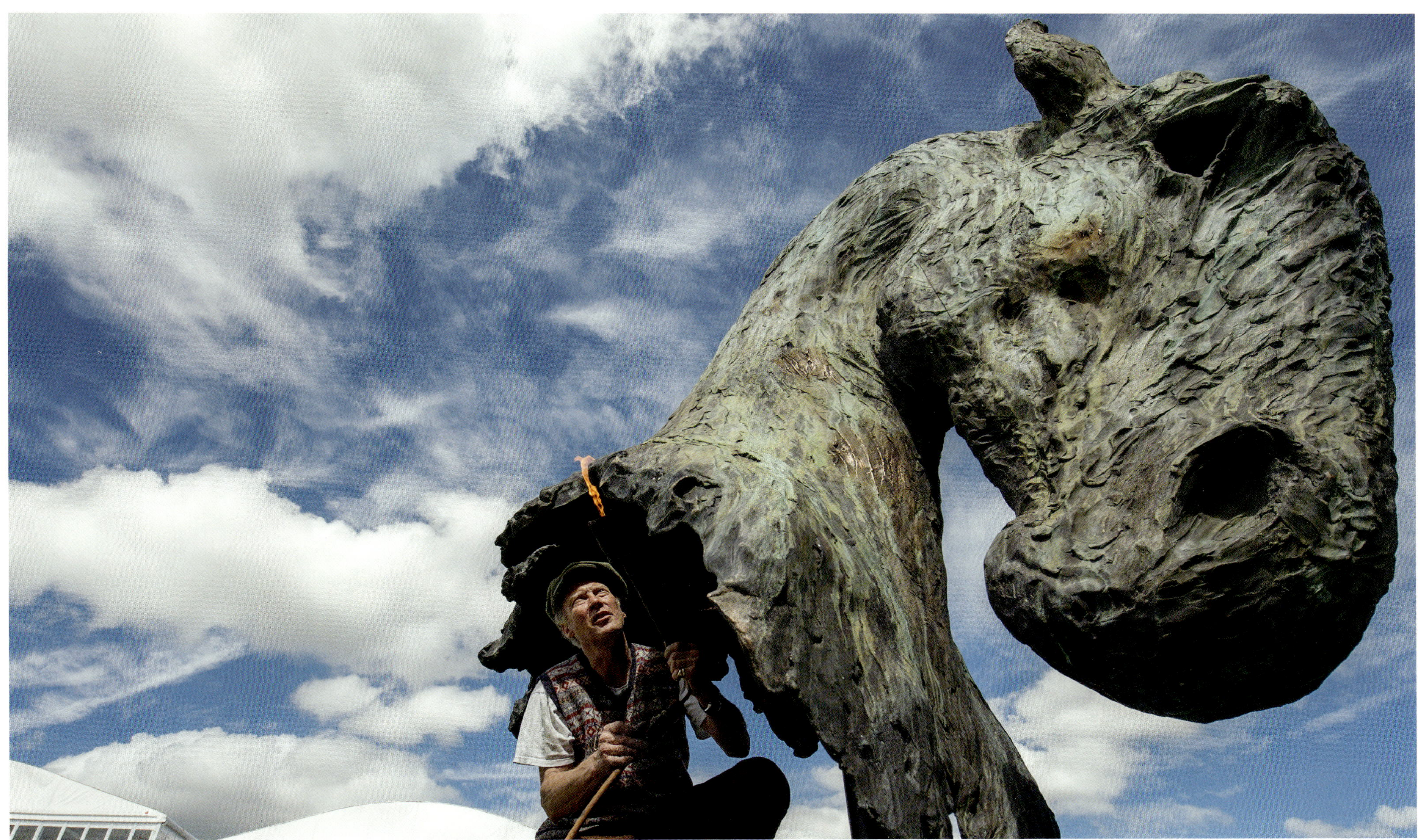

The man behind the head
Nic Fiddian-Green's distinctive
horses' heads have become one
of the most recognisable sights
in contemporary equine sculpture.
But we usually see the heads not the
man. Here he is working on the eve
of Royal Ascot 2013.

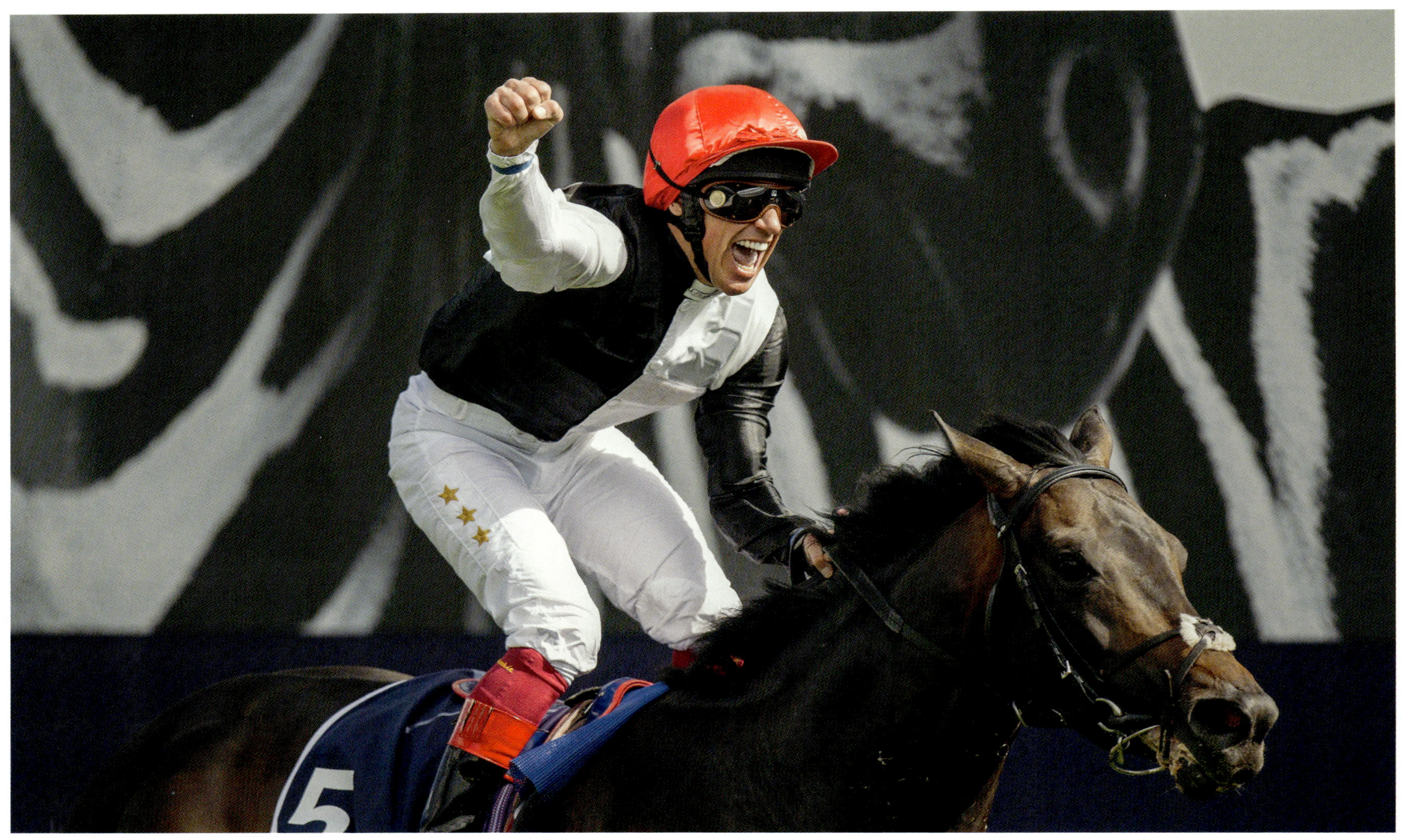

Derby delight
Colour co-ordinated. Frankie
celebrates as he and Golden Horn
pass the post in the 2015 Derby.
Sponsors' logos and a jockey's
silks, cap and boots rarely blend
as perfectly as this.

Epsom Downs on Derby Day
Helter-skelter, merry-go-round,
open top buses, green-groomed turf
and horses flashing by in a splash of
colour and noise. Three centuries on,
Derby Day is still a timeless moment
in the nation's story.

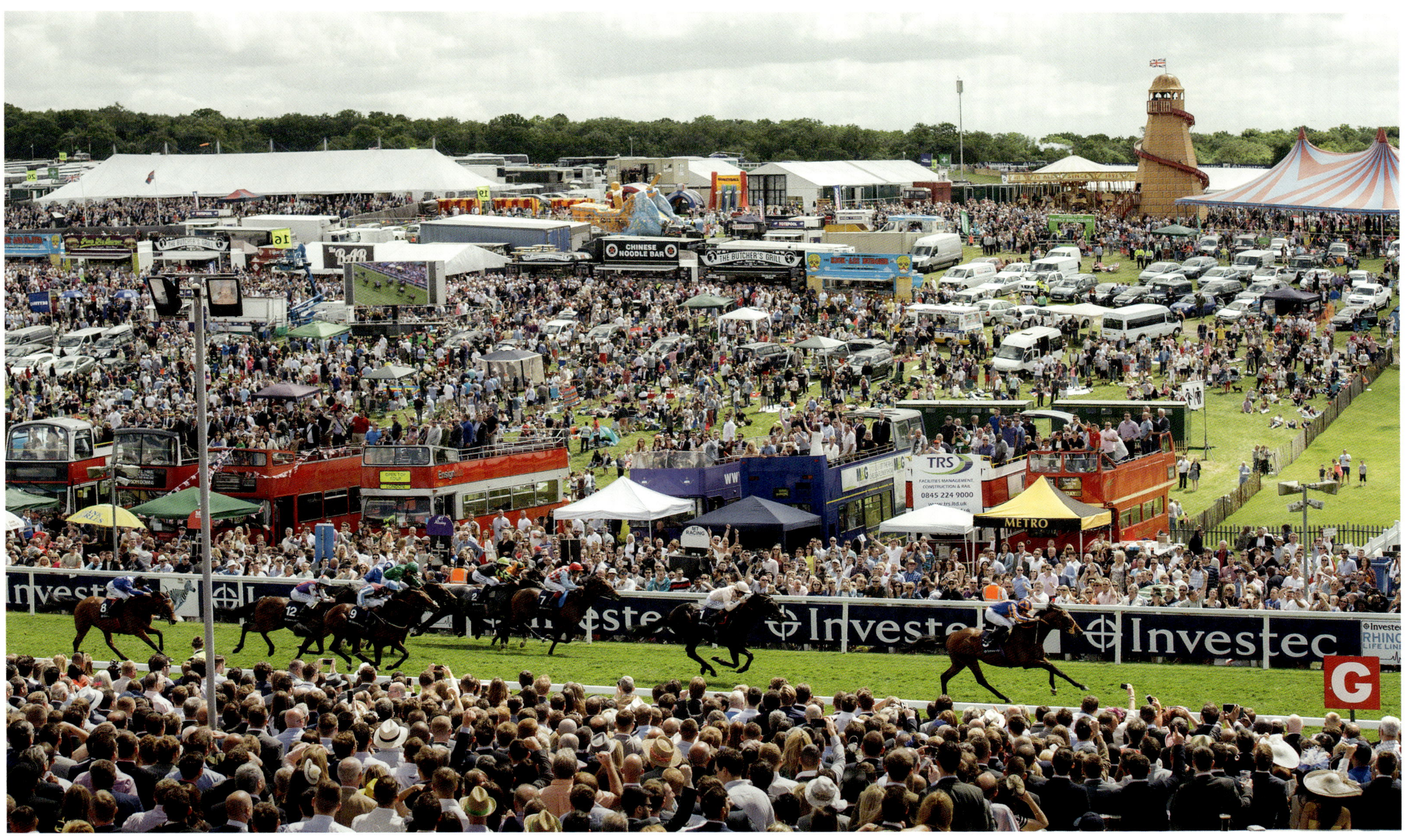

CHINESE NOODLE BAR
THE BUTCHER'S GRILL
THE BUTCHER'S GRILL
THE BAR
TRS
FACILITIES MANAGEMENT,
CONSTRUCTION & RAIL
0845 224 9000
www.trs.ltd.uk
M&G
OPEN TOP TOUR
Investec
Investec
Investec
METRO
G

July

Boats and manes

Horse and boat power on a Monday evening. The runners wing past Windsor Marina before the final run back to the winning post.

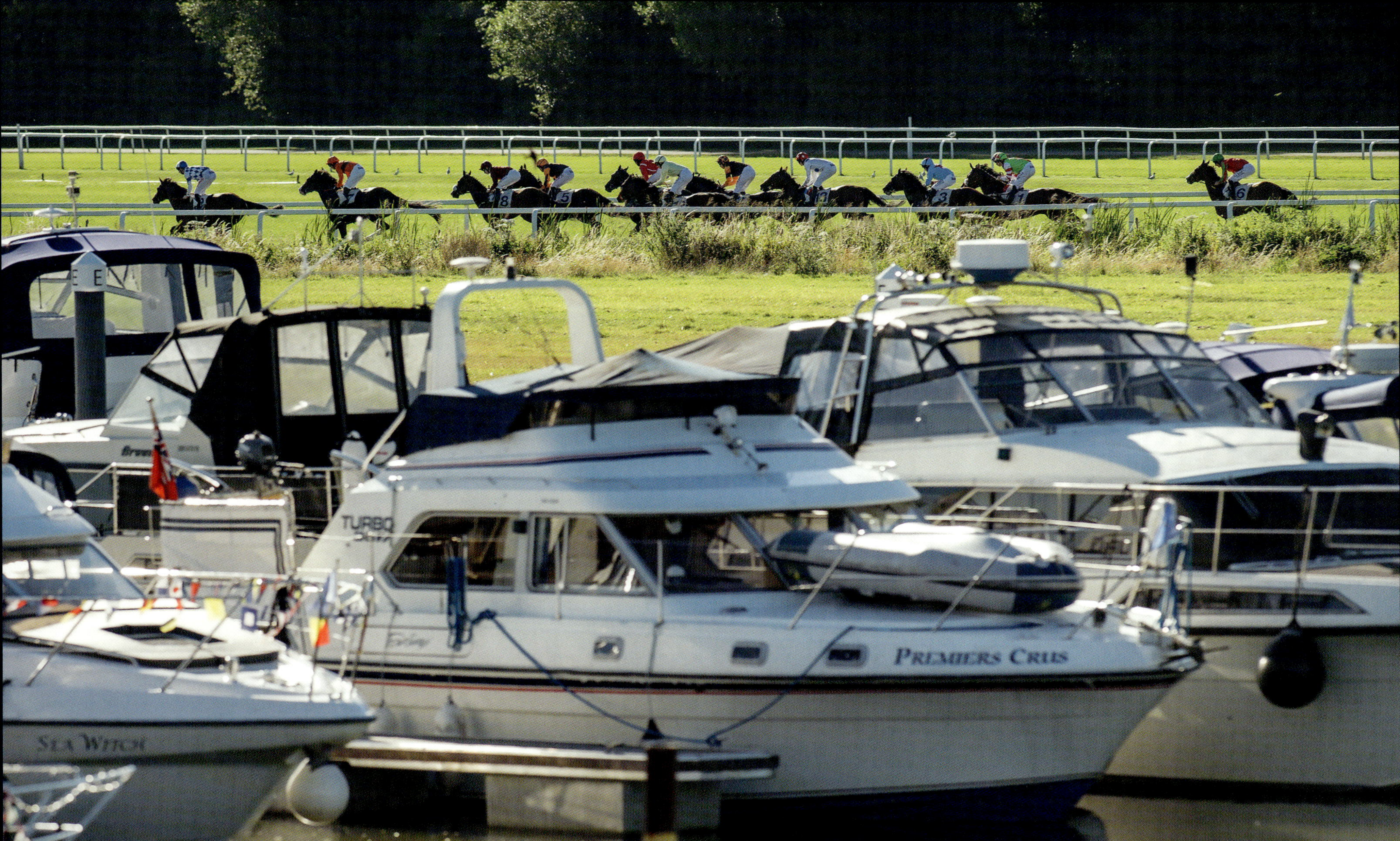

SEA WITCH
TURBO
PREMIERS CRUS

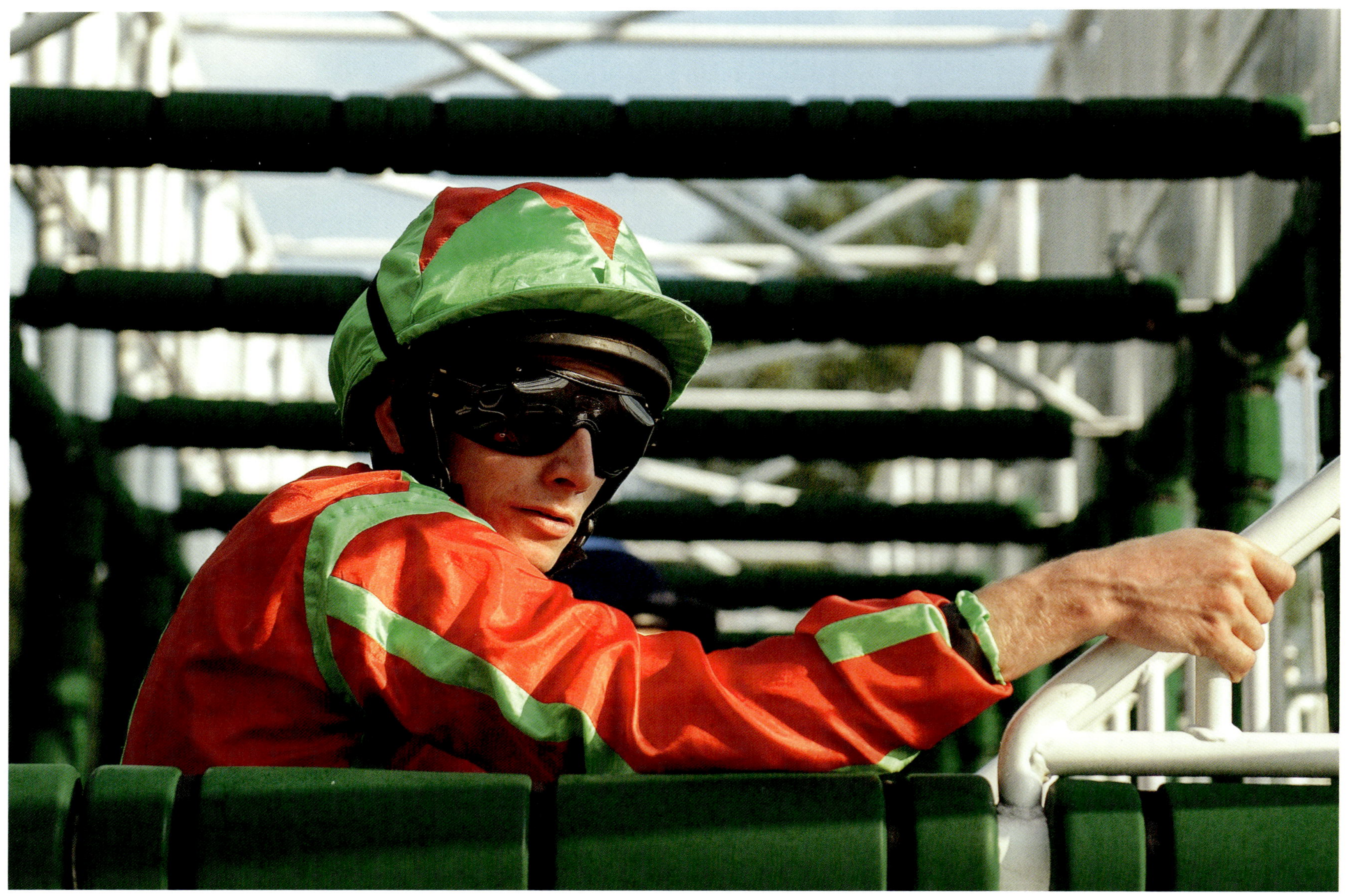

Calm and then collection
Ryan Moore sits quietly on Danz
Choice before leaping out of the
stalls (opposite) and going on to
victory at Sandown.

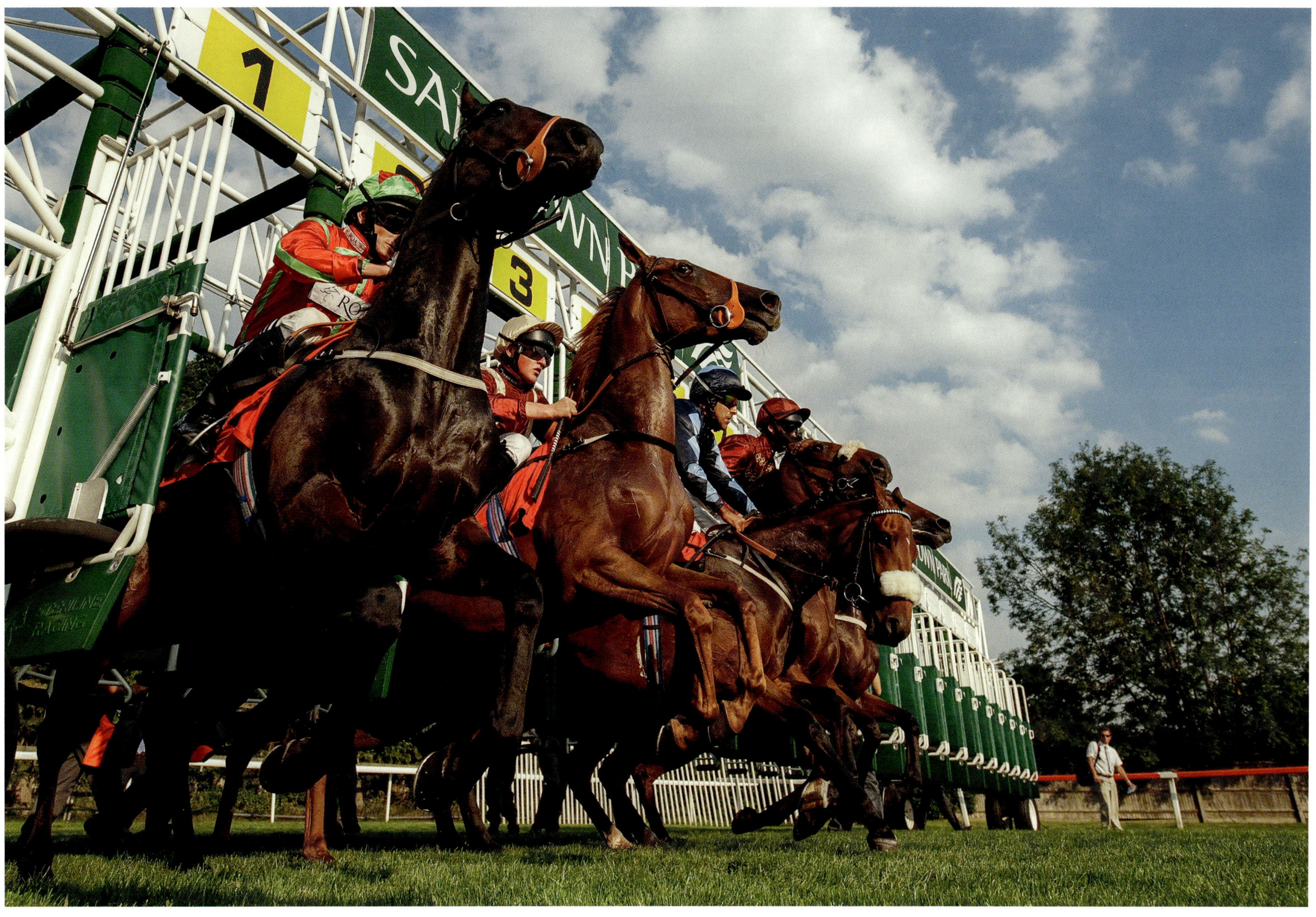

1
SA
3
WN P

Wash down for New Approach
Stallion men Ken Crozier (left) and
Darren Palmer get doused as stallion
New Approach shakes himself at
Dalham Hall. New Approach won the
2008 Derby and ten years later his
son Masar was to do the same.

King of the range
Dubawi is top of the Dalham Hall
Stud stallion roster and carries
himself as if he knows it. In his place
plenty of what glitters actually
turns to gold.

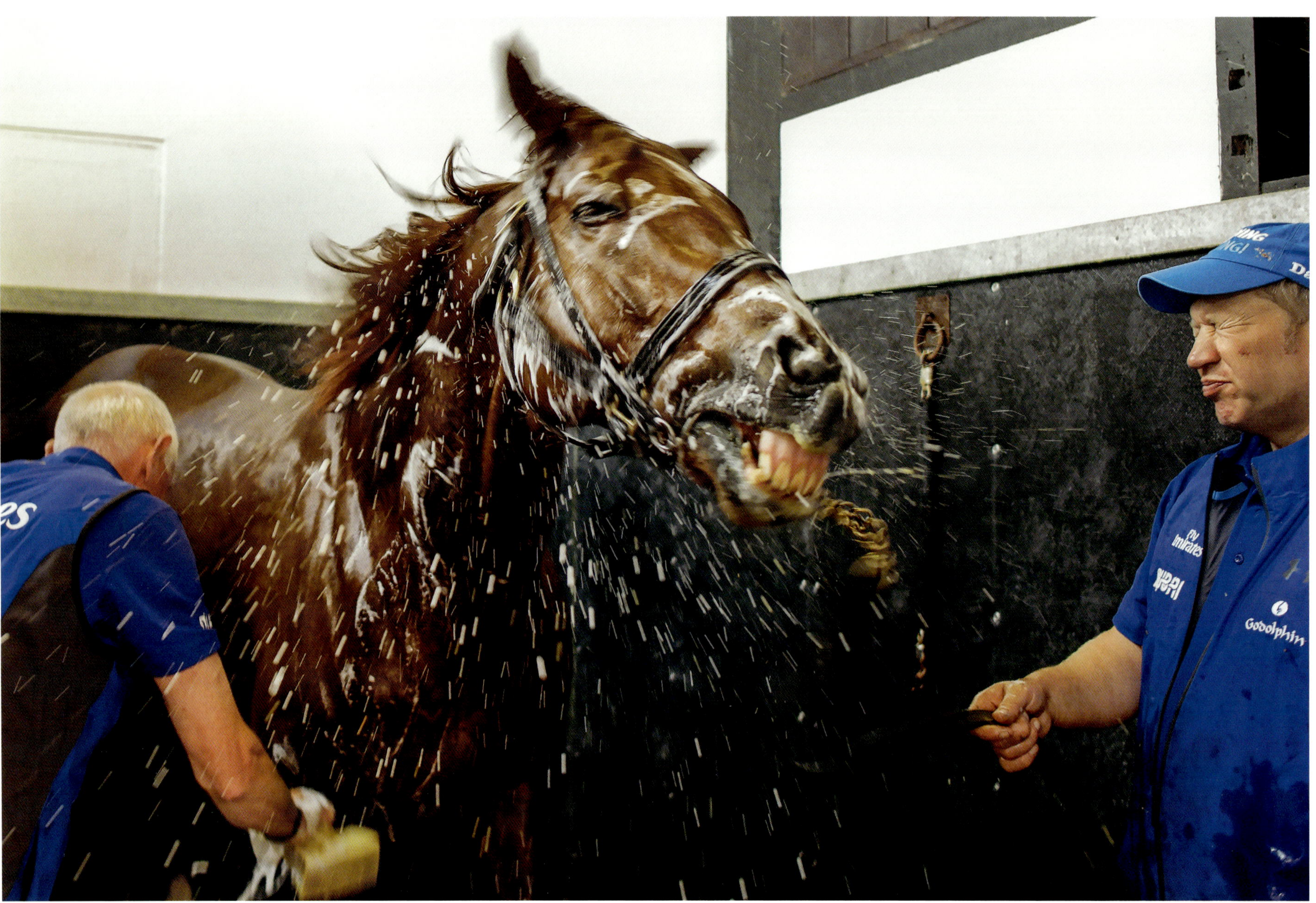

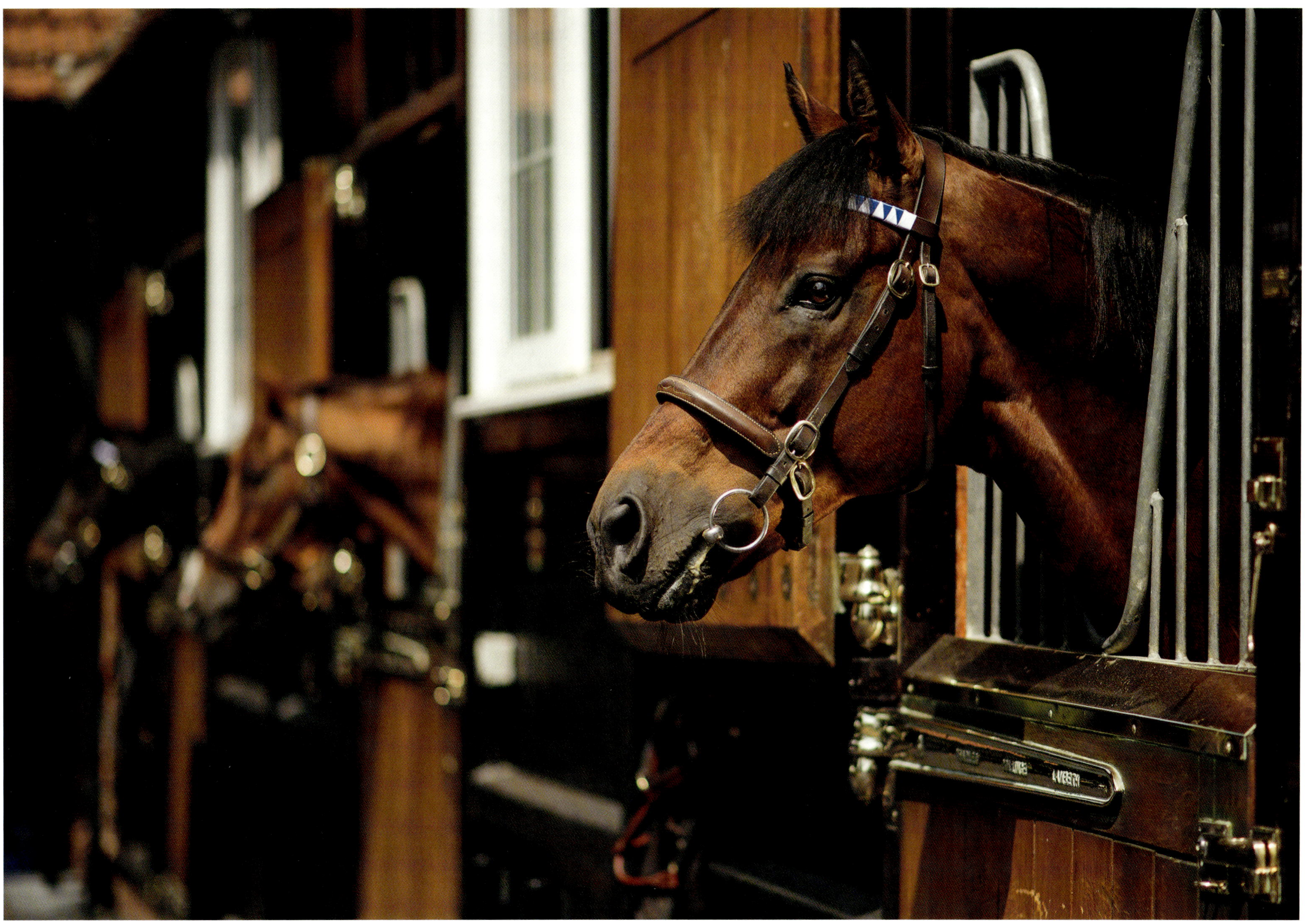

Yorkshire glory
Mark Johnston's horses returning
from exercise at Middleham with the
Yorkshire Dales as a backdrop. The
stable has won more races than any
other in British racing history.

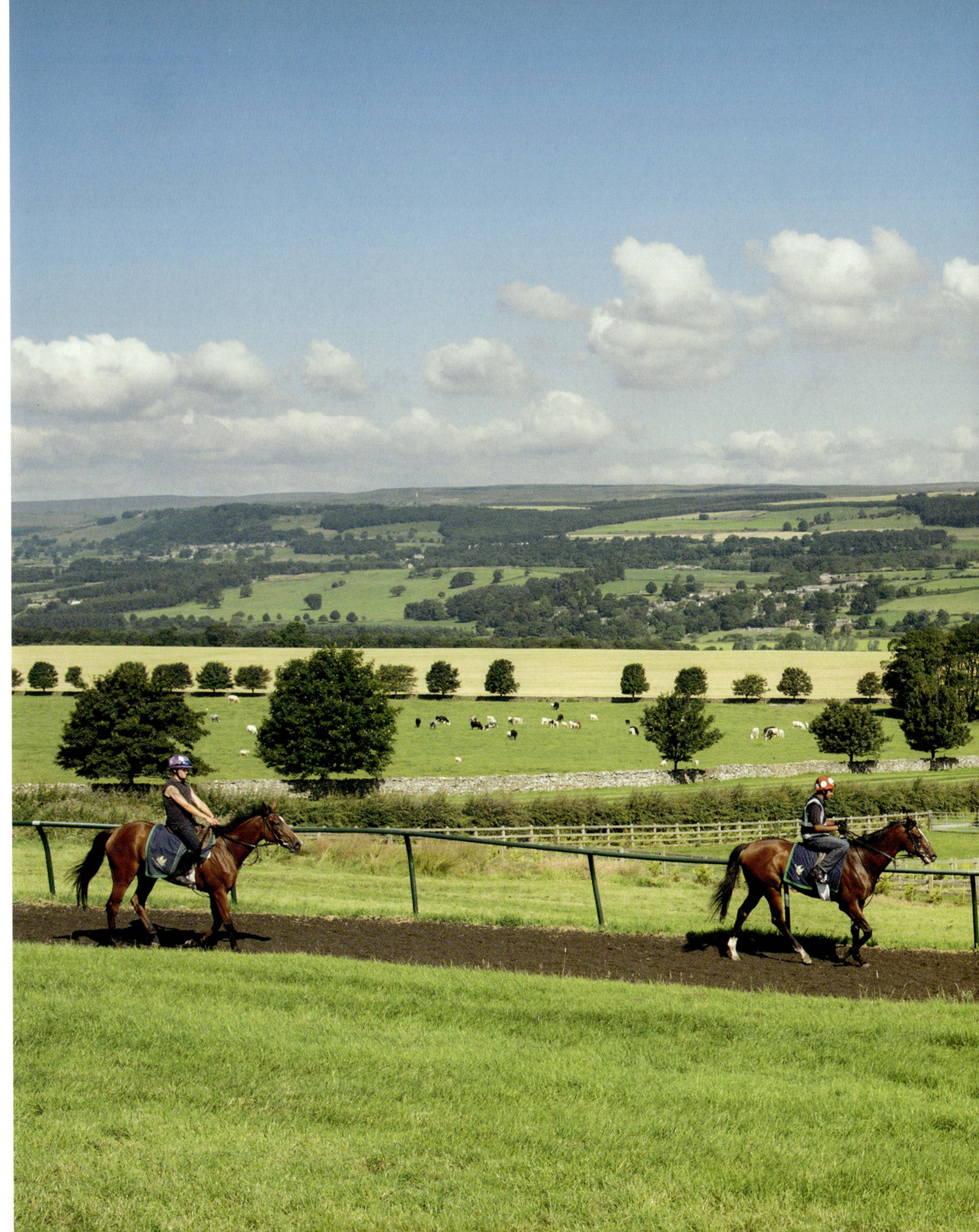

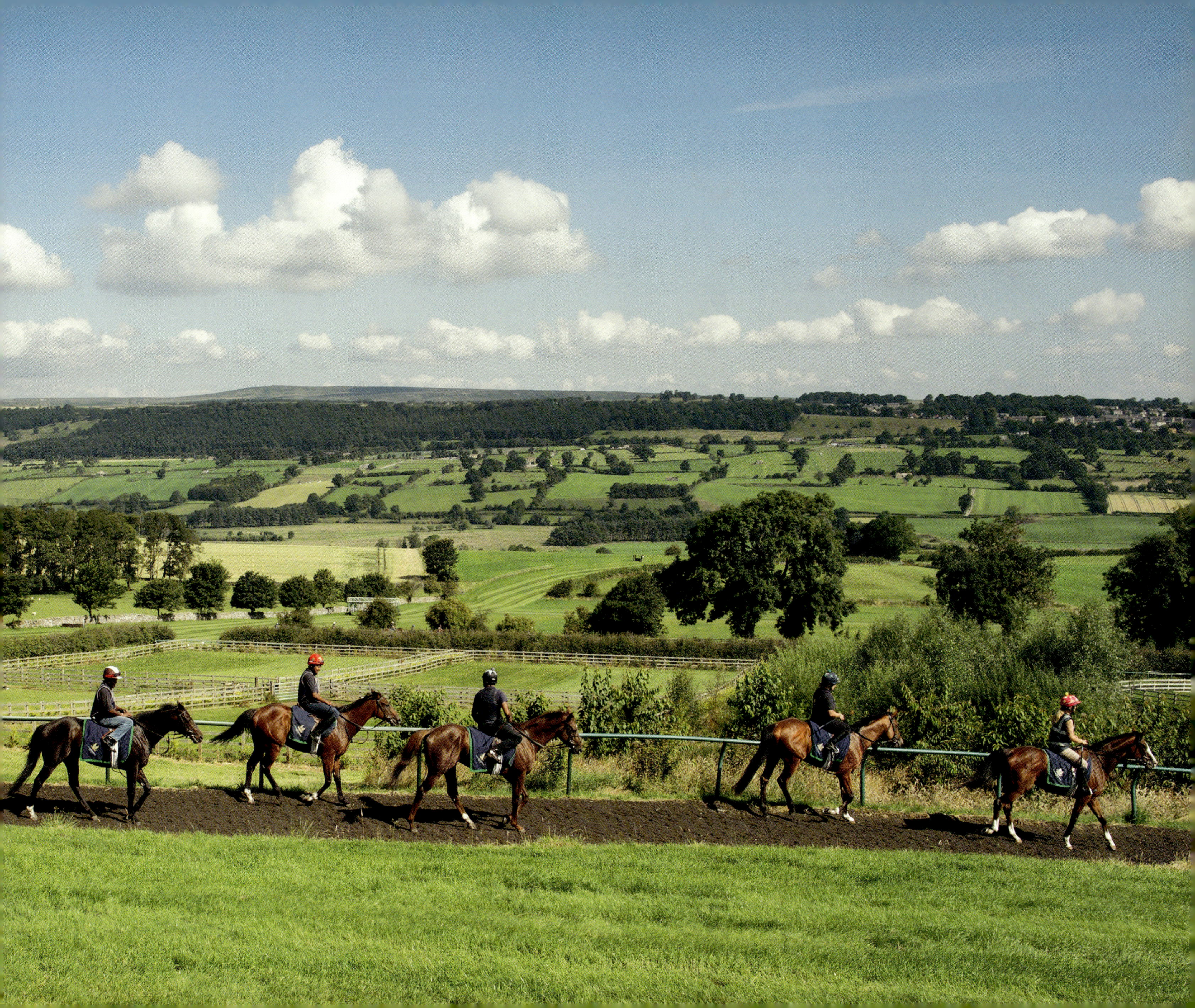

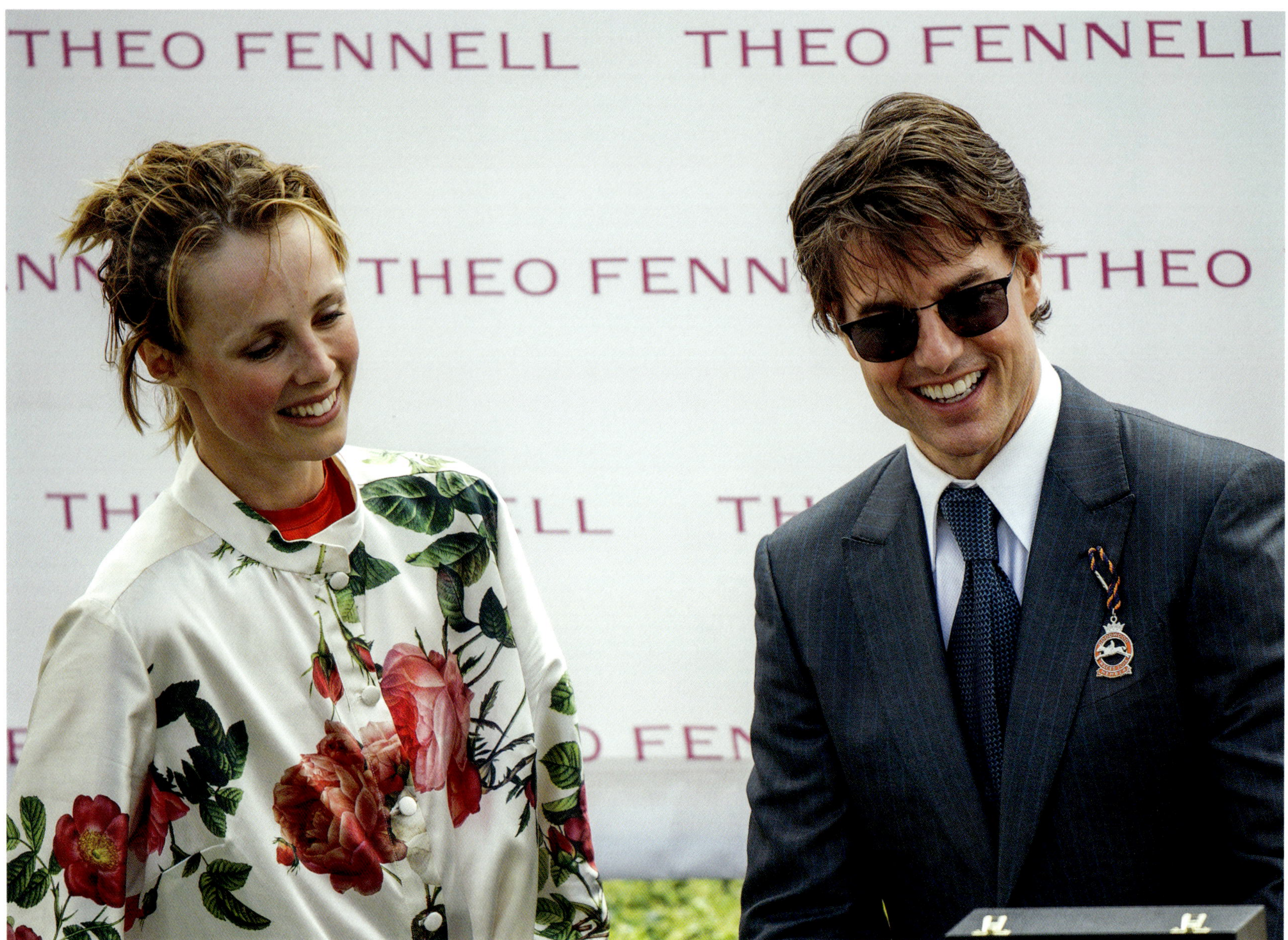

Mission easily possible
American megastar Tom Cruise
presents supermodel Edie Campbell
with her trophy for winning the
Charity Ladies Race at Goodwood.

Cool down
Travelling head girl Jitka Krajmerova
leads the appropriately named
Seaside Sizzler past the newly
installed cooling fans at Ascot
in 2016.

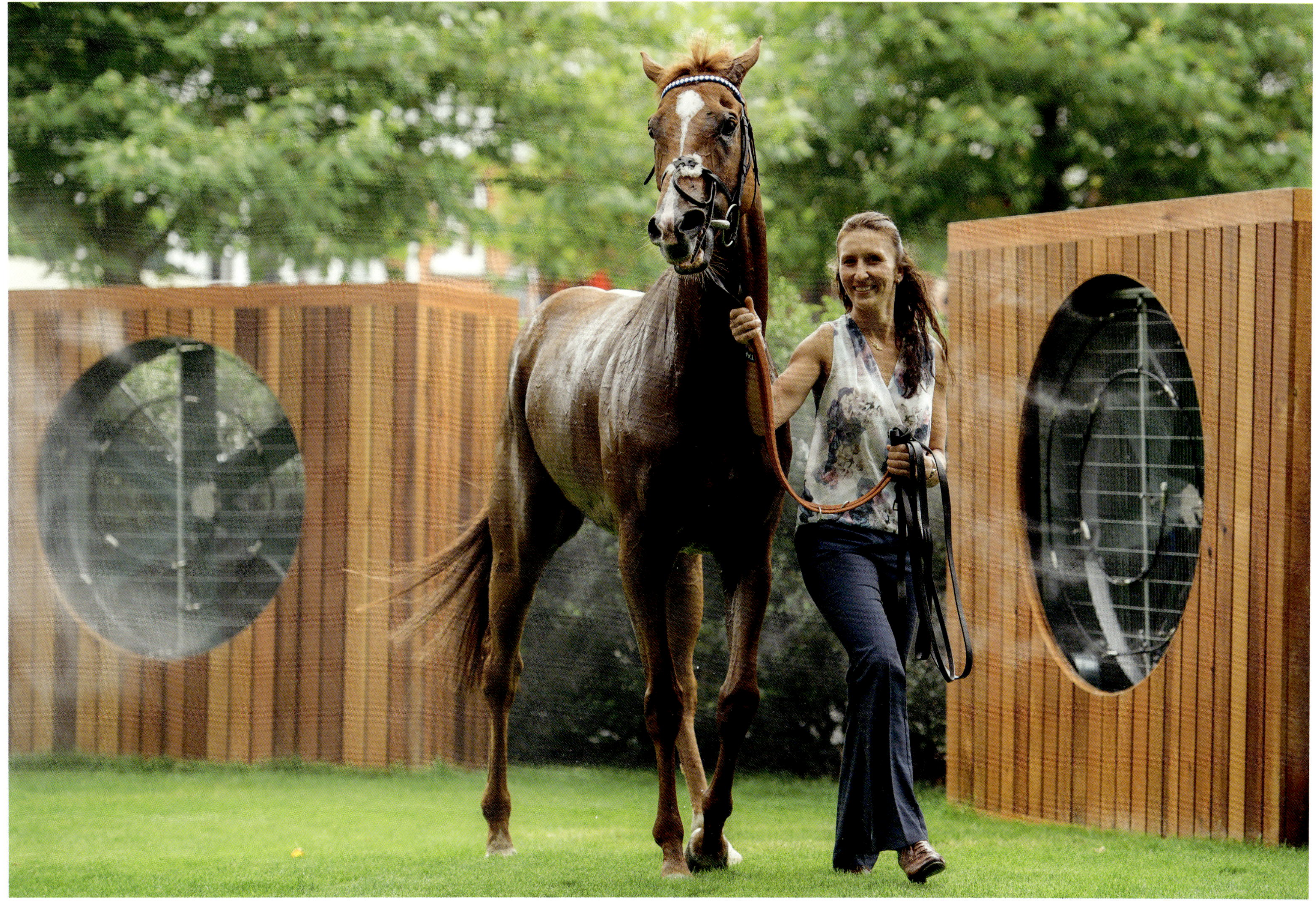

Power on the hoof
The massive Alpha Centauri storms
home under Colm O'Donoghue
to win the Falmouth Stakes at
Newmarket's July Meeting. The
three-year-old filly is bigger than
most jumps horses but this and her
Royal Ascot victory stamped her
as a special star on the Flat.

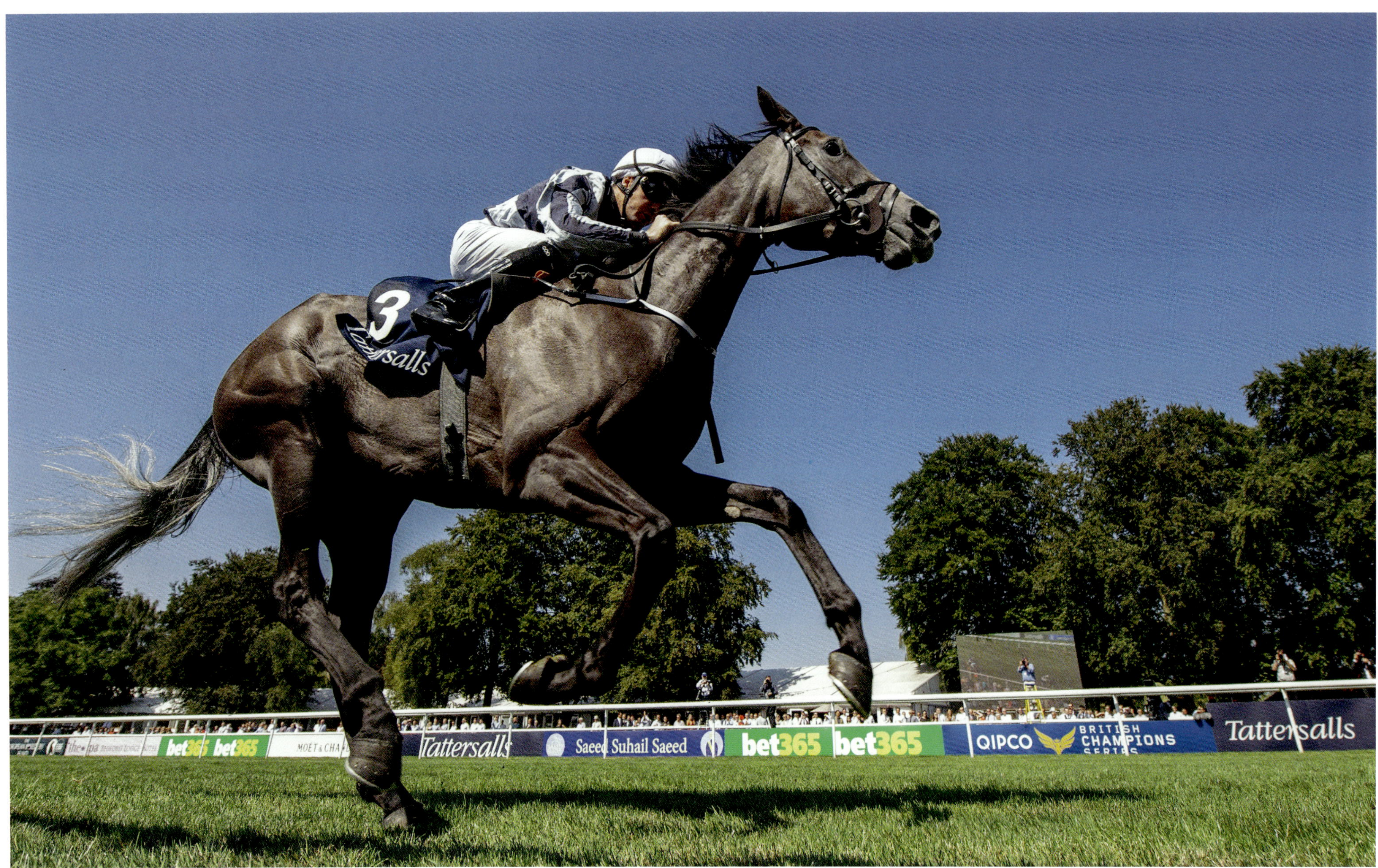

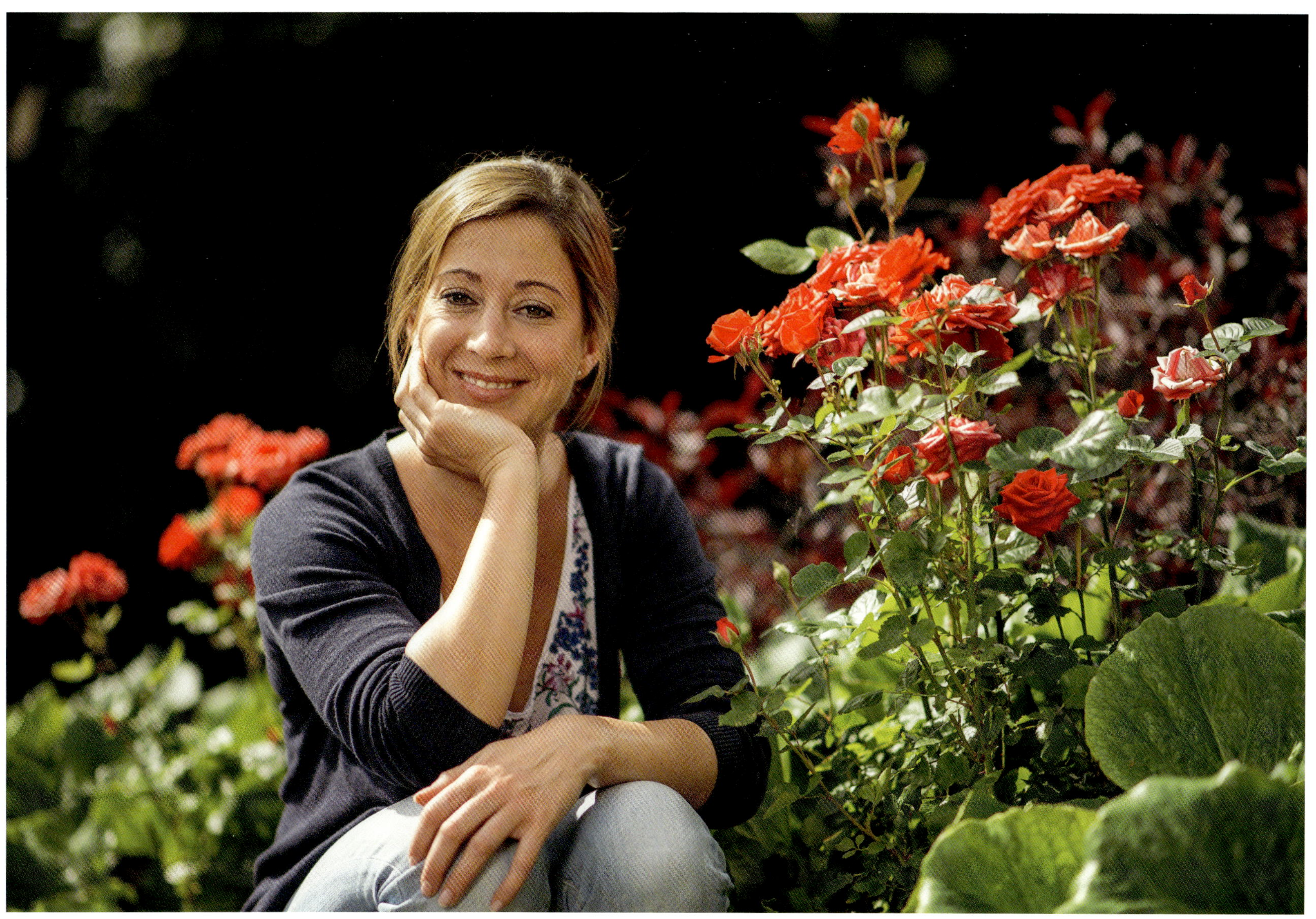

Hayley Turner
Mould-breaking jockey Hayley
Turner sits by the roses in her
Newmarket garden. Hayley is very
proud of her prowess in the 'man's
world' of the racetrack but she
guards her femininity too.

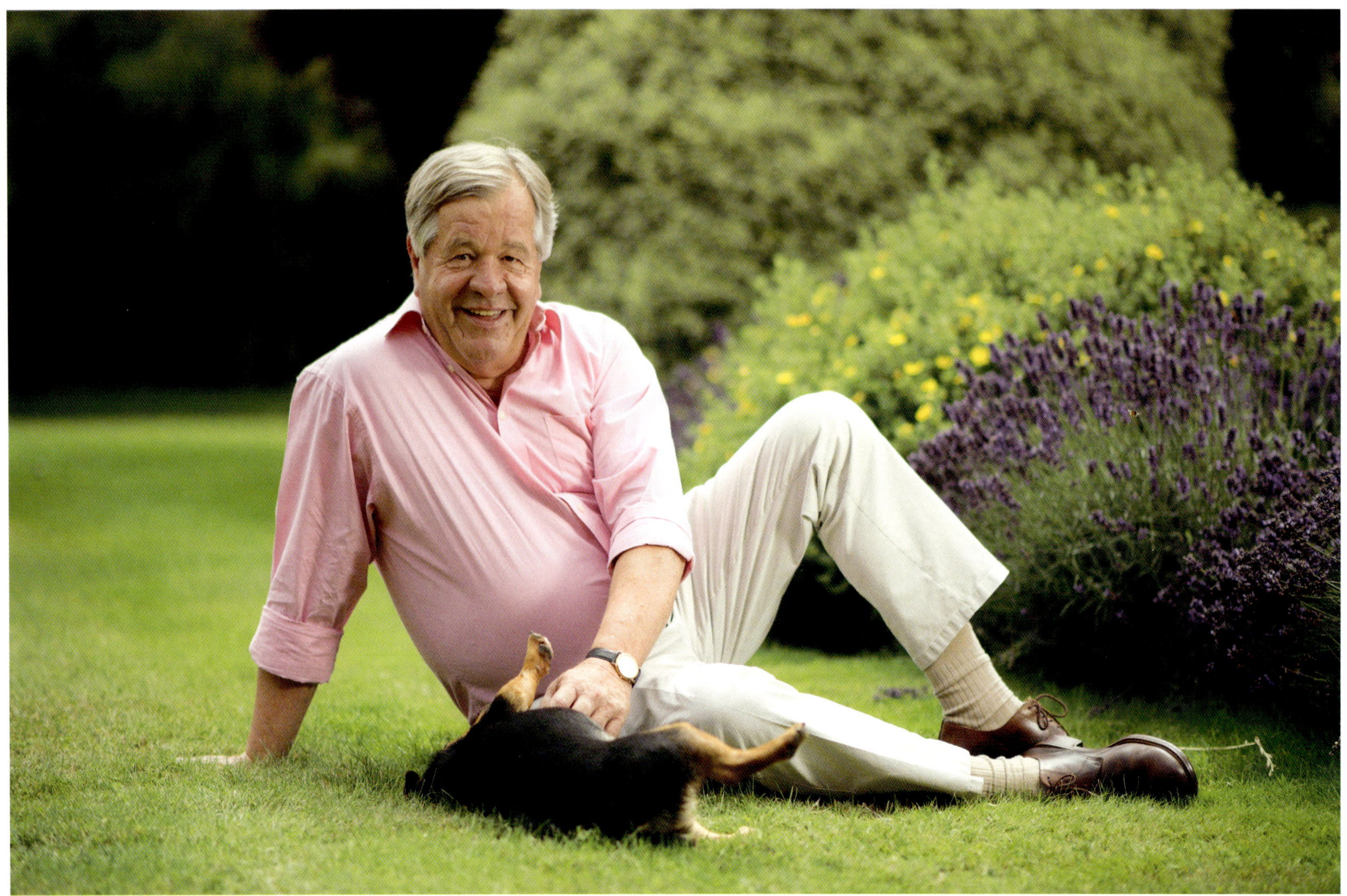

Michael Stoute
On the racetrack, Sir Michael Stoute can be focused to the point of brusqueness. This picture shows that back in his garden he can be a different fellow.

Spectacles
Rose-tinted. The July Course has its own 'old mixed with new' atmosphere. It even shines out in reflection.

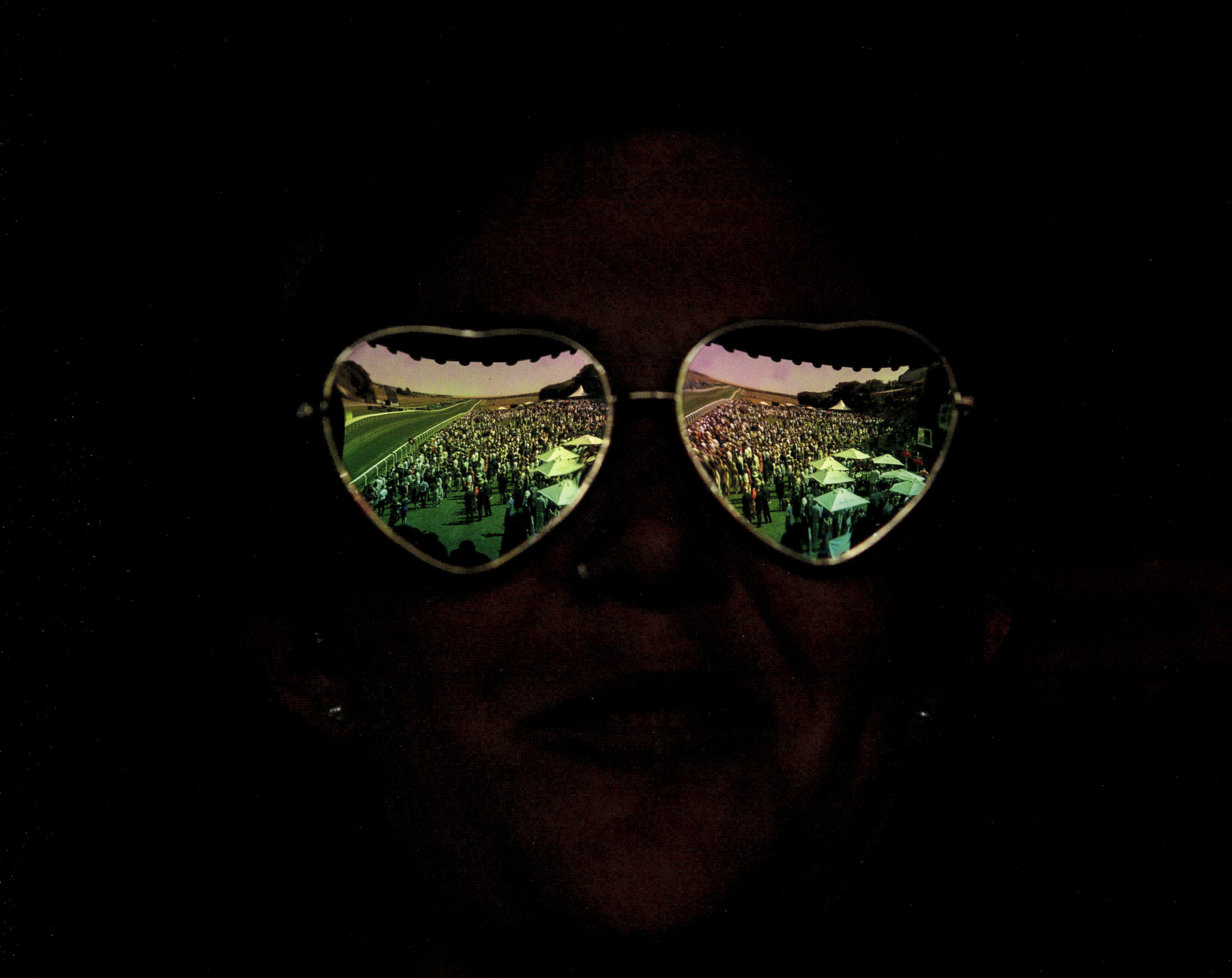

August

Sunburst at Goodwood
A view through the leaves as the runners reach the top of the hill. British racing has some wonderful settings but few better than out in the country at Goodwood.

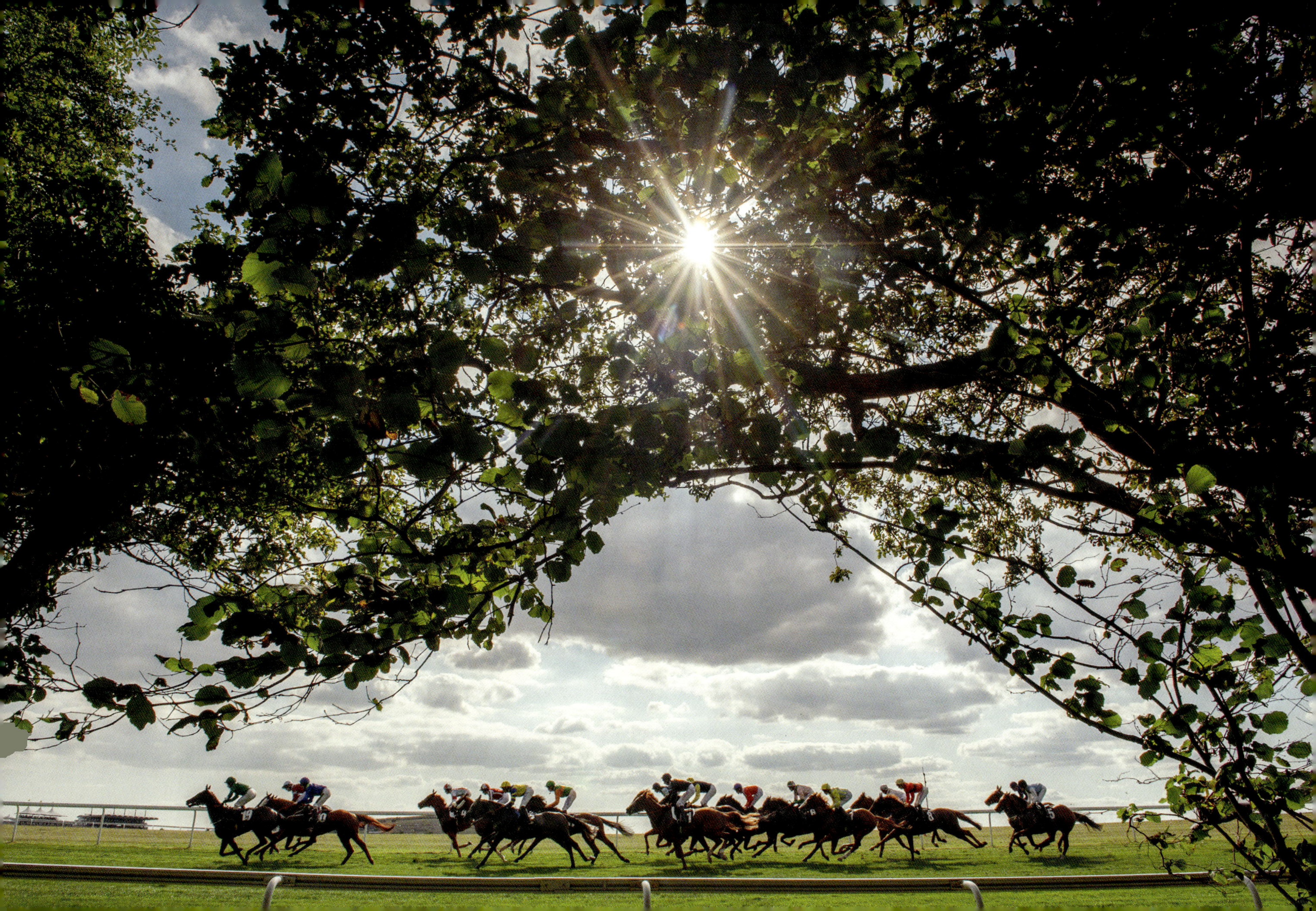

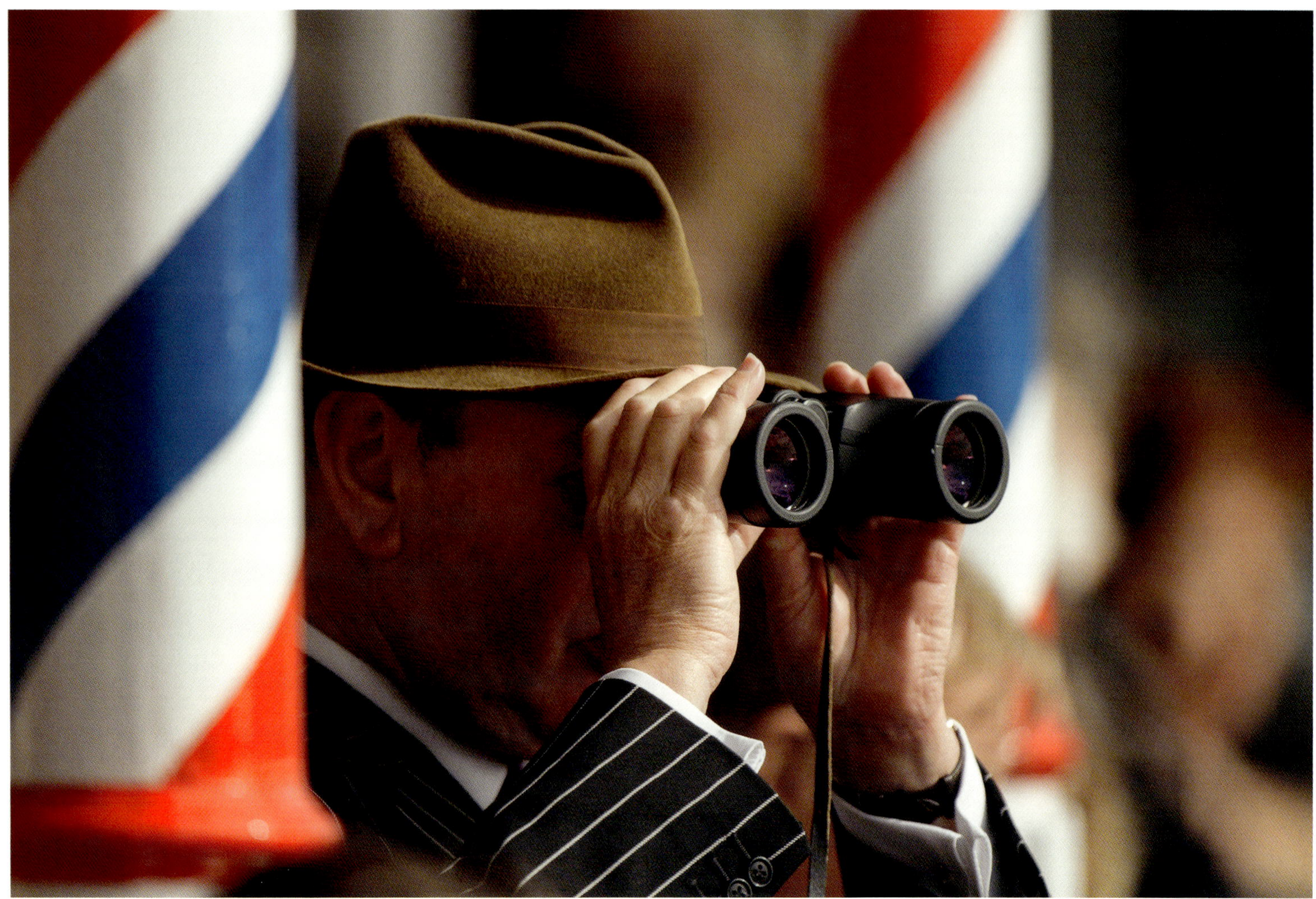

The blur of action
I love to photograph the 6f start
at Goodwood as the dark woodland
background gives up no distractions.
Shooting against the light and using
a slow shutter speed gives this great
impression of speed and colour.

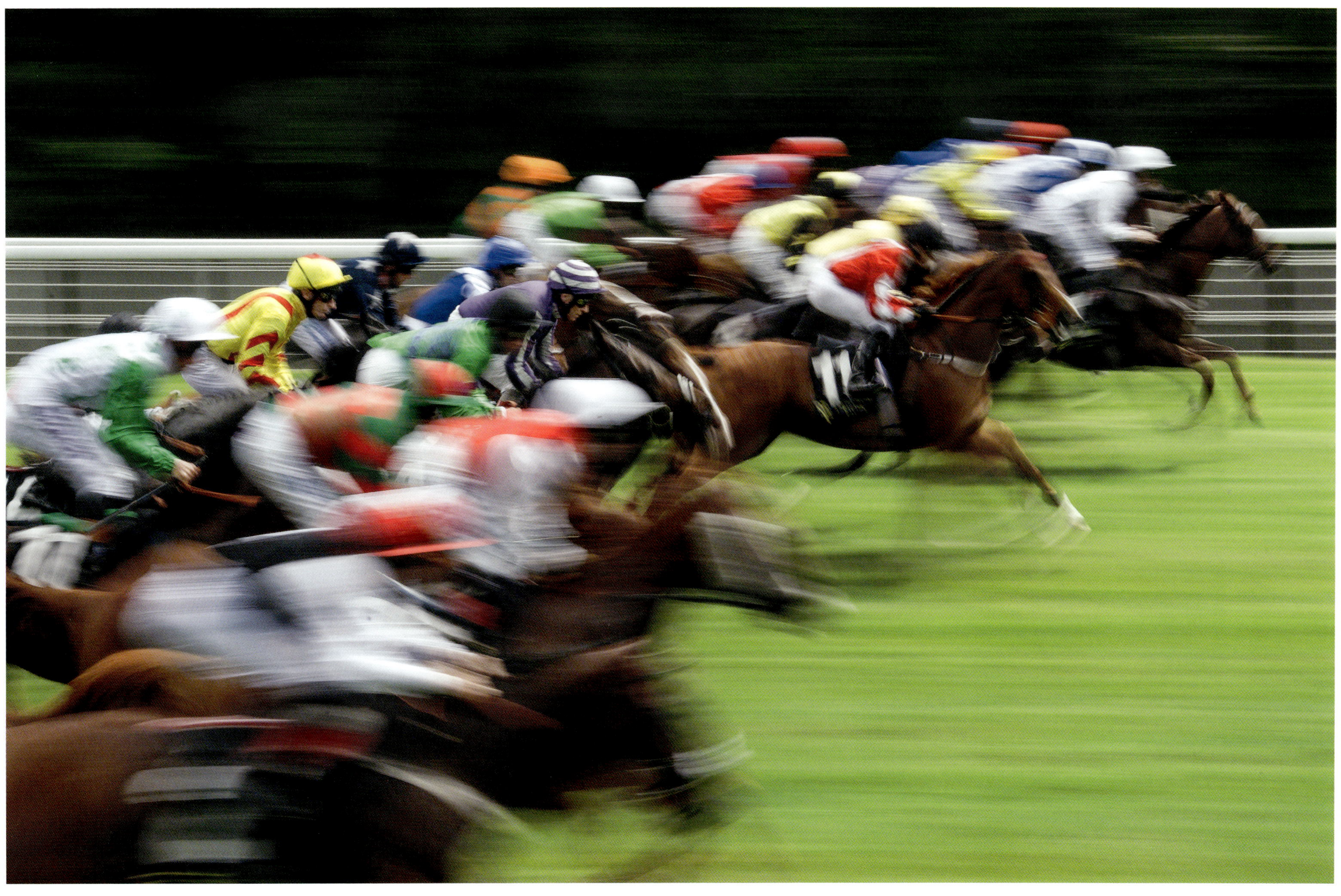

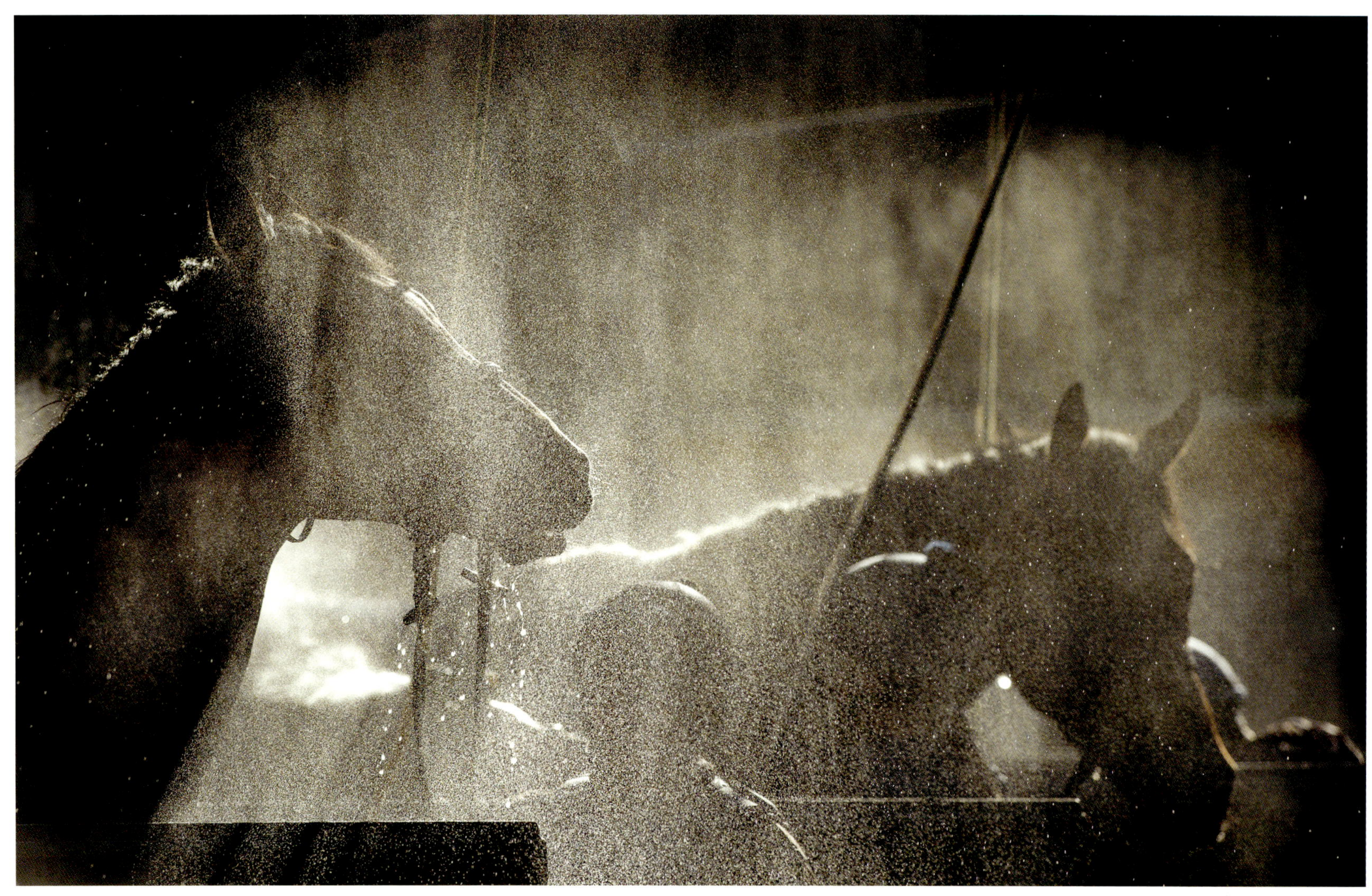

Cooling off in summer 1
Horses being hosed off after exercise
at Richard Hannon's yard. The way
they are standing gives a sense of
enjoyment of the cooling process.
Whereas opposite …

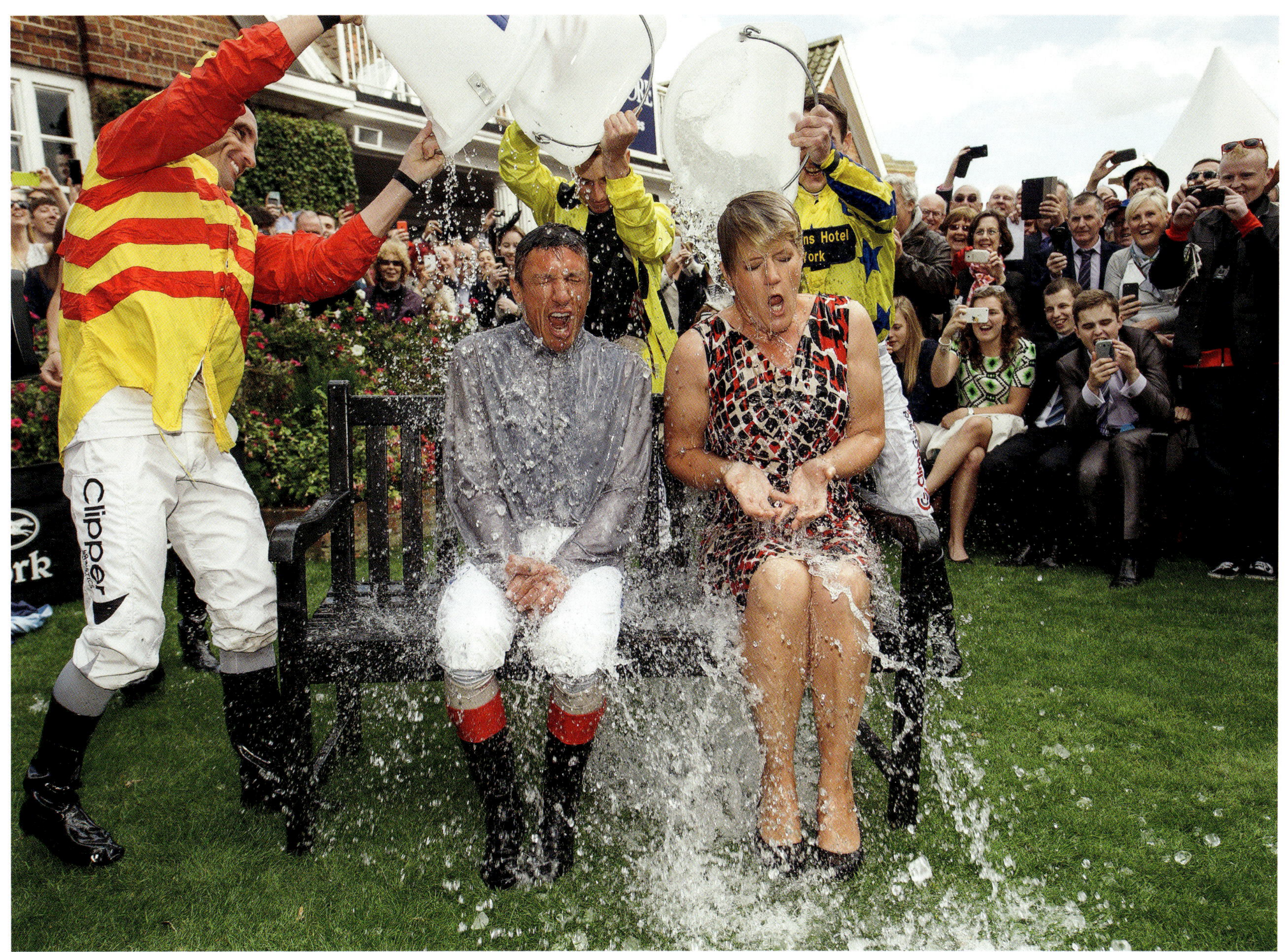

Cooling off in summer 2
The Ice Bucket Challenge was a
fund-raising idea for motor neurone
disease that went viral in the summer
of 2014. Here Clare Balding and
Frankie Dettori do their bit outside
the old weighing room at York.

Colt in a cage
This pen looks a bit like a chicken run
but it is a good idea for it gives green
grass and open-air freedom without
allowing the space for a horse to
gallop and injure itself. It also makes
a great picture.

The finishing touch
This is not any old wrist grooming
any old mane. For the horse is dual
Derby winner Australia and the wrist
belongs to trainer Aidan O'Brien.
Brick walls usually ruin a background
but this one blends beautifully with
Australia's red chestnut coat colour.

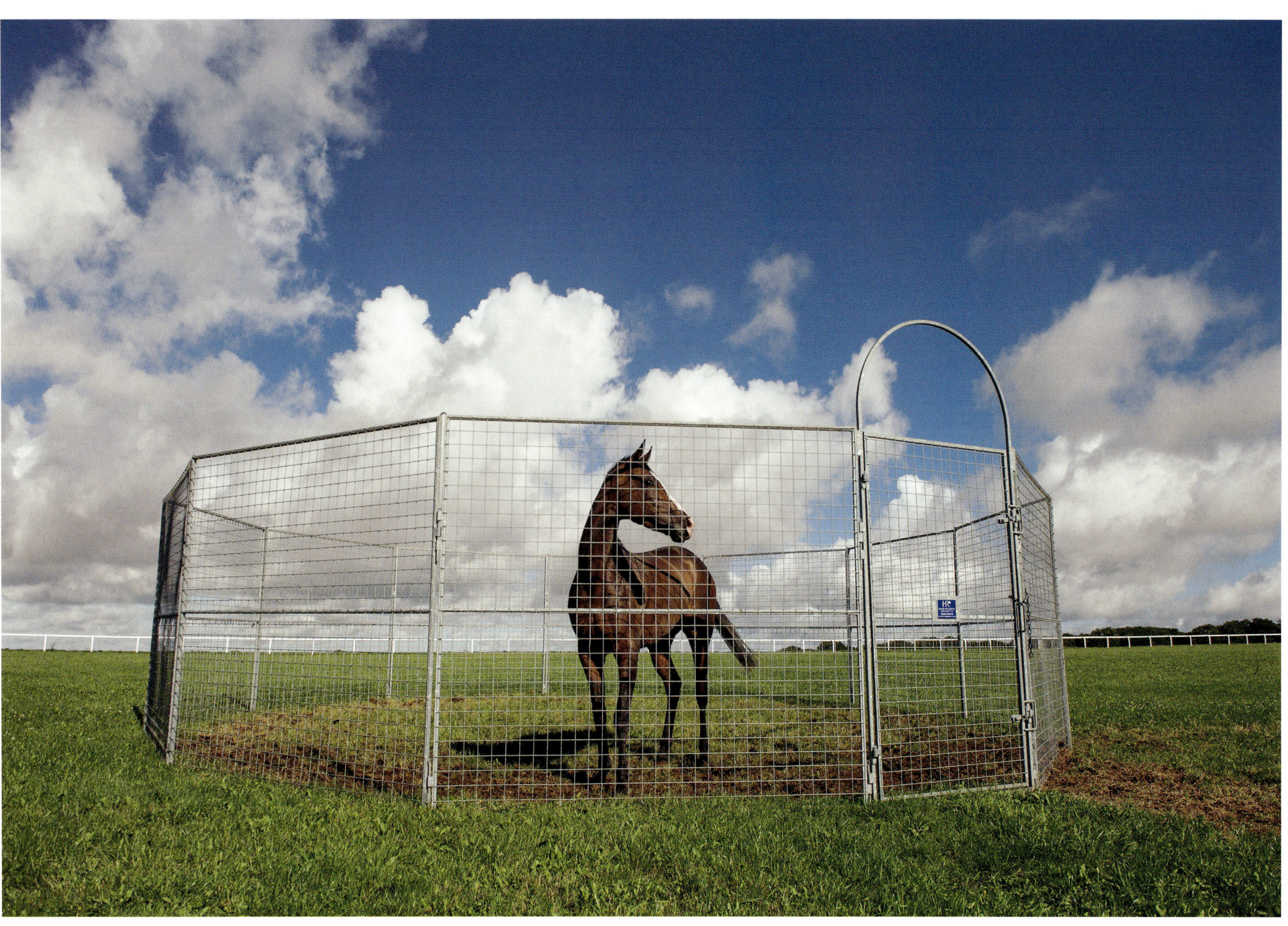

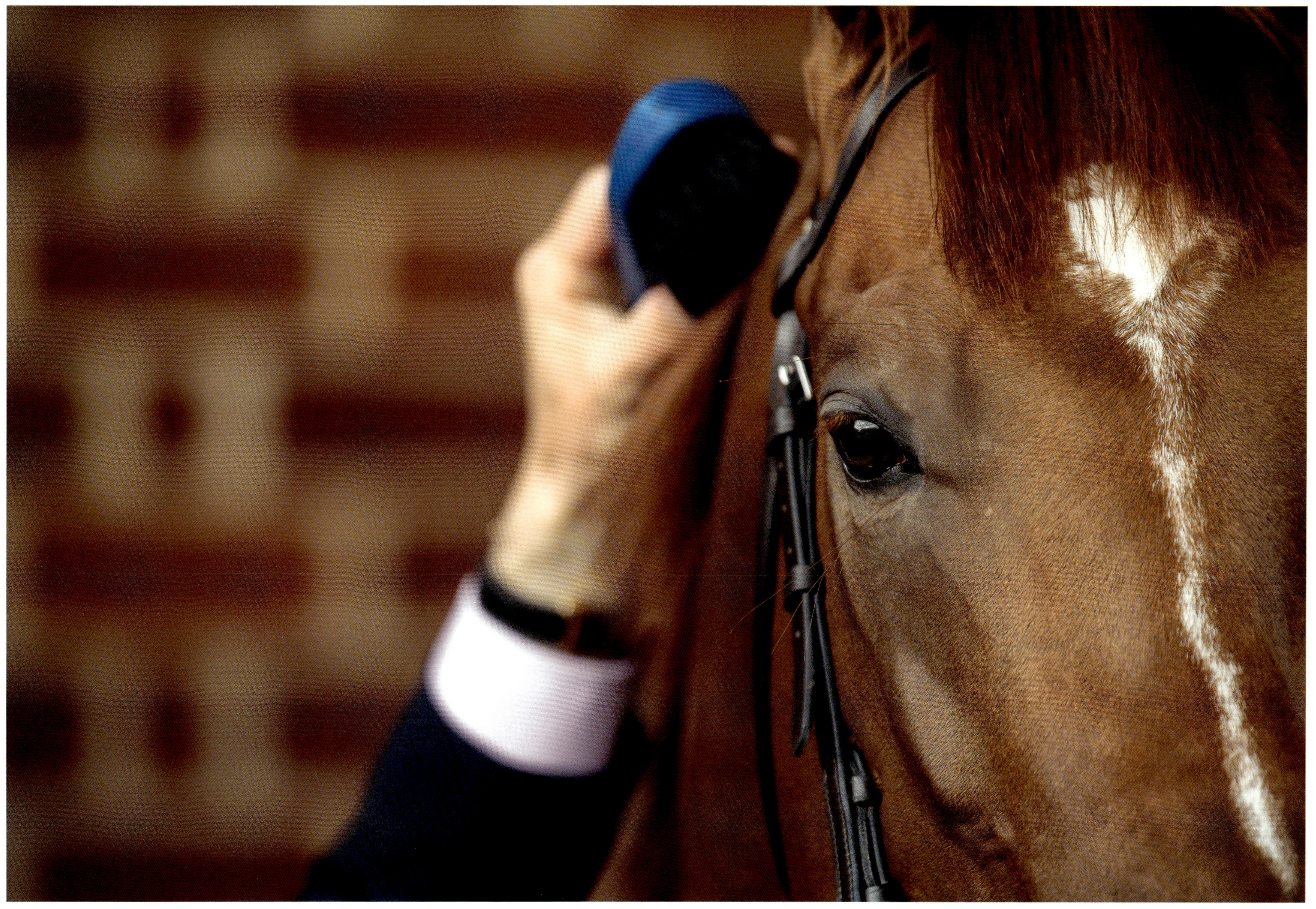

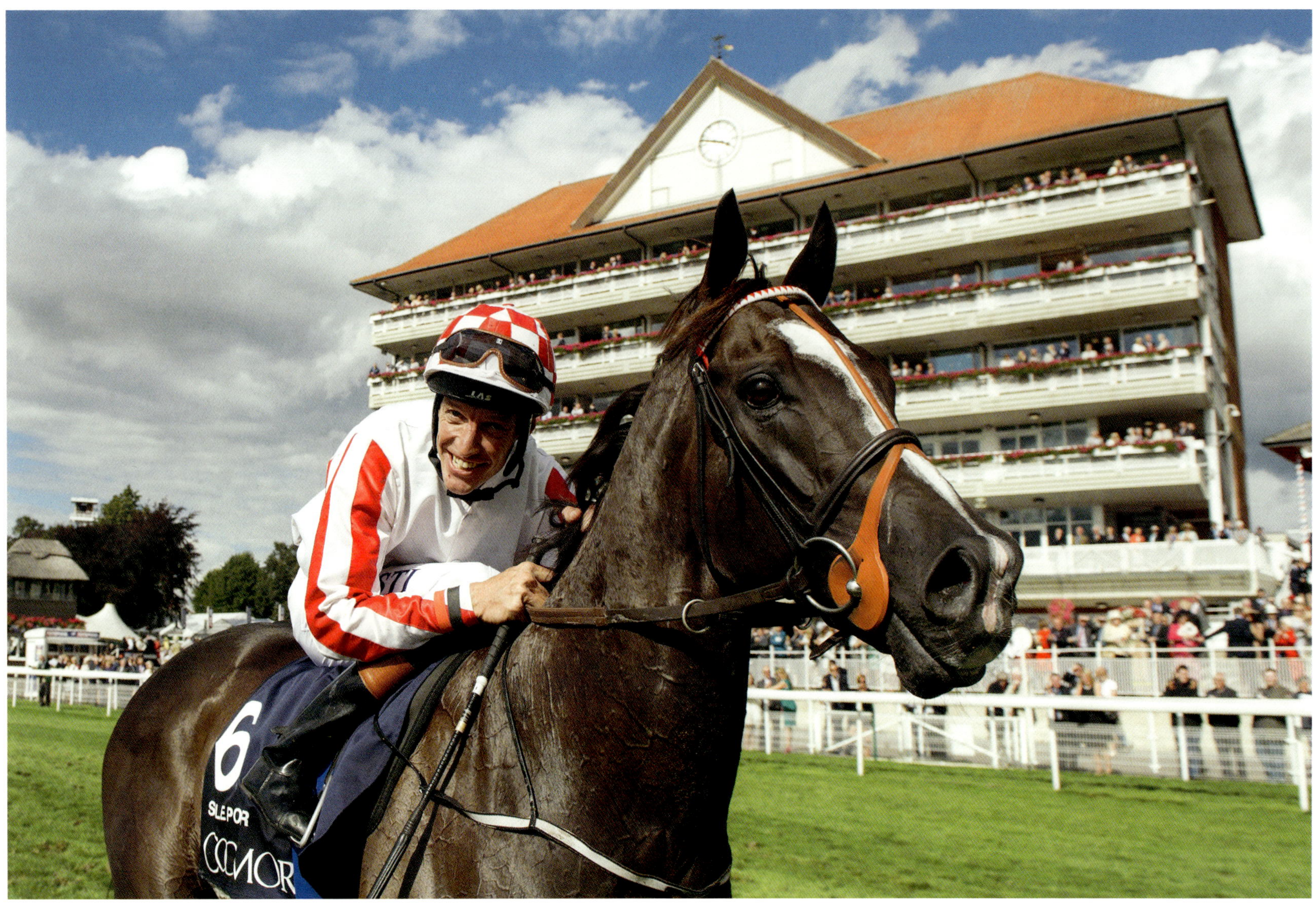

Smile of triumph
Richard Hughes had just delivered
one of his signature late, late finishes
to win the 2014 Nunthorpe on Sole
Power. That is real delight written
across his face.

Thunder threatens
As the runners raced towards the
finish of the 2017 Stewards' Cup, the
darkest of thunderstorms loomed.
It was as good a mix of sunshine and
cloud as you will ever see.

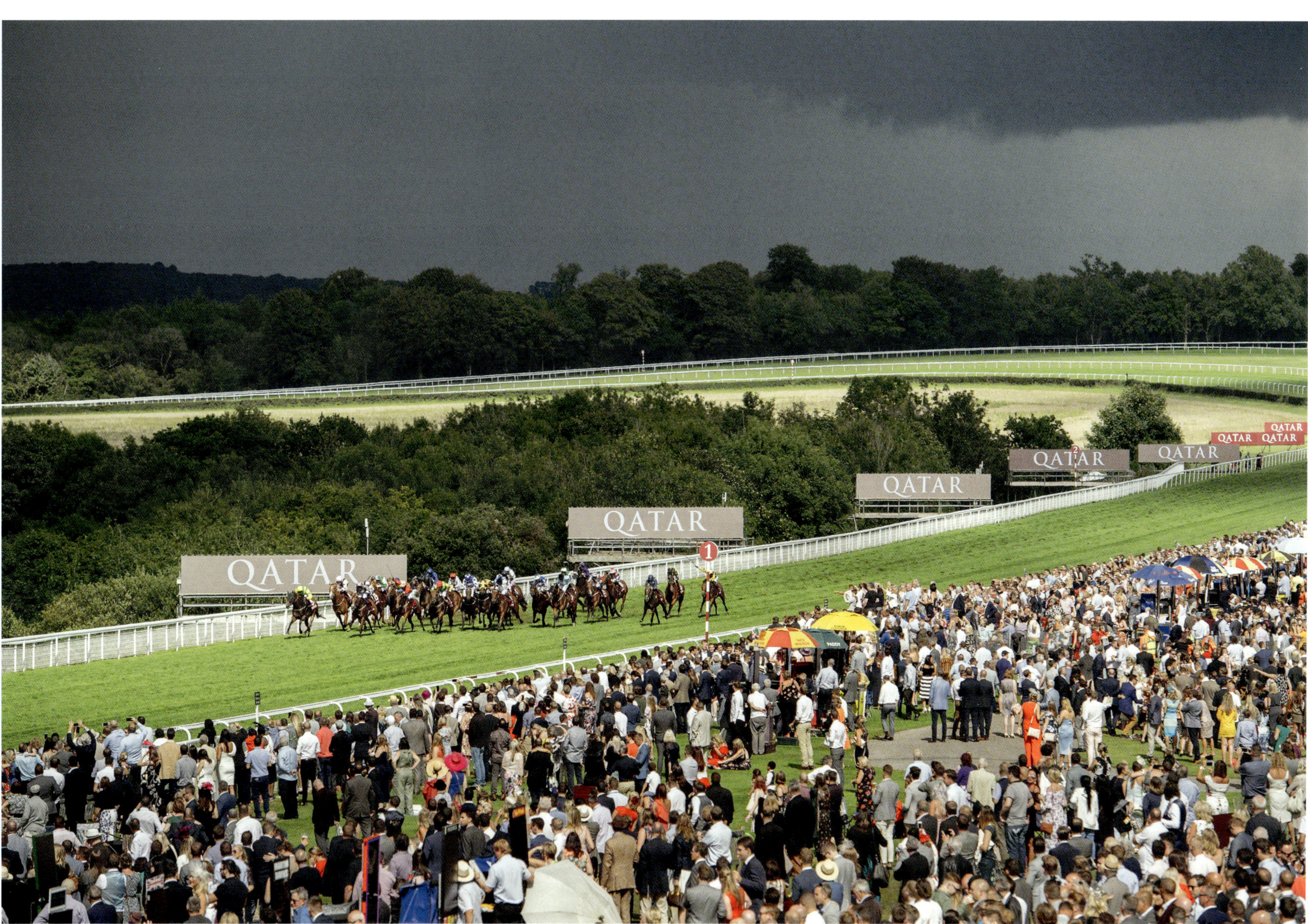

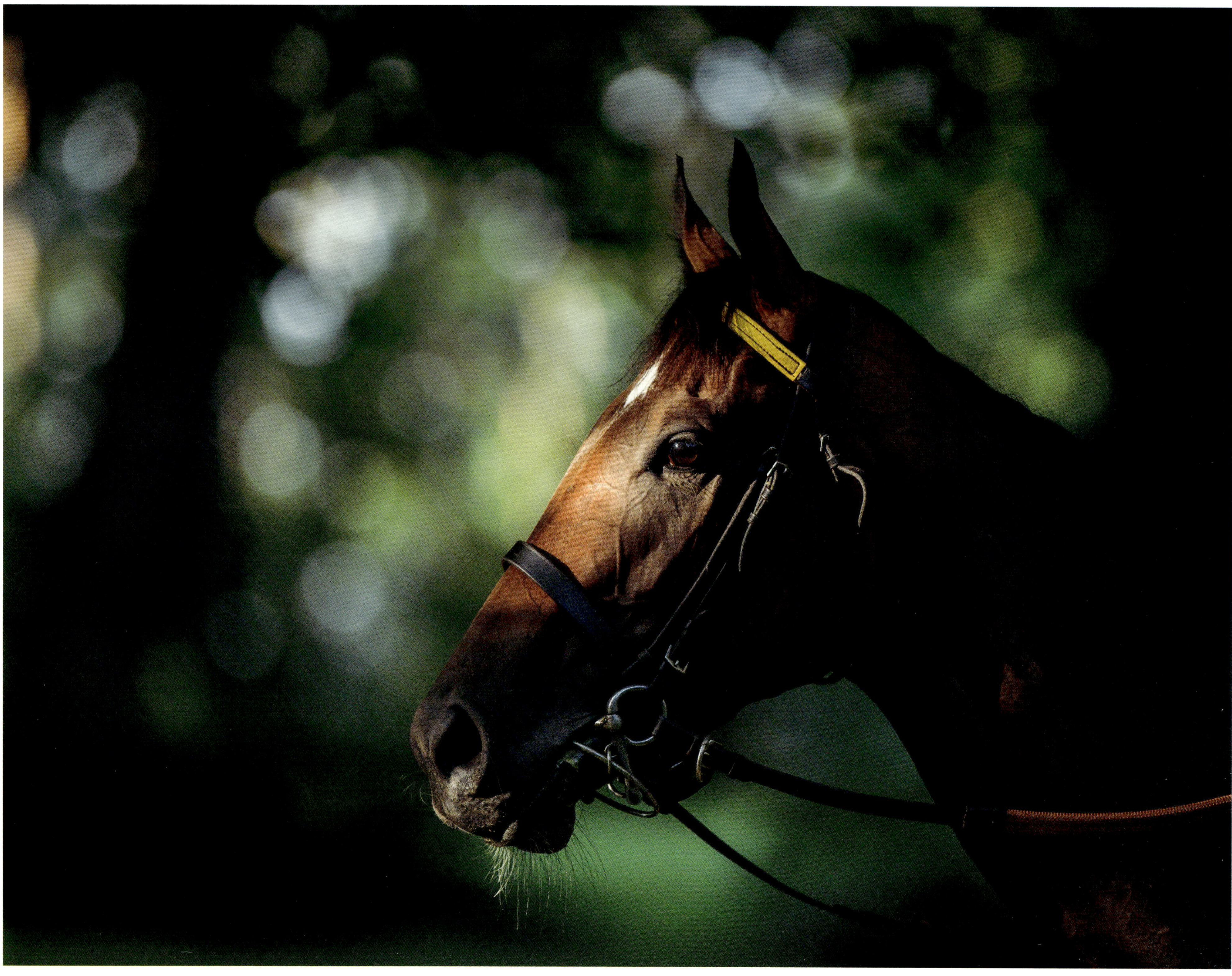

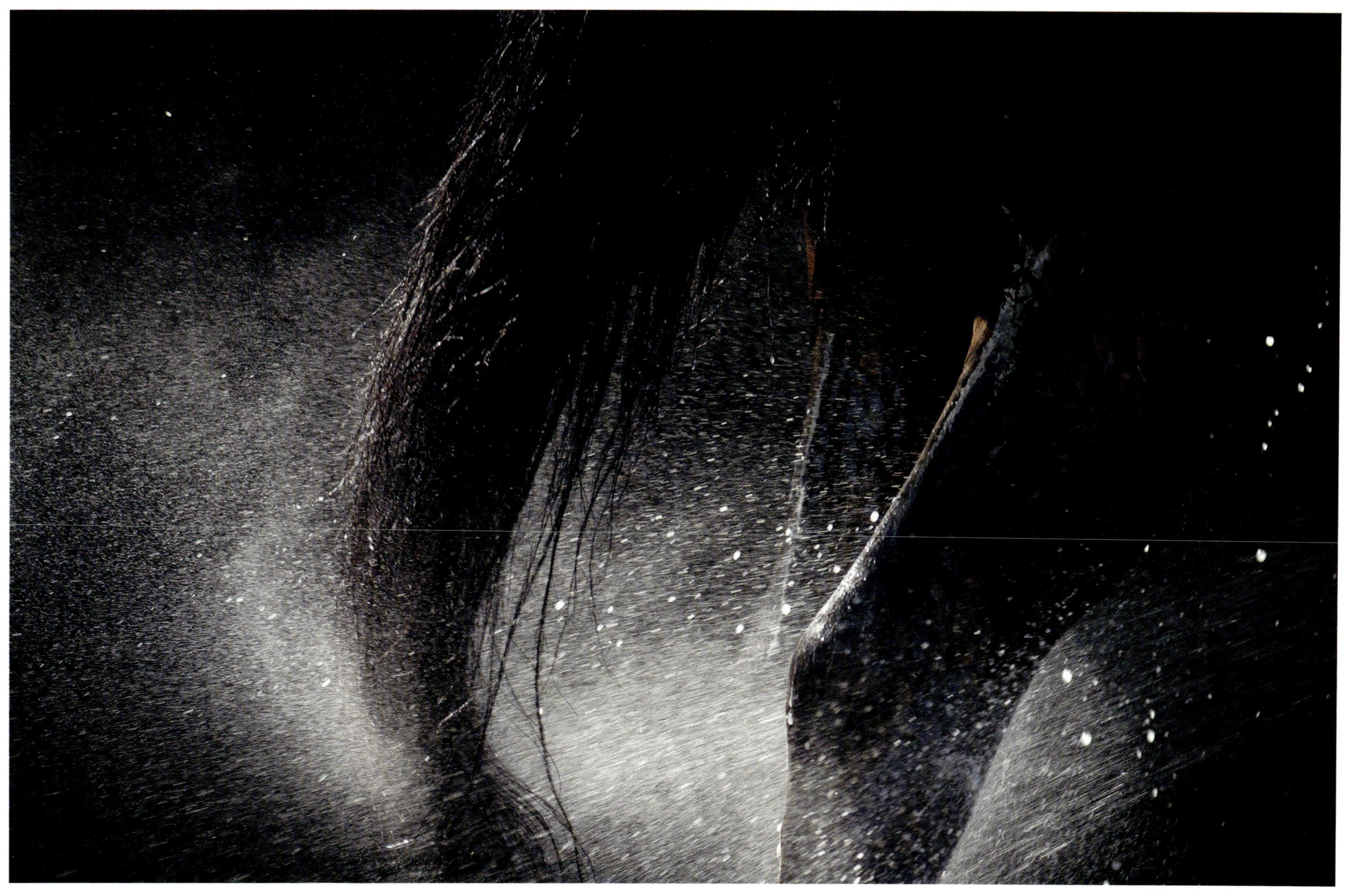

The beauty of the thoroughbred
The top sprint filly Marsha poses
in the woods at Newmarket. I don't
often do head portraits but she was
such a stunner and gave us this.

Water in the tail
There is something sensuous
about water washing horses down
in midsummer. This shot after the
Melrose Handicap at York only has
droplets and tail and hind leg but you
can feel the impact.

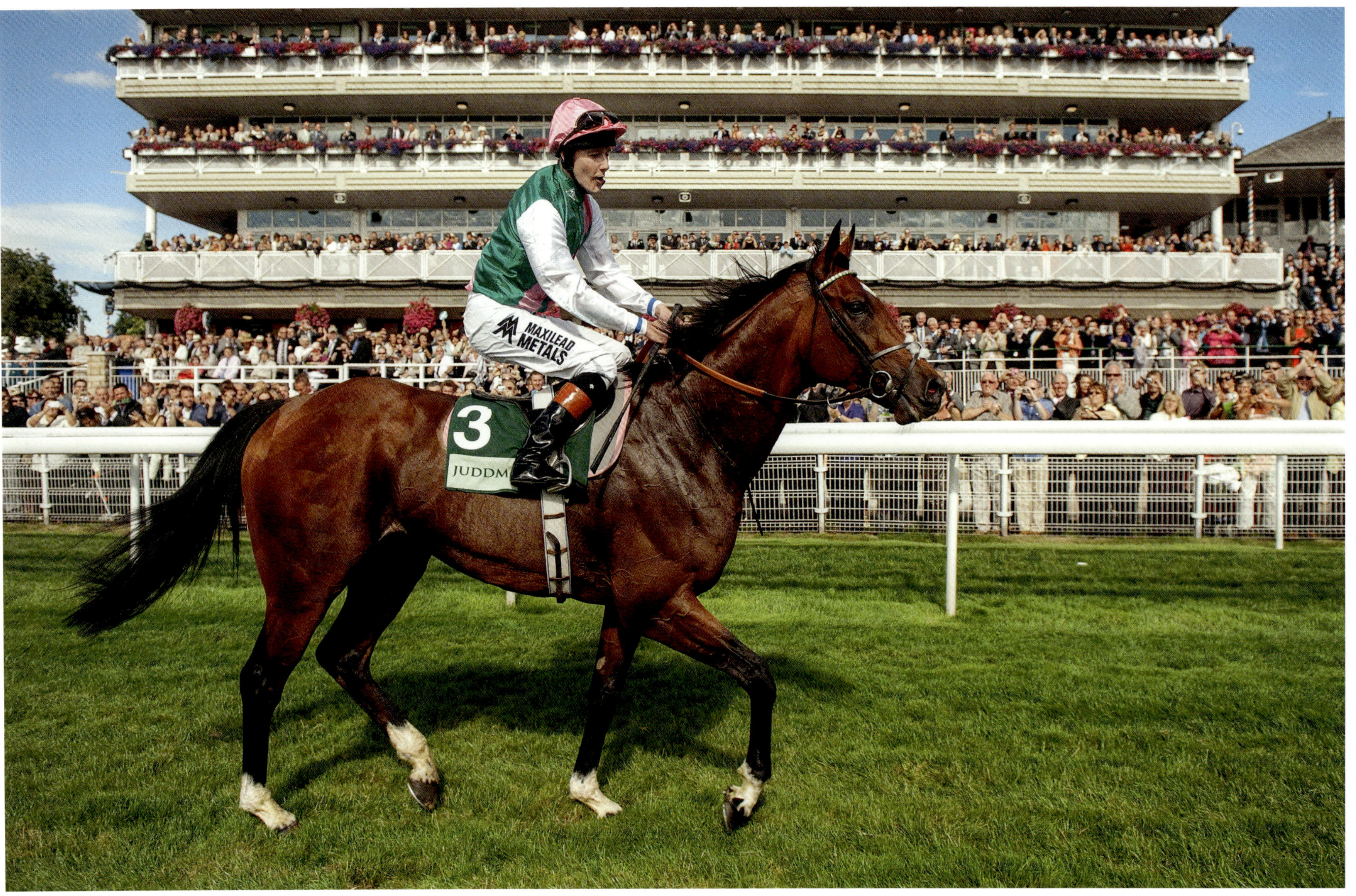

Simply the best
Frankel had just produced the most impressive of all his victories in York's Juddmonte International and the awe still hangs on Tom Queally's lips. Look closely because this is the best horse you will ever see.

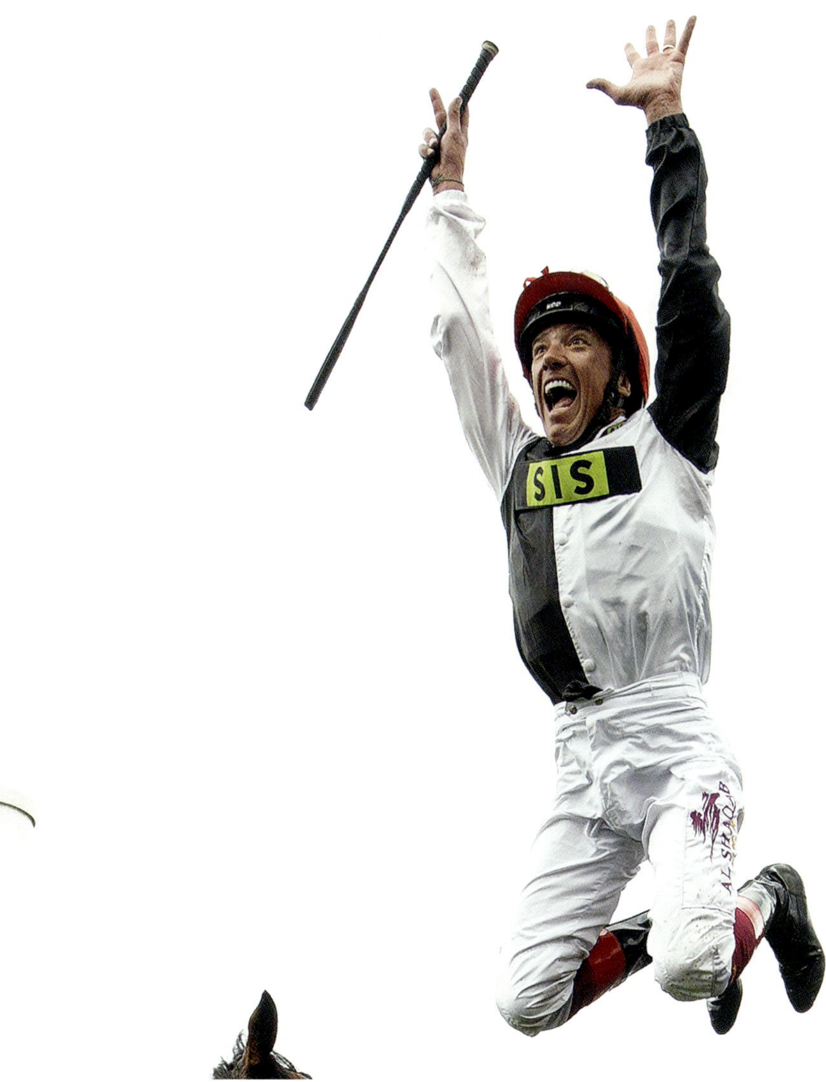

Dettori in white and black
He had just won the Great Voltigeur
on Cracksman but this image is
all about black and white contrast
given by the colours and the sky.
The colour is left to Frankie's face.

September

Shadows and light at Lingfield
Late afternoon in September gives
the most wonderful shadows.
Shooting into shade needs as black
a background as possible. That's
what makes this work.

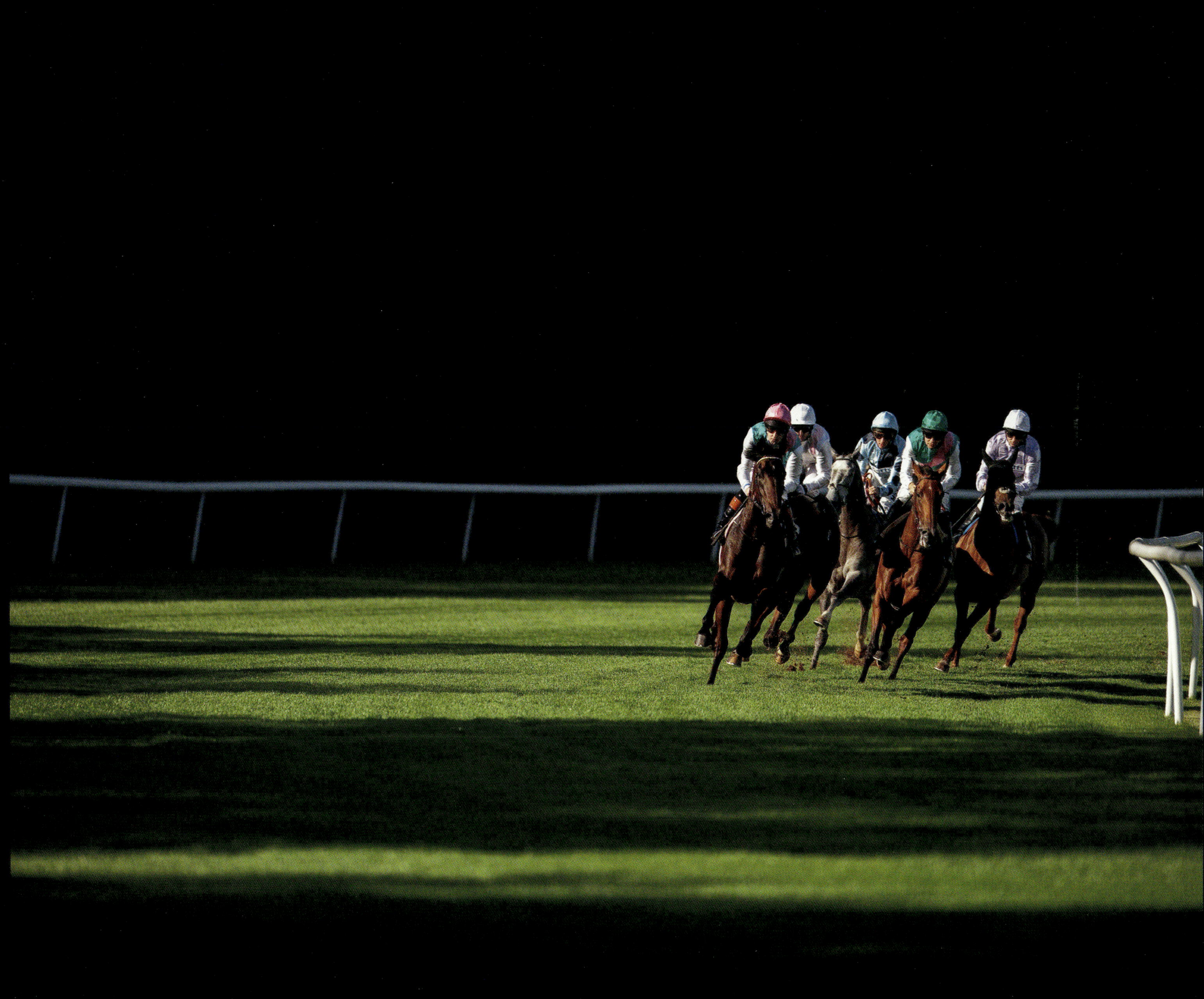

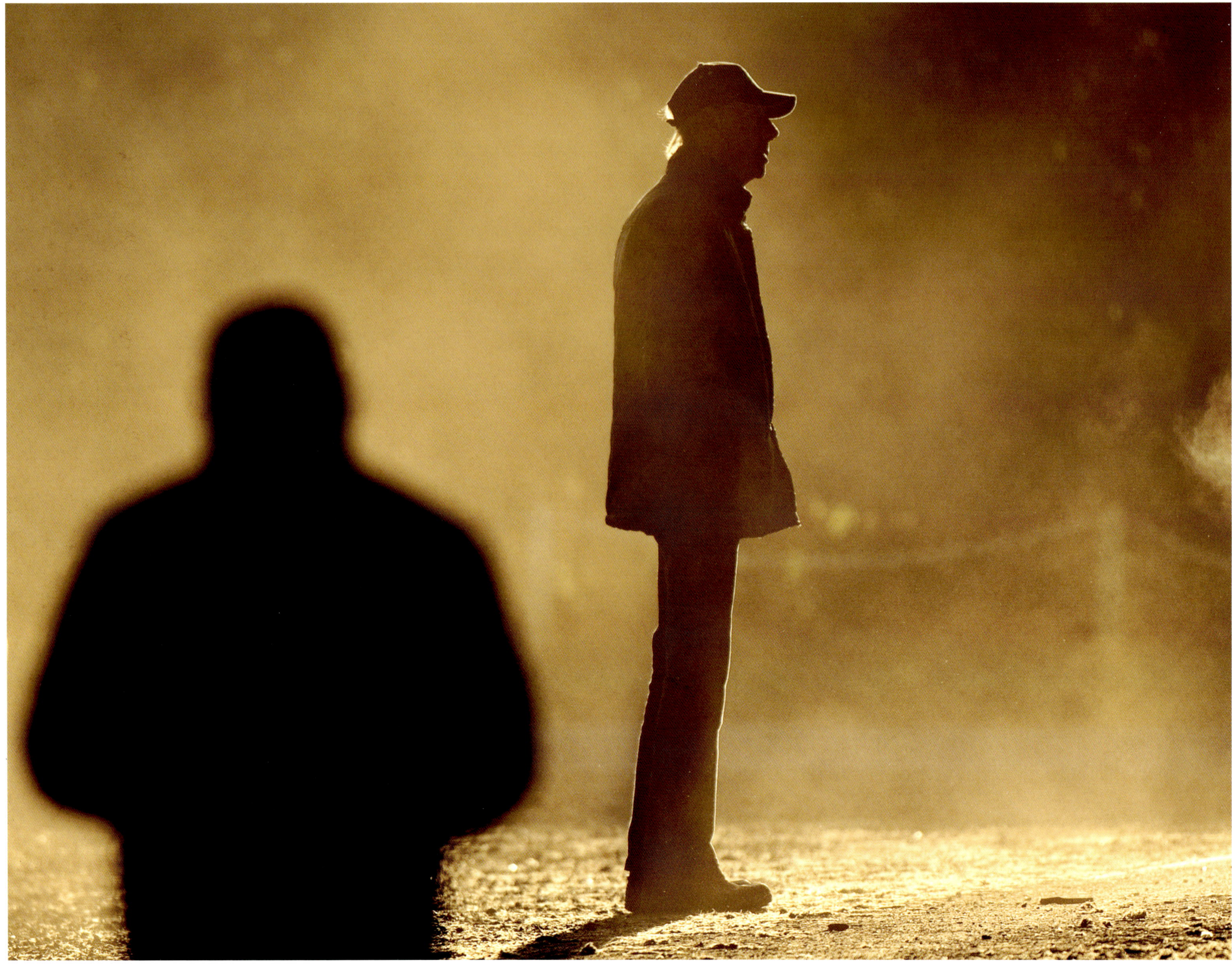

Henry's last September
Henry Cecil was to die next June
but in September 2012 he was still
supervising a string that included
Frankel. That's what he lived for.

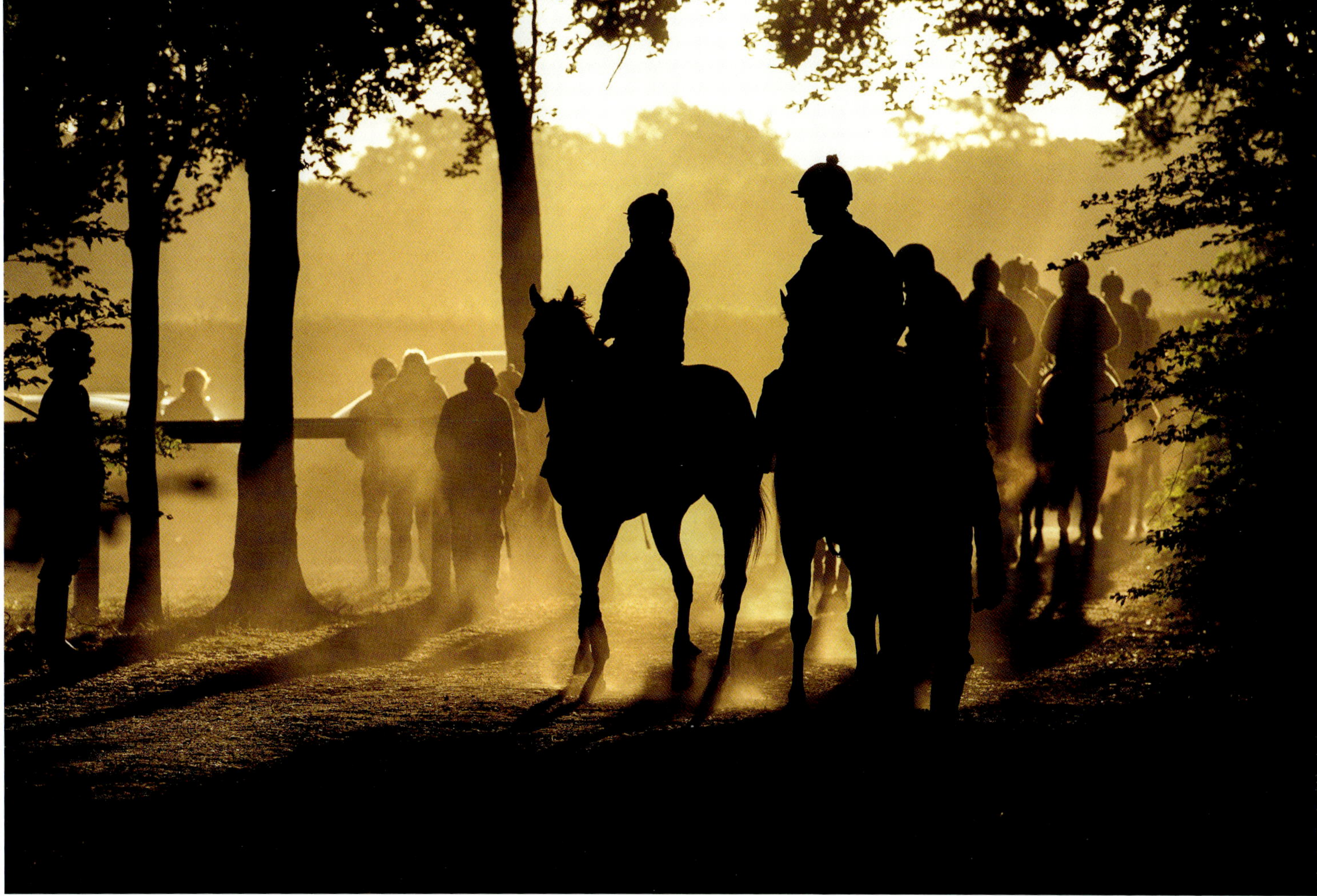

The string in the shadows
The Henry Cecil string file off
through the woodland after working
on the Al Bahathri gallop. The picture
shows how much activity surrounds
a big stable on work mornings. What
makes it is the dust and golden
September light.

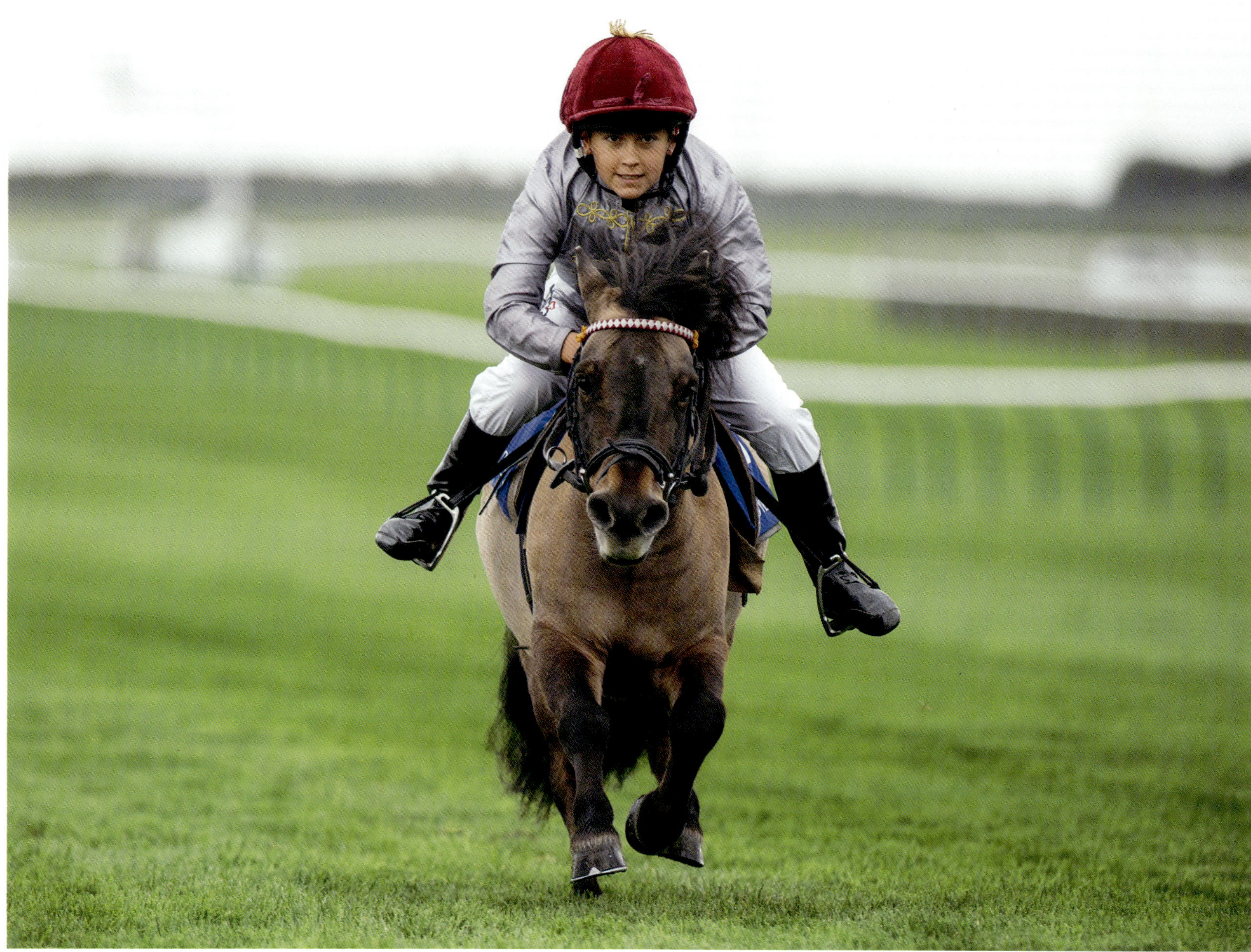

Rocco Dettori in action
Twelve-year-old Rocco Dettori rides
a finish on the impressively named
Mahagadartin Beeswax in the
Shadwell Stud Shetland Pony Grand
National at Newmarket. Like father,
not quite yet like son?

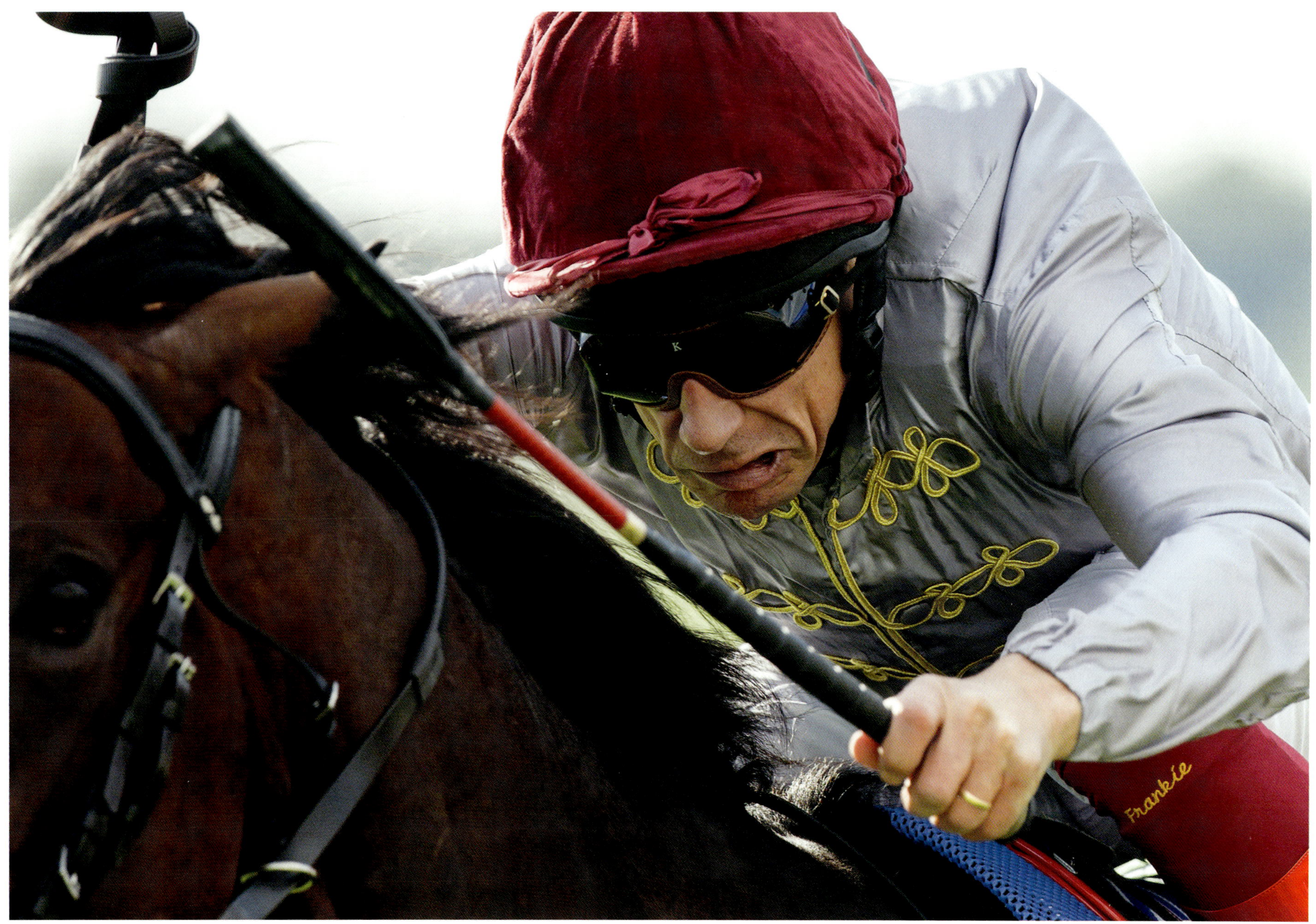

Much more than a showman
Frankie Dettori wins the Middle Park
Stakes on Shalaa. Underneath all
the showmanship you can see the
extraordinary balance and clamped-
in compulsion that makes him such
an exceptional jockey.

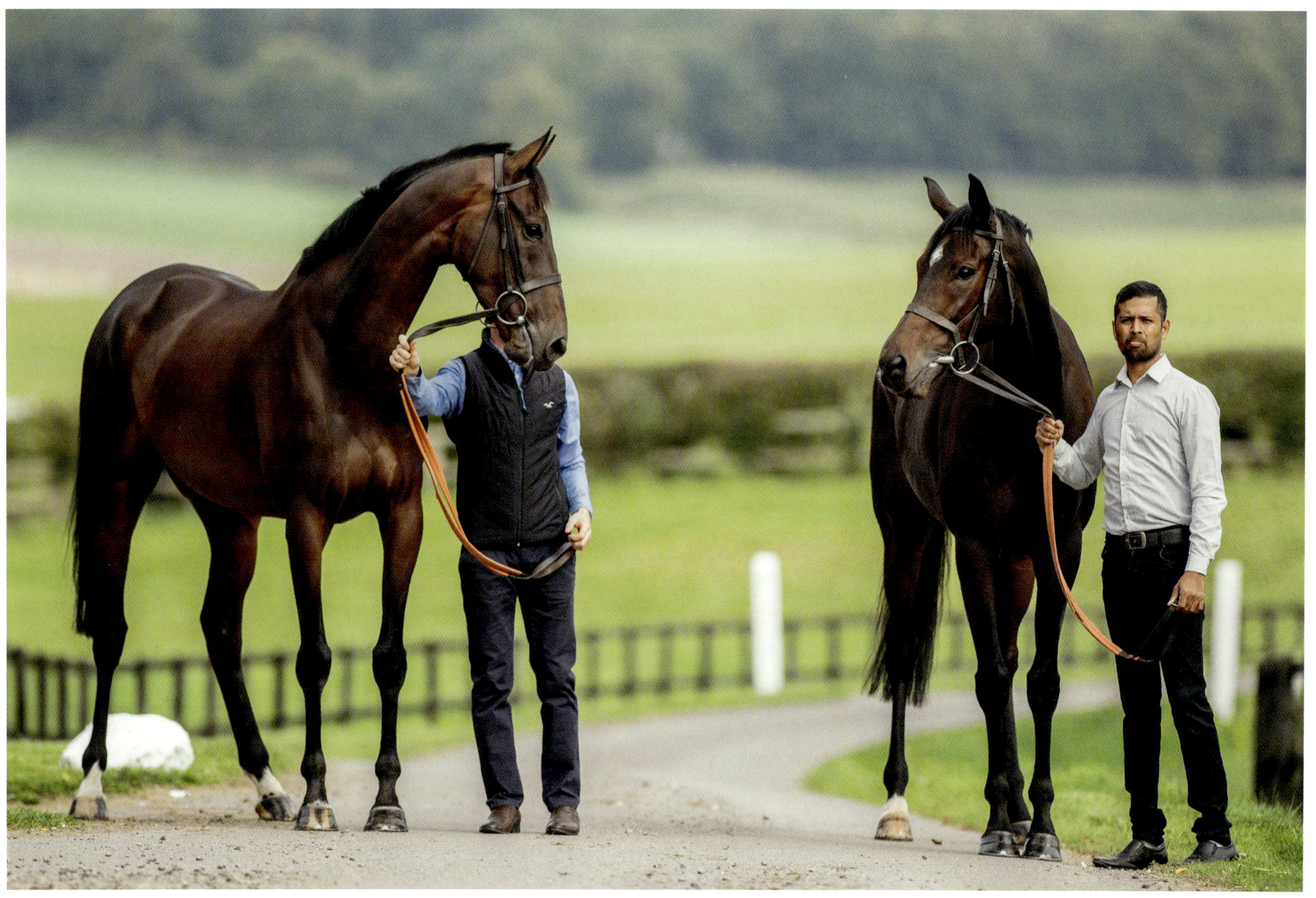

Two stars, different sizes
Might Bite (left with Dave Fehily) and
Altior (Mohammed Hussain) were the
final two turns at Nicky Henderson's
Open Day and were to deliver in the
season ahead.

Under the arm
It's so often hard to see the horses
in the huge expanse at Newmarket
that I liked the idea of looking under
this racegoer's arm. As he shielded
his eyes he was giving us the frame
to our picture.

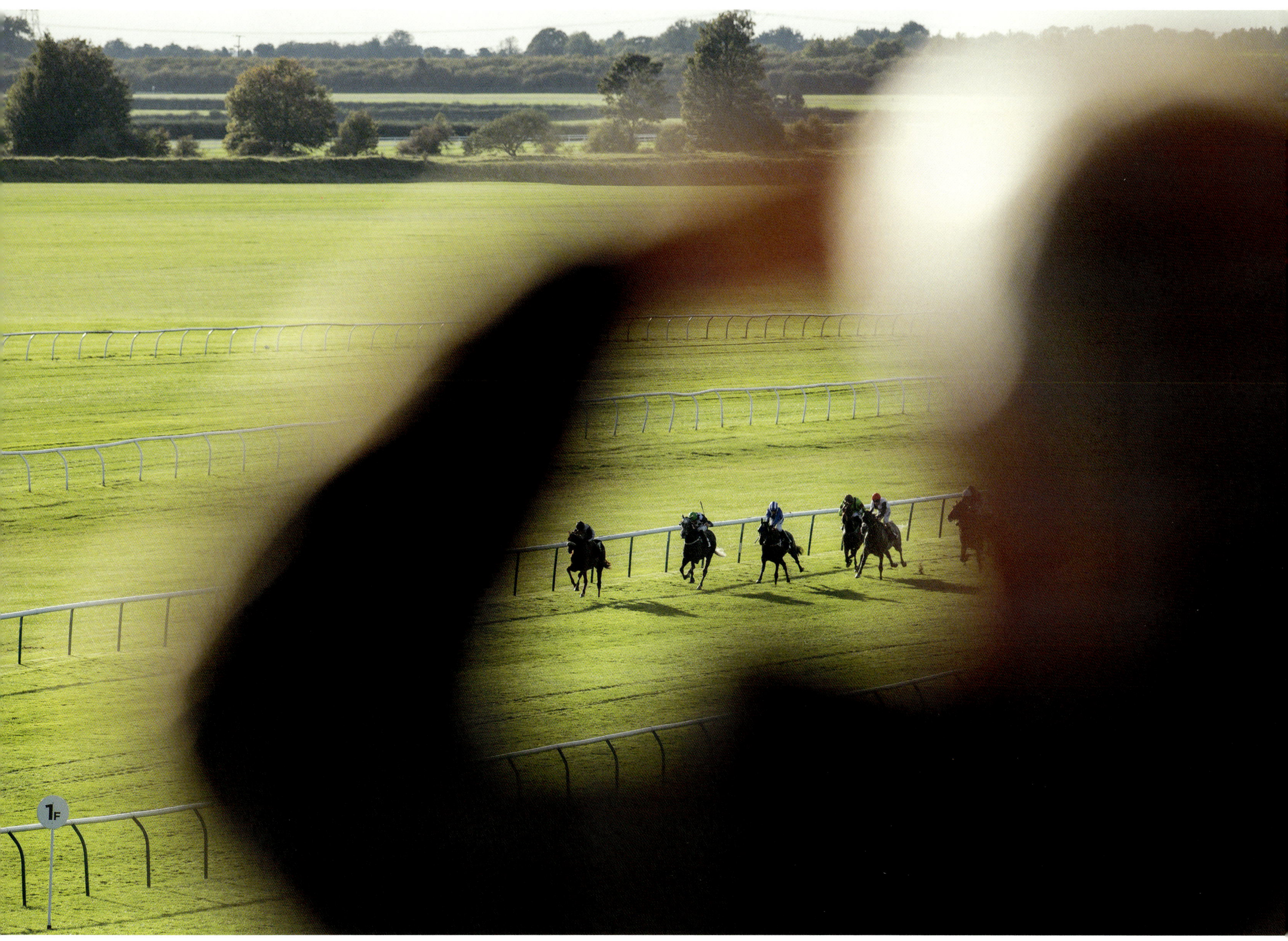

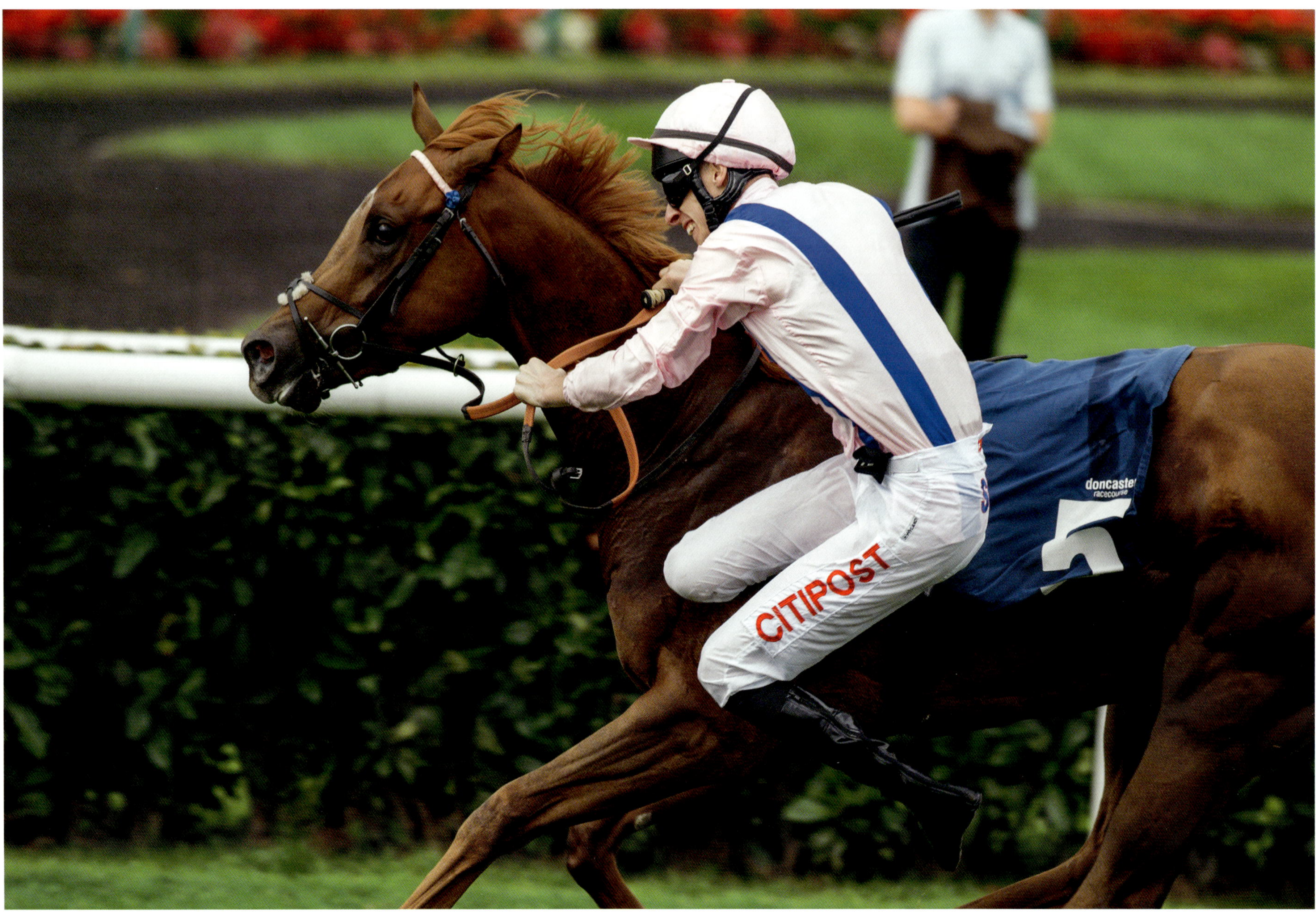

Last yards disaster
Just before the Doncaster winning post, Cotai Glory jinked to the right, George Baker's saddle slipped and suddenly we have this image of him gently sliding down the side. At full gallop the landing was a lot bumpier than this looks.

How many decades?
51-year-old French star Gerald Mosse has seen 35 years as a jockey and his distinctive white gloves have won some major victories all over the world. His move to Newmarket in 2018 means we see much more of his famous profile.

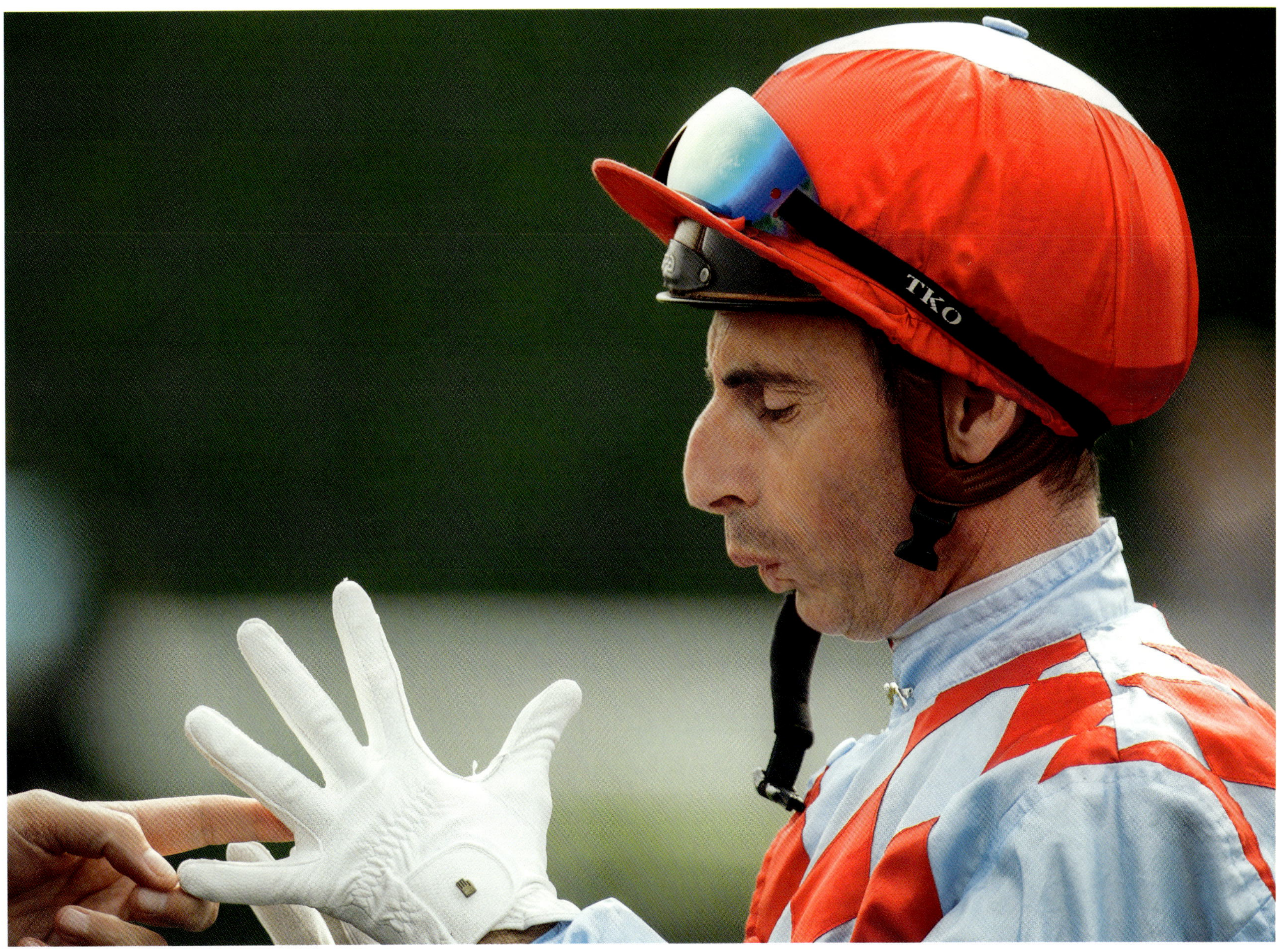

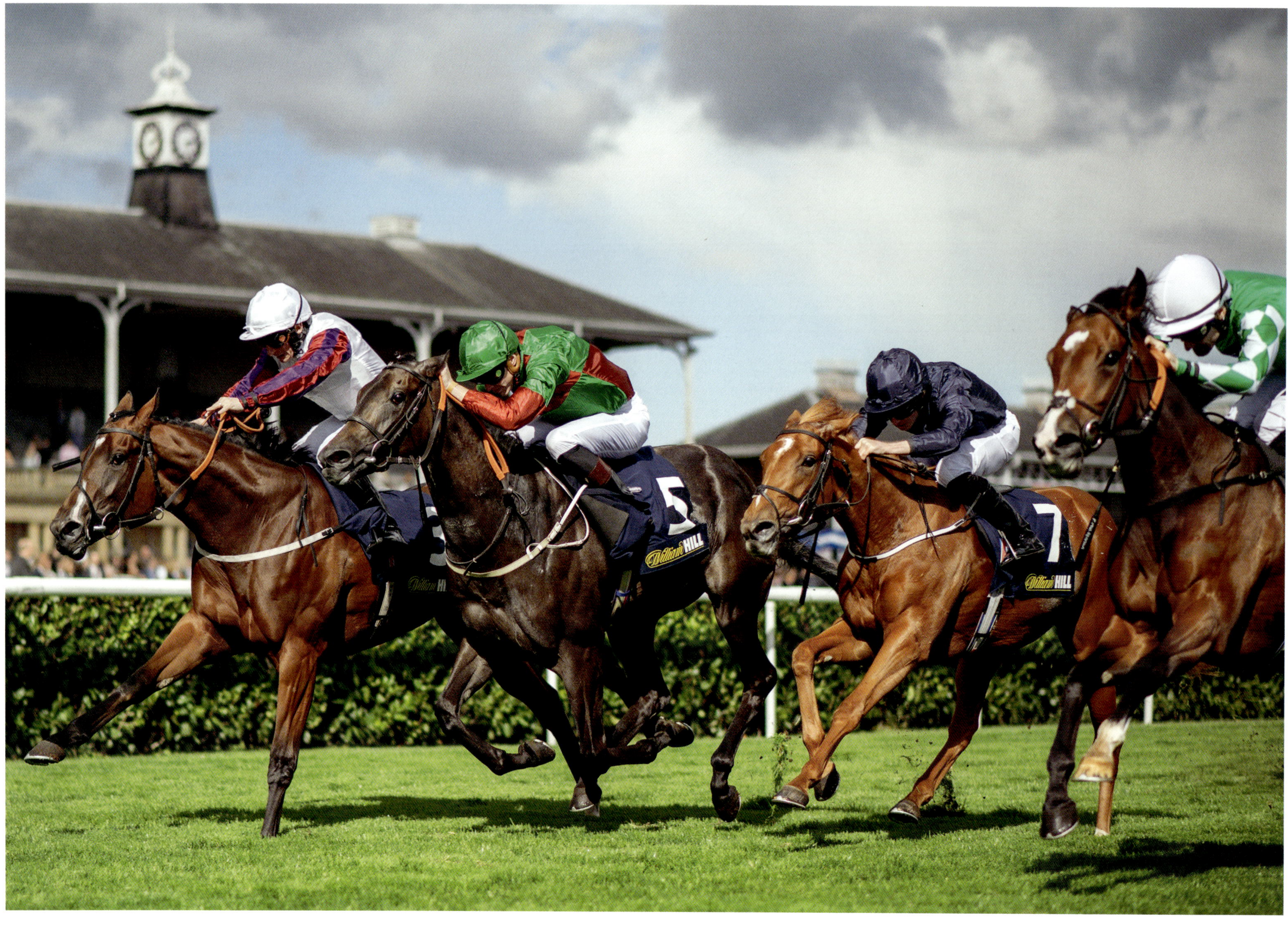

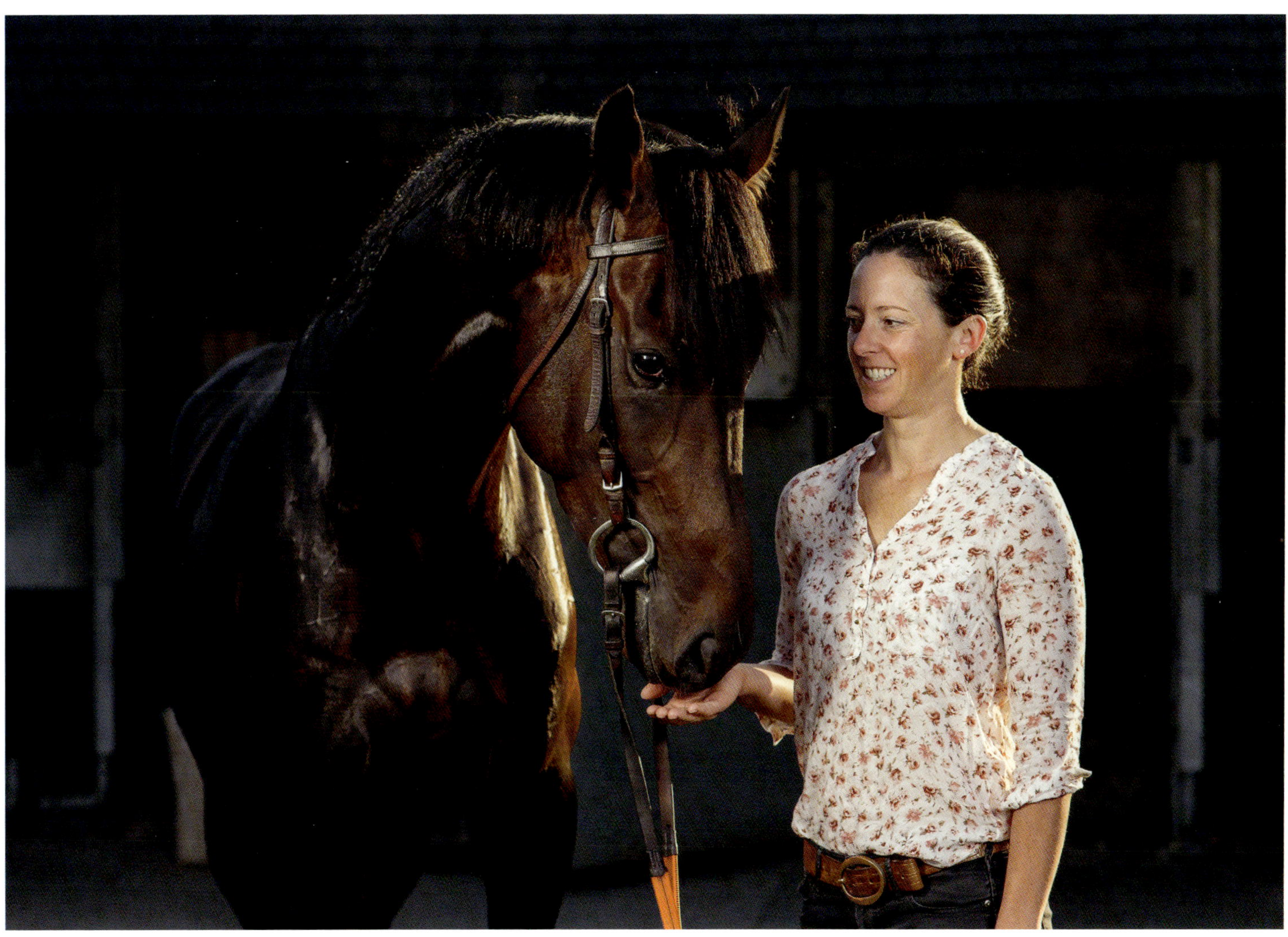

Four way finish
Doncaster has an impressive new stand but the old one and its clock tower remains the most iconic. Here it provides a perfect counterpart to Laurens' victory in the May Hill Stakes for two-year-old fillies.

Classic pride
Harbour Law's 22-1 victory in the St Leger may have surprised many but it brought great happiness to trainer Laura Mongan and to Epsom which had not housed a classic winner for almost 50 years. That shows.

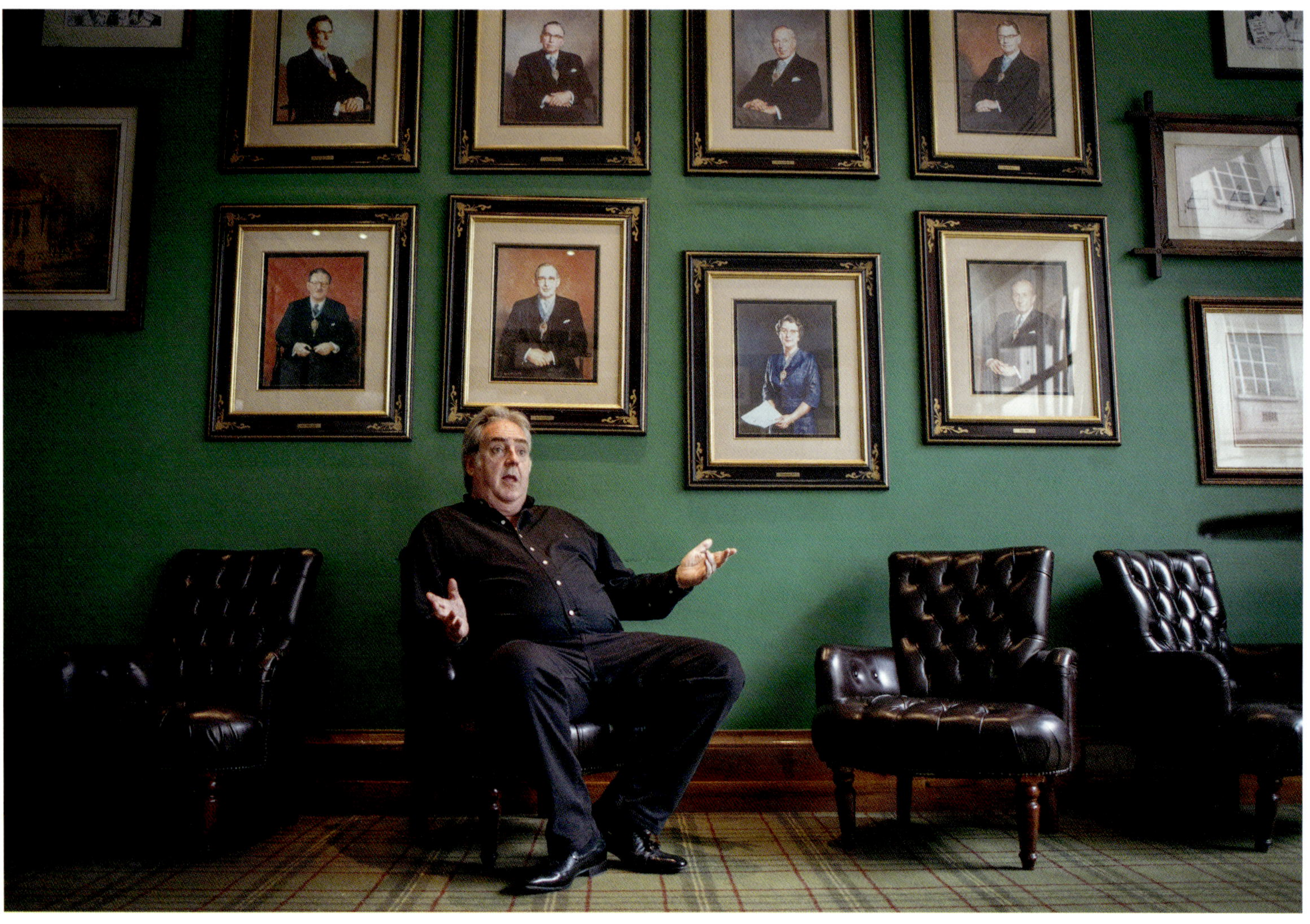

It was like this
Legendary punter Harry Findlay
holds forth about his new book
Gambling For Life. We hadn't seen
him since his raucous heyday as part-
owner of Denman. Let's say he had
not dropped silent.

B******t
How convinced is Silviniaco Conti?
Paul Nicholls' top chaser sticks his
tongue out as UKIP leader Nigel
Farage tries the chat-up smile.
Note the champagne.

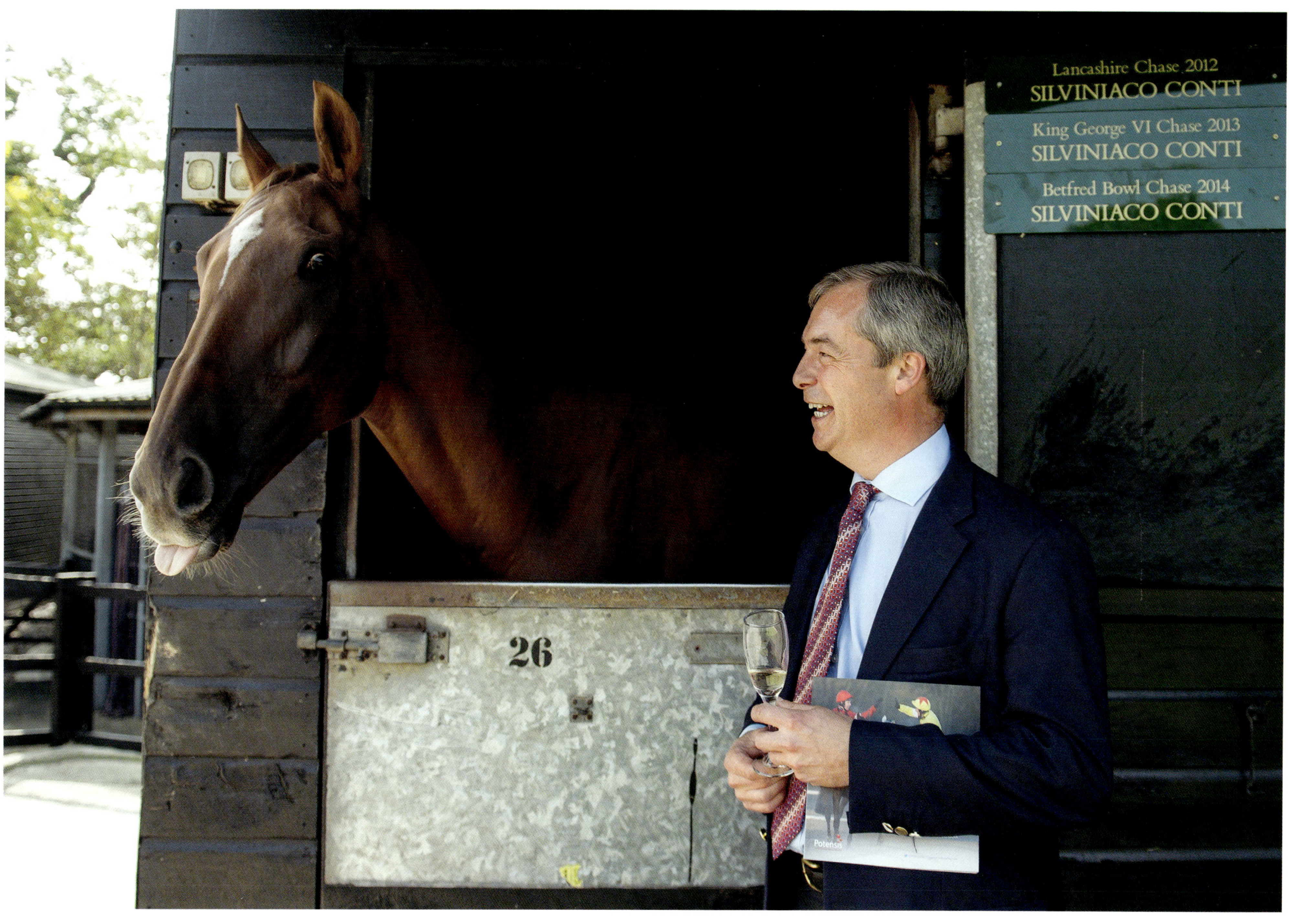

Lancashire Chase 2012
SILVINIACO CONTI
King George VI Chase 2013
SILVINIACO CONTI
Betfred Bowl Chase 2014
SILVINIACO CONTI
26

October

Soaring silhouettes
Jumpers at Stratford late in the afternoon. At this time of year, we begin to realise that their game will soon be centre stage.

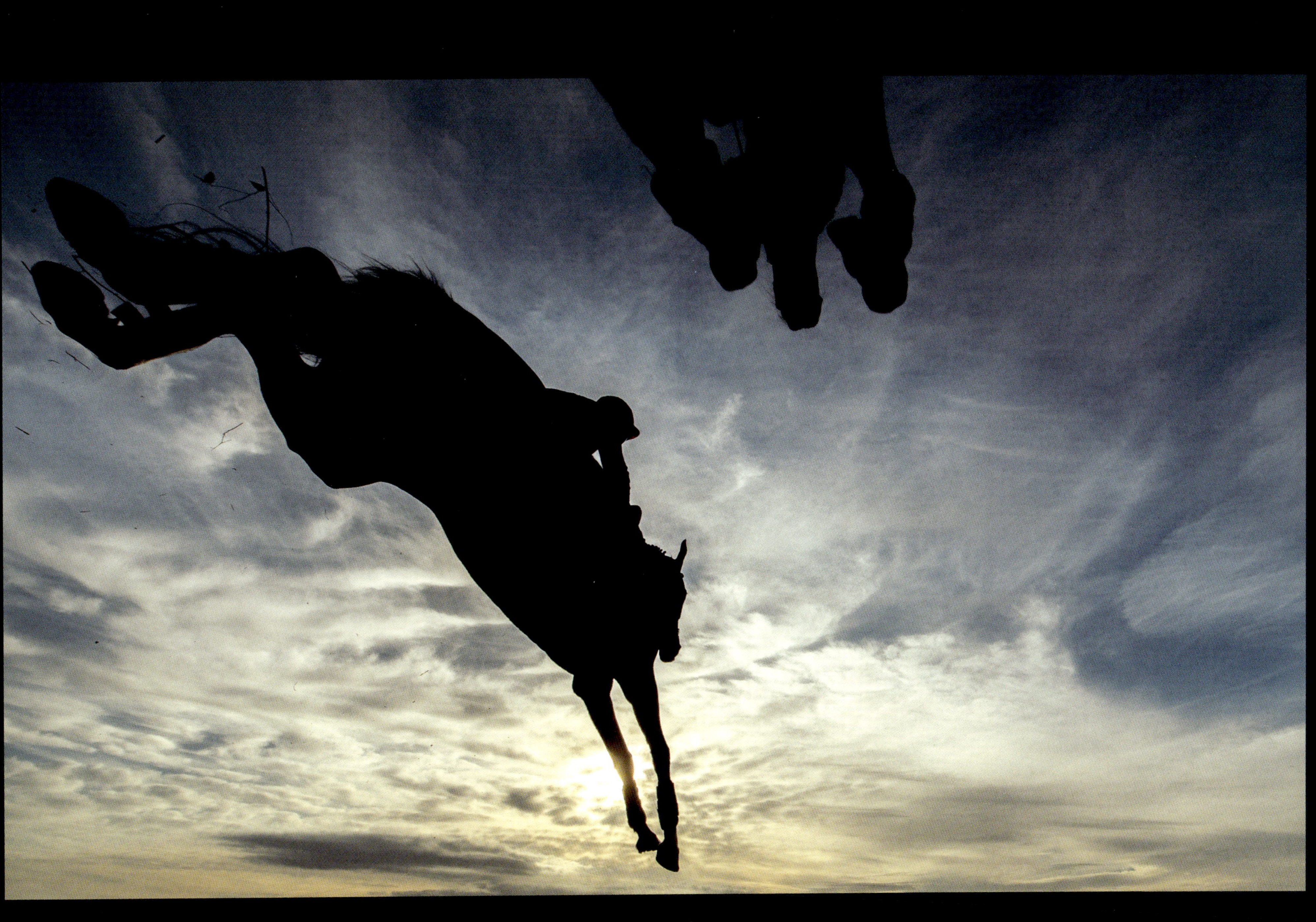

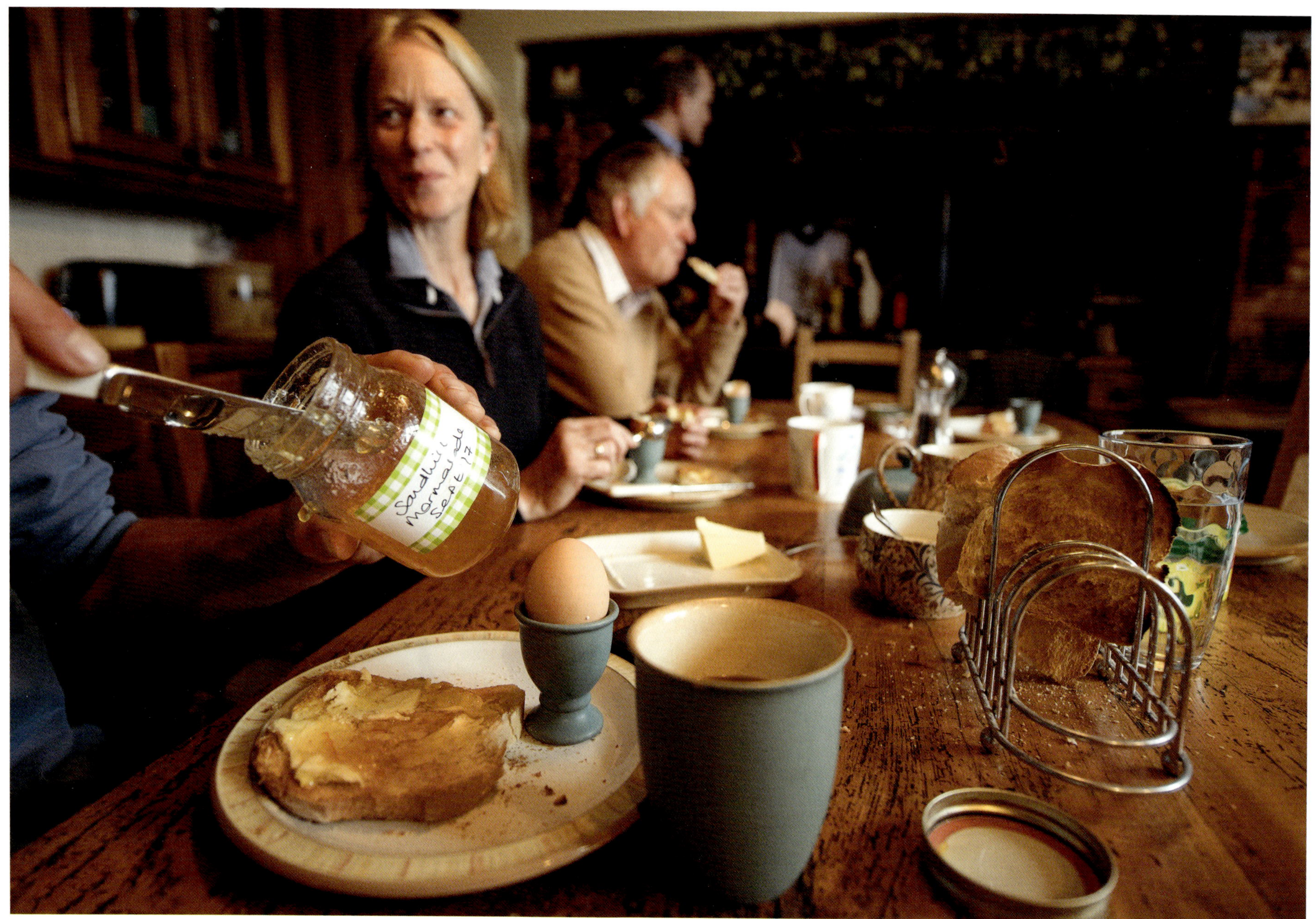

Breakfast table at Philip Hobbs' yard
Breakfast is always the same and
delicious at Philip Hobbs' Sandhill
Stables near Minehead in Somerset.
Toast, marmalade and boiled
egg. Check the marmalade –
it's home-made.

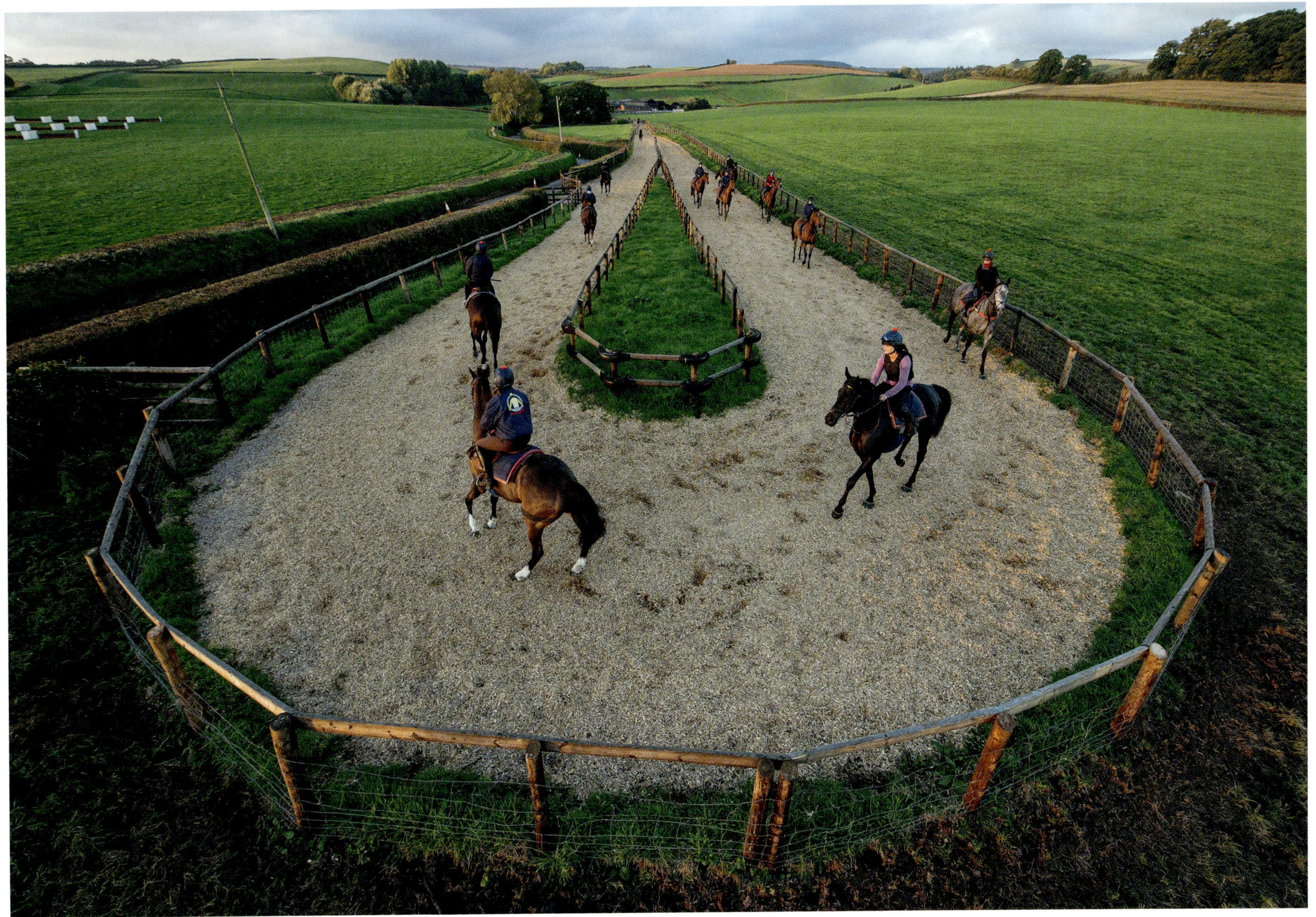

Turning in
This shot comes courtesy of fellow photographer Michael Steele who had commandeered a bucket loader to give us height at the bottom of Philip Hobbs' gallop. Who ever thought that horses turning should make a teardrop?

On the boil
Sharper mornings give steamier shadows, especially at the Seven Barrows schooling ground with horses ready to test their jumping.

Absolutely Fabulous
Peter O'Sullevan's memorial service at St Luke's Church in Chelsea brought the A-listers out in tribute. Rory Bremner mimicked a final O'Sullevan commentary and Sir Terry Wogan and Joanna Lumley did the readings. They, like the rest of us, revered him.

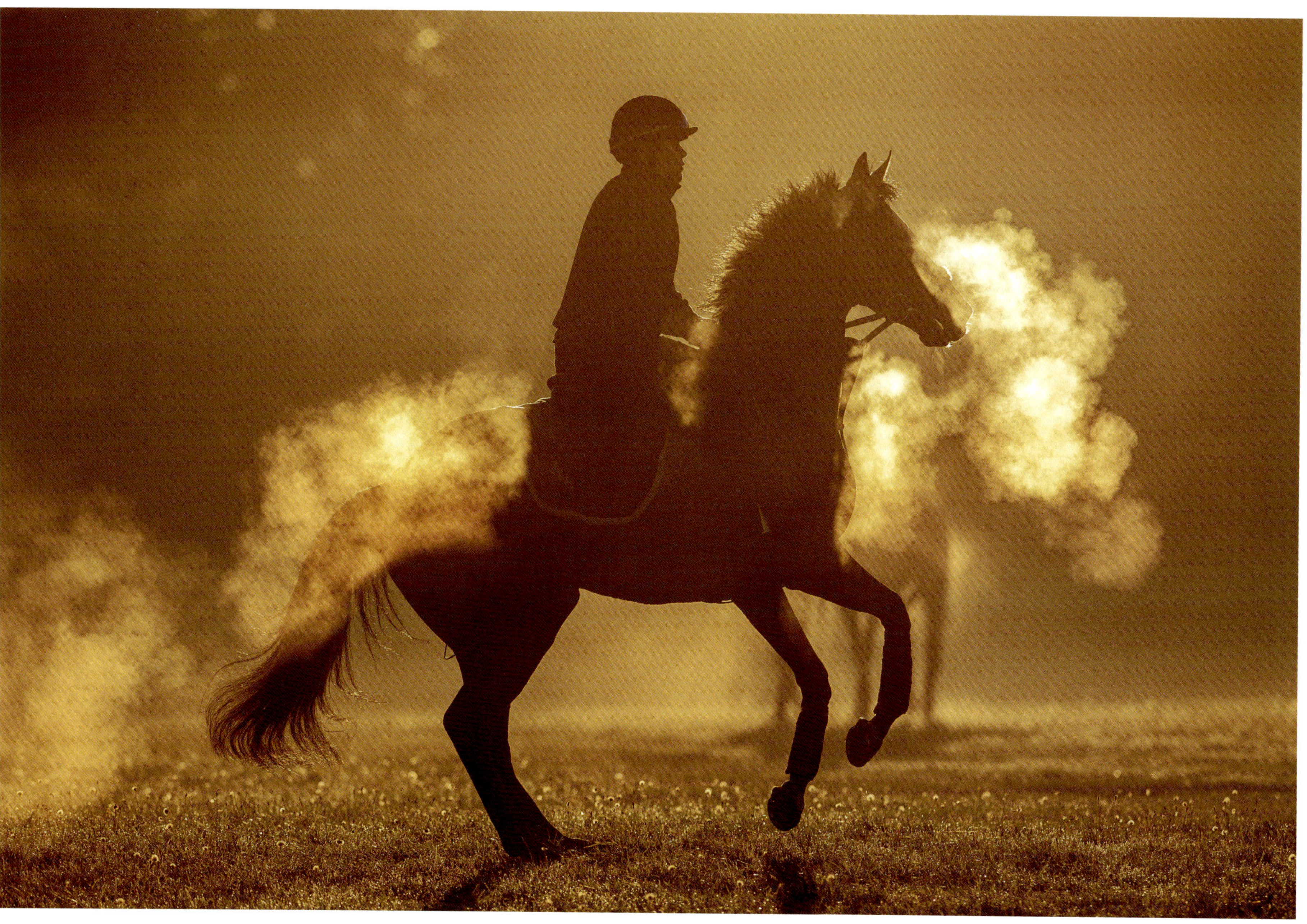

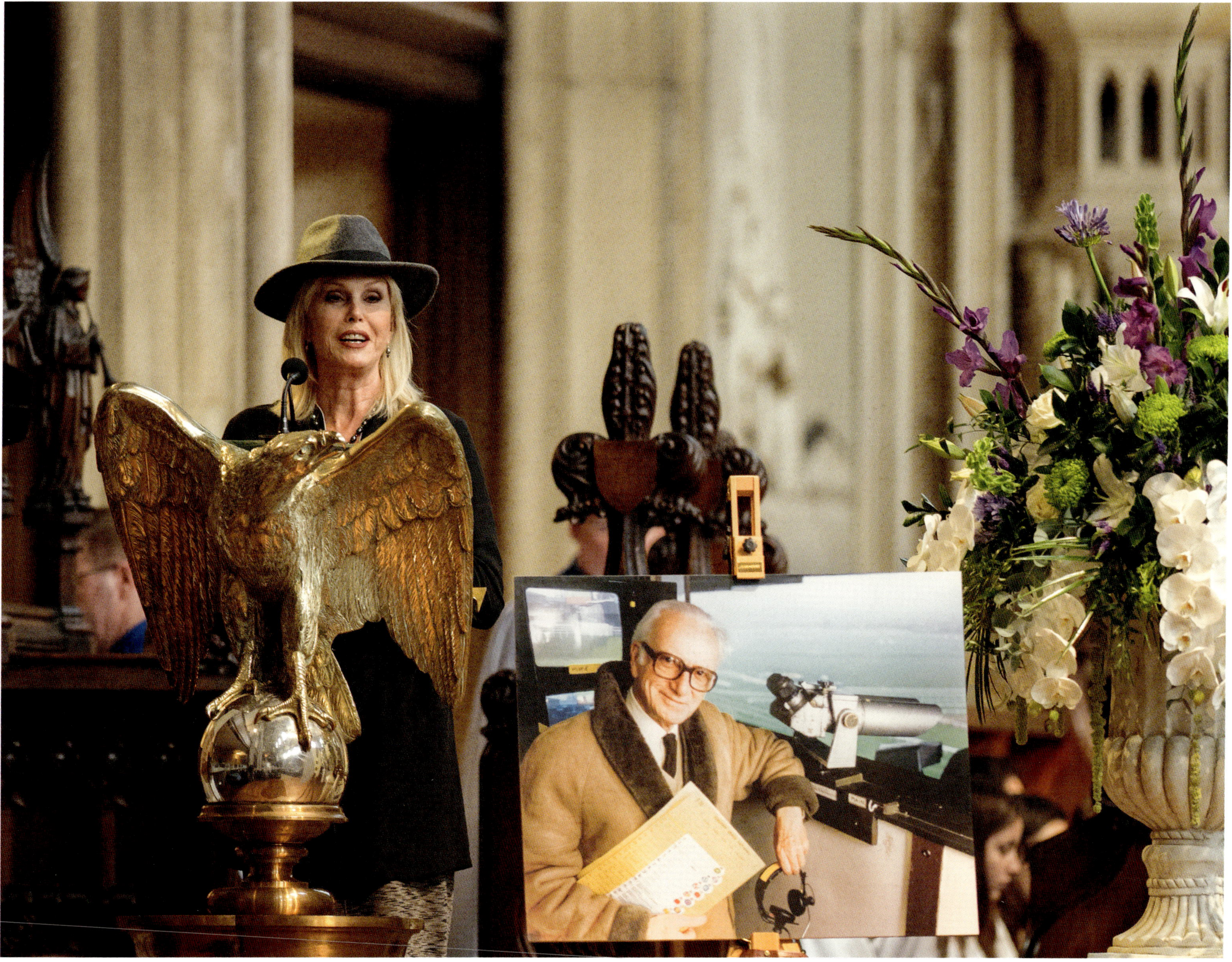

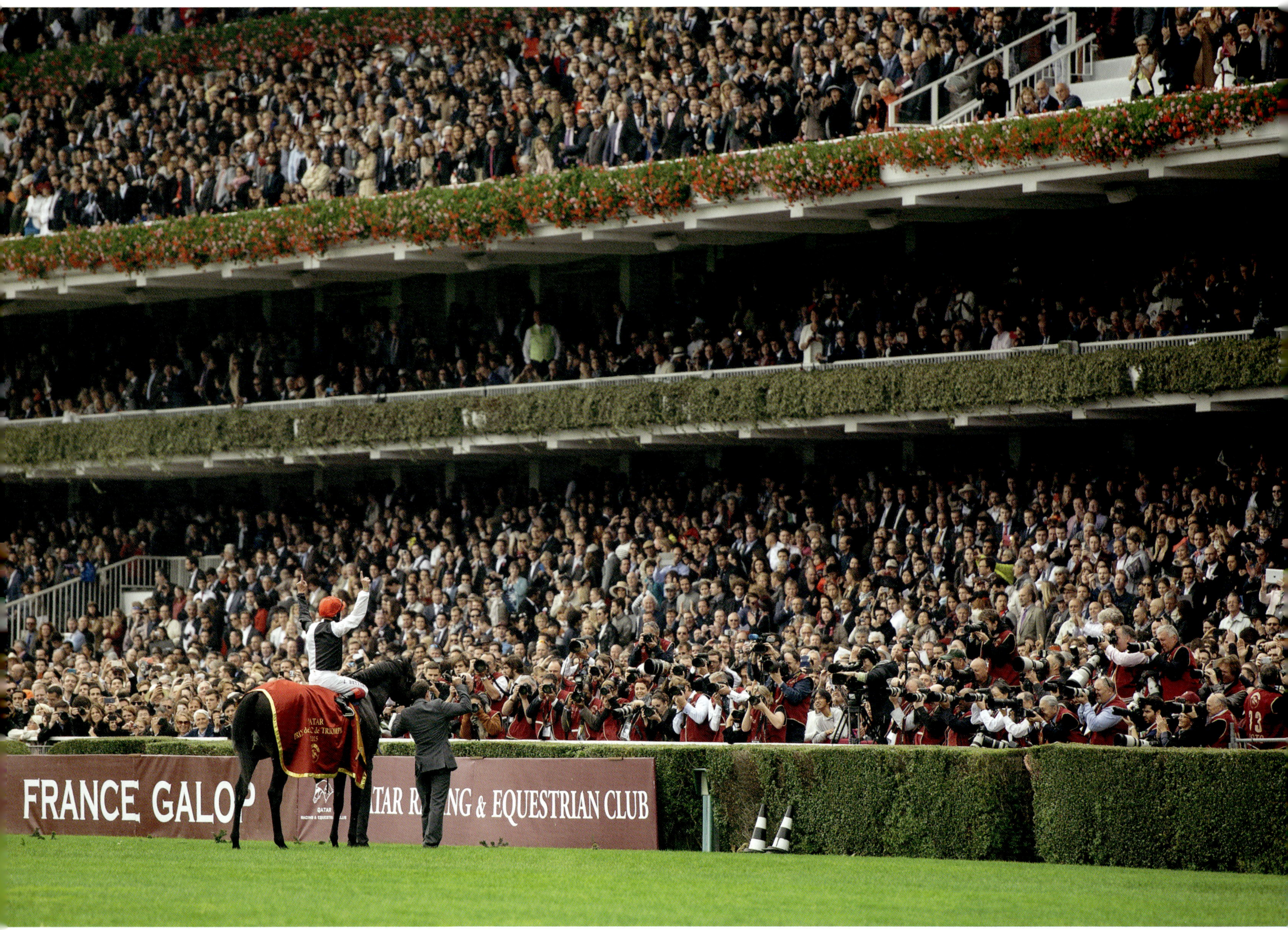

FRANCE GALOP
QATAR RACING & EQUESTRIAN CLUB

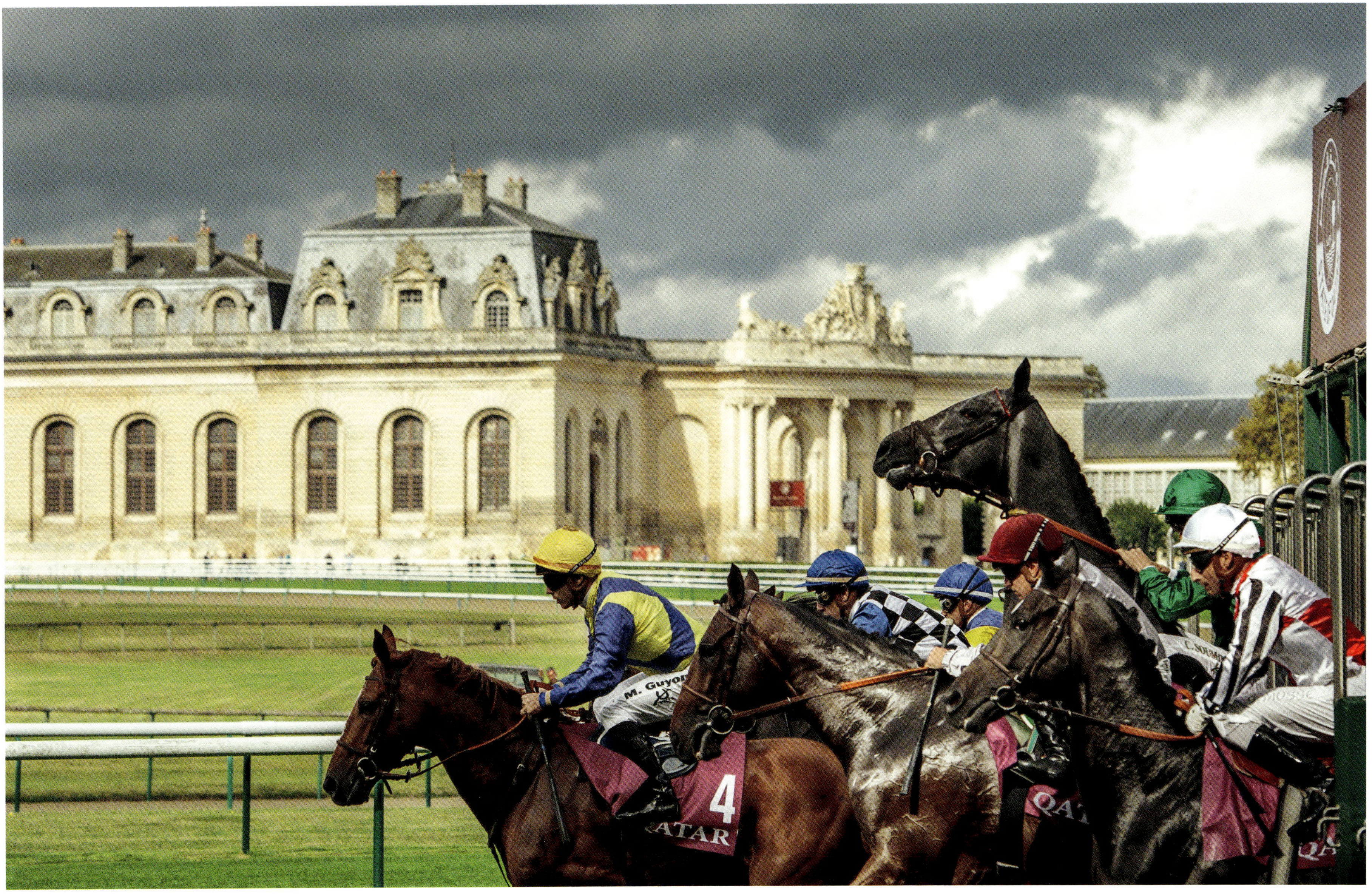

The final salute
The last 'Arc' at 'Old Longchamp'.
Frankie Dettori and Golden Horn
salute the crowds massed for the
2015 Prix de l'Arc de Triomphe.
The stands were to be demolished
the next day. It was a great sign-off.

History and histrionics
The grey filly Minamya rears leaving
the stalls for the Prix Chaudenay
at Chantilly. In the background are
Les Grandes Écuries – the stables
built because the Prince de Condé
thought he would be reincarnated
as a horse.

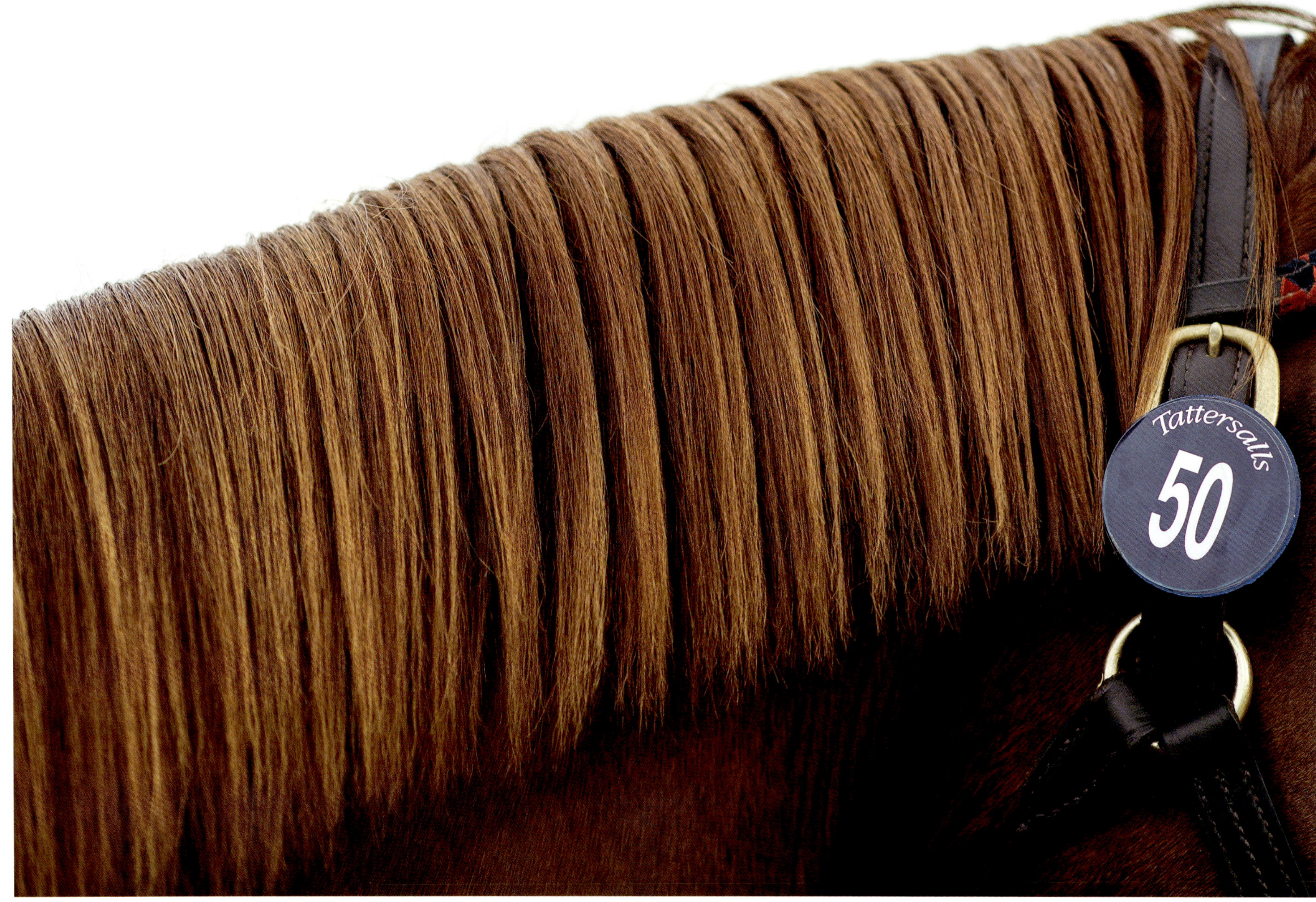

Not a hair out of place
The 'Book One Sale' at Tattersalls
is the most prestigious yearling sale
in Europe with unraced, un-galloped
youngsters making seven figures.
Worth spending some time – as
here – on a hairdo.

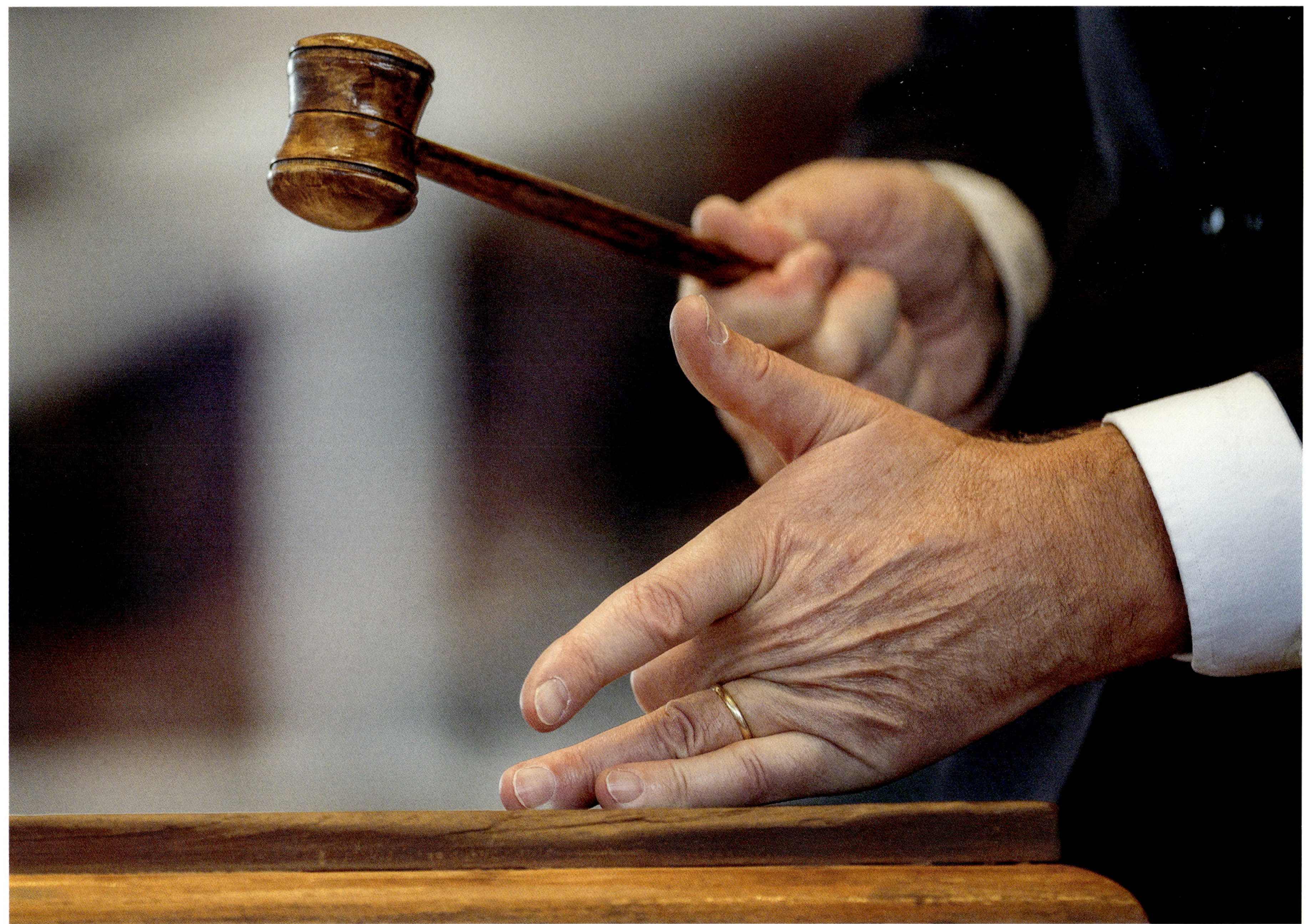

Going, going …
Auctioneer John O'Kelly has cracked
his gavel on some of the biggest
bloodstock sales ever made. In
October 2013, he knocked down a
yearling Galileo filly at Newmarket
for a cool 5 million guineas.

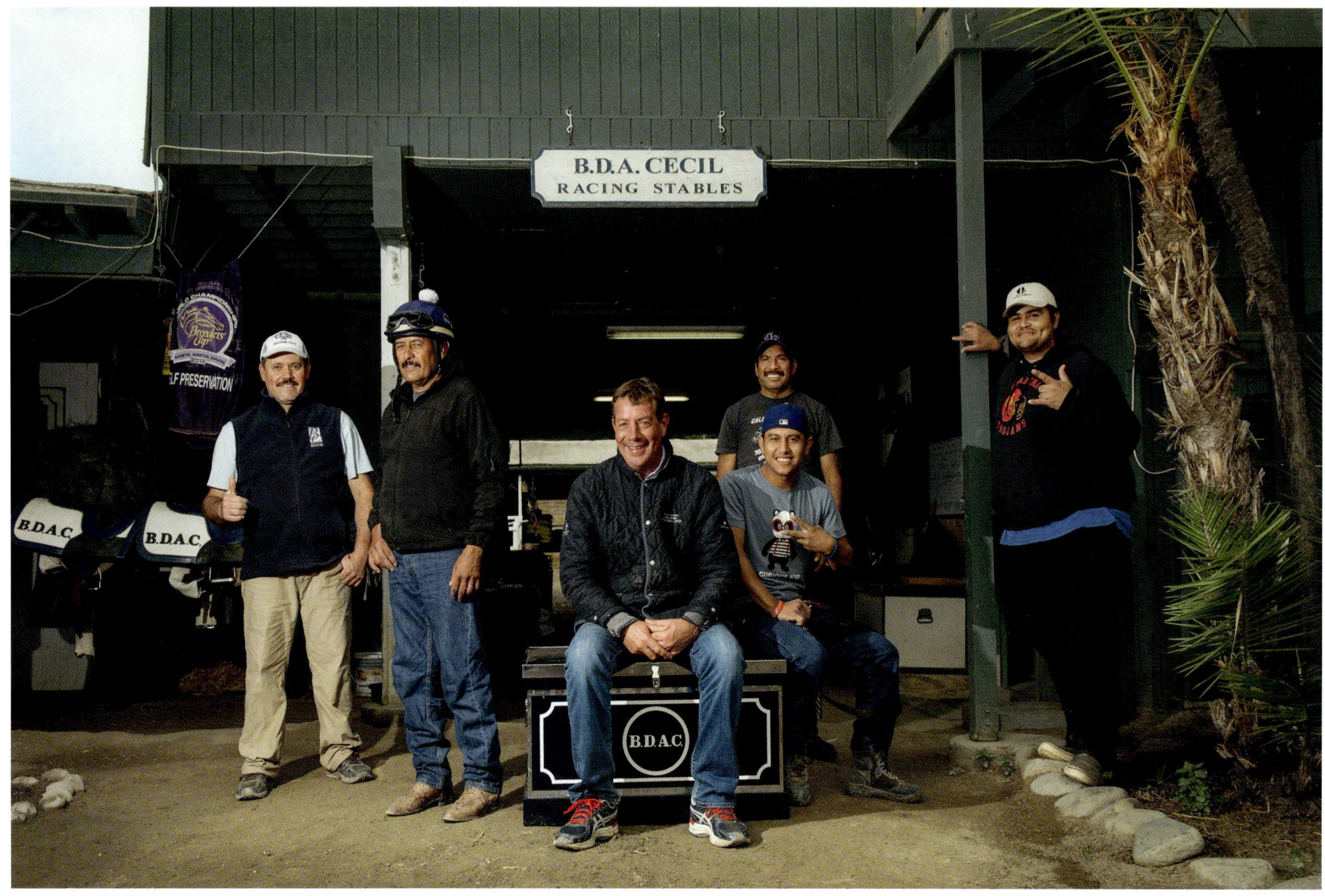

Teamwork

Henry Cecil's nephew Ben Cecil runs a happy training ship at Santa Anita but his team is mostly Mexican. This was a few days before Donald Trump's election so the future president's talk of a wall on the border was very unsettling.

Celestial light

The Les Aigles training grounds at Chantilly are amongst the most beguiling in the world. Add October mist and sun through the trees and you get something truly spectacular.

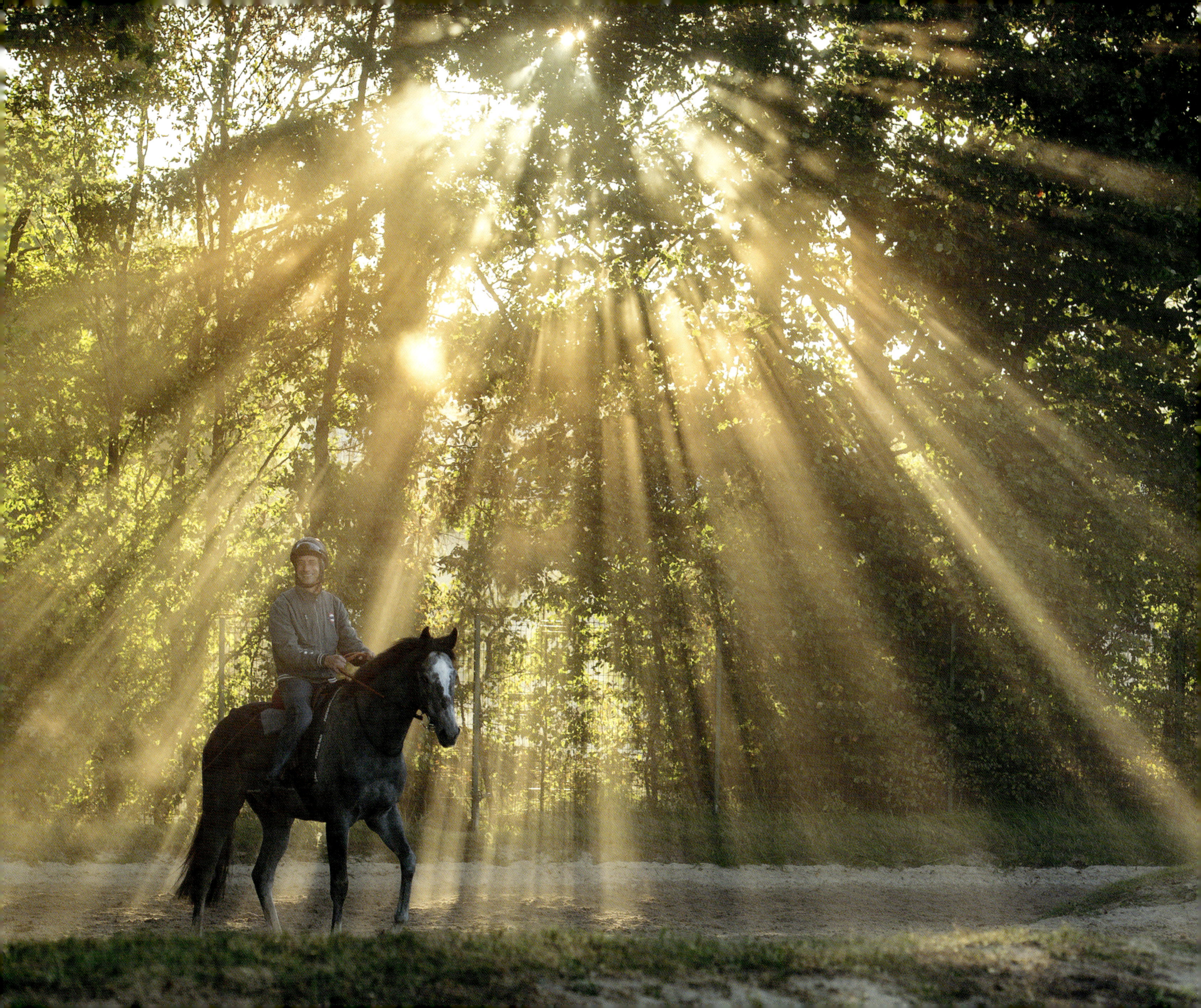

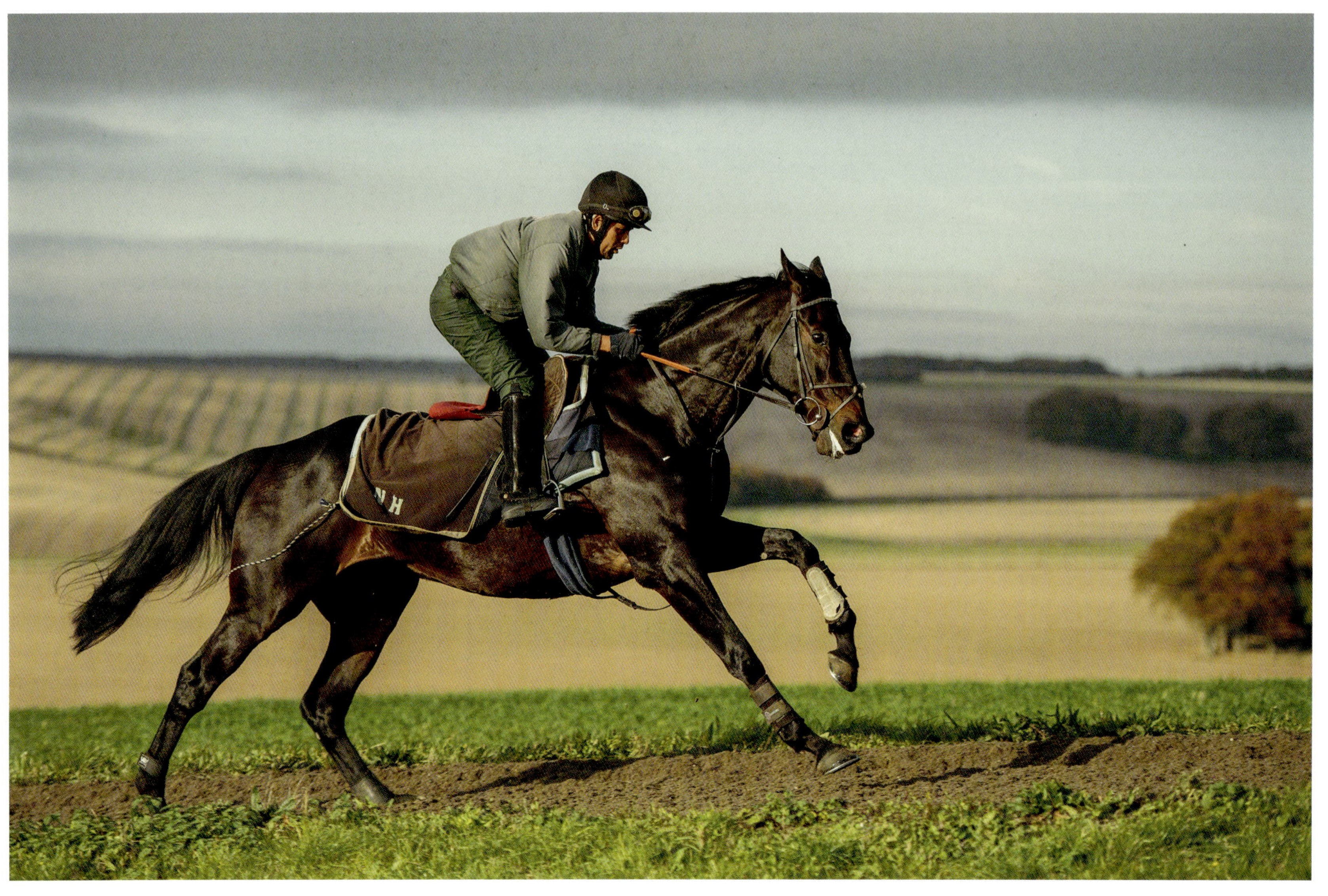

Monarch of Mandown
Sprinter Sacre: a symbol of power
and grace. His long-standing ally
Sarwar Mohammed takes the
champion chaser up the gallops
above Lambourn. It's my favourite
picture of him.

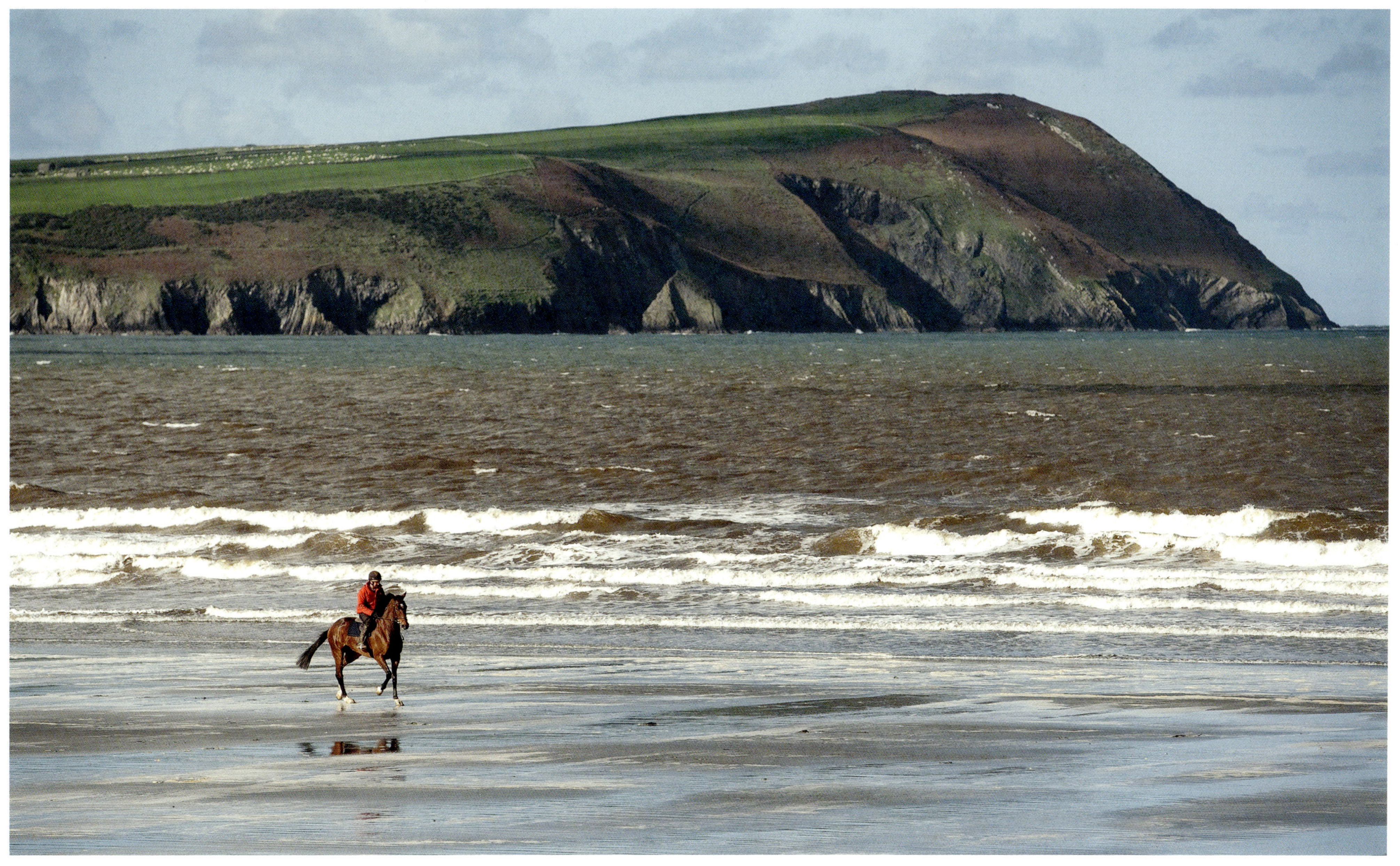

Lone ranger in the surf
By October, Newport Sands in
Pembrokeshire have emptied of
holidaymakers to leave Rebecca
Curtis' horses to exercise alone.
Here Cheltenham winner Teaforthree
and Alan Latter trot on the fringe of
the surf.

November

From the roof
The Breeders Cup Mile start at Santa
Anita. The elevation makes the
picture. They are fifty yards from the
start, the colours are rich against the
sand of the track and the winner is
to be Tamarkuz, nearest to us in the
blue silks of Sheikh Hamdan.

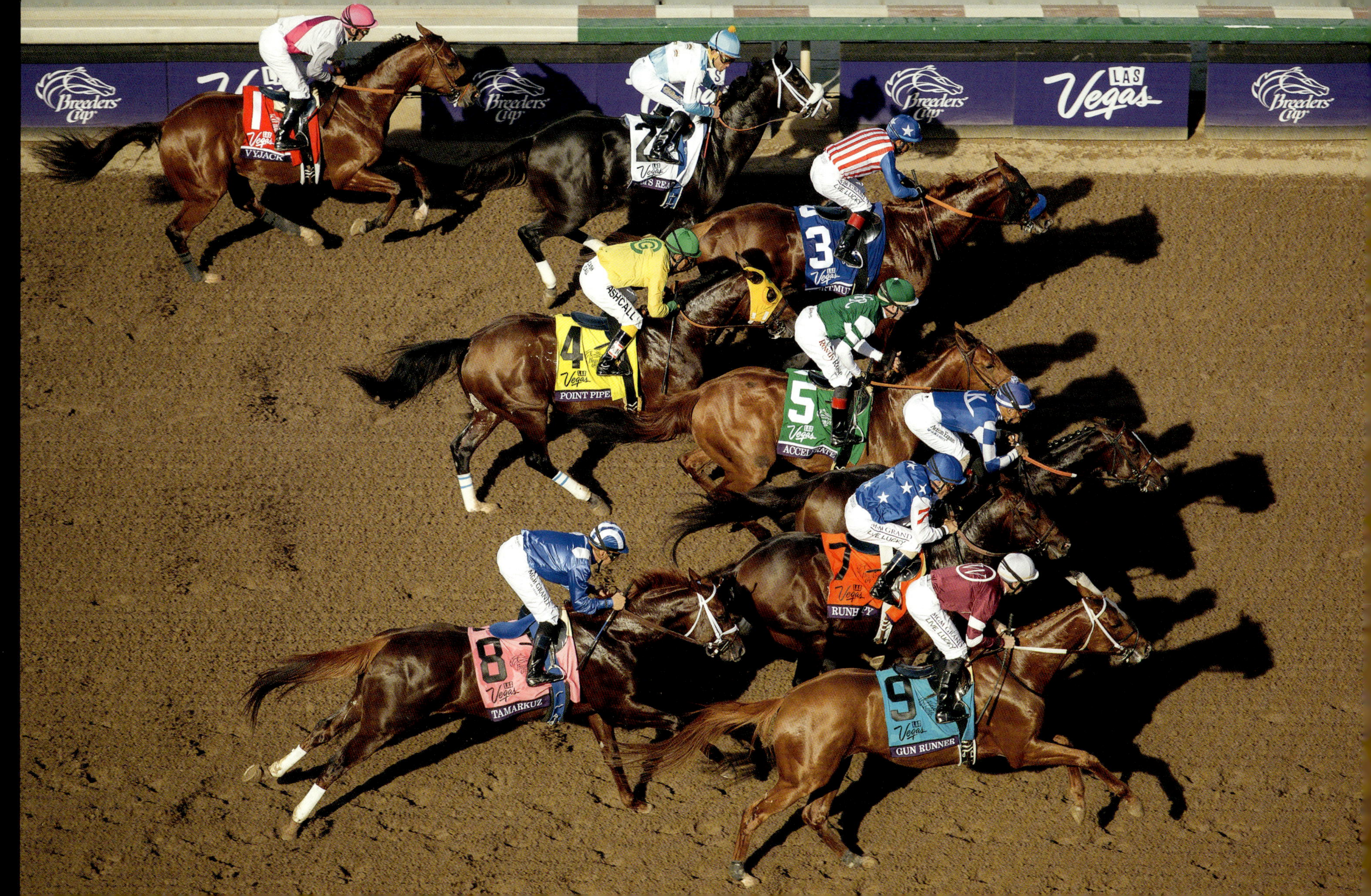

Breeders' Cup
LAS Vegas
VYJACK
ASHCALL
POINT PIPE
3
4
5
ACCELERATE
7
RUNHAPPY
8
TAMARKUZ
9
GUN RUNNER

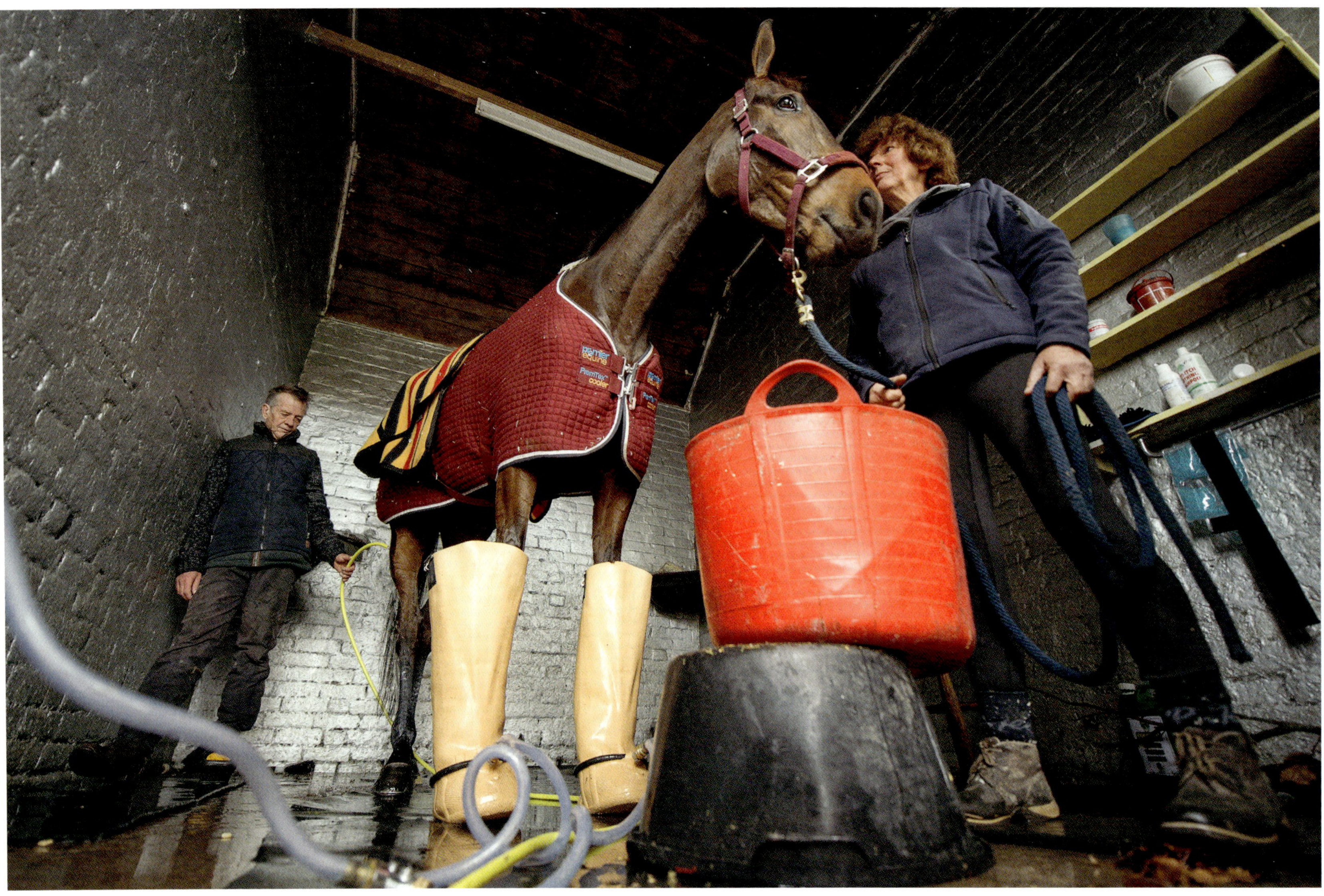

Ice boots

Poor old Coneygree became almost as famous for his battles against injury as he did for winning the 2015 Cheltenham Gold Cup. Here Sally Golding holds the bridle while his legs have the ice treatment and trainer Mark Bradstock looks on.

Hind legs hiccup

A bizarre leap from If In Doubt and Barry Geraghty during the 2015 Hennessy Gold Cup. It looks as if he has been trained to tuck his legs up like a showjumper.

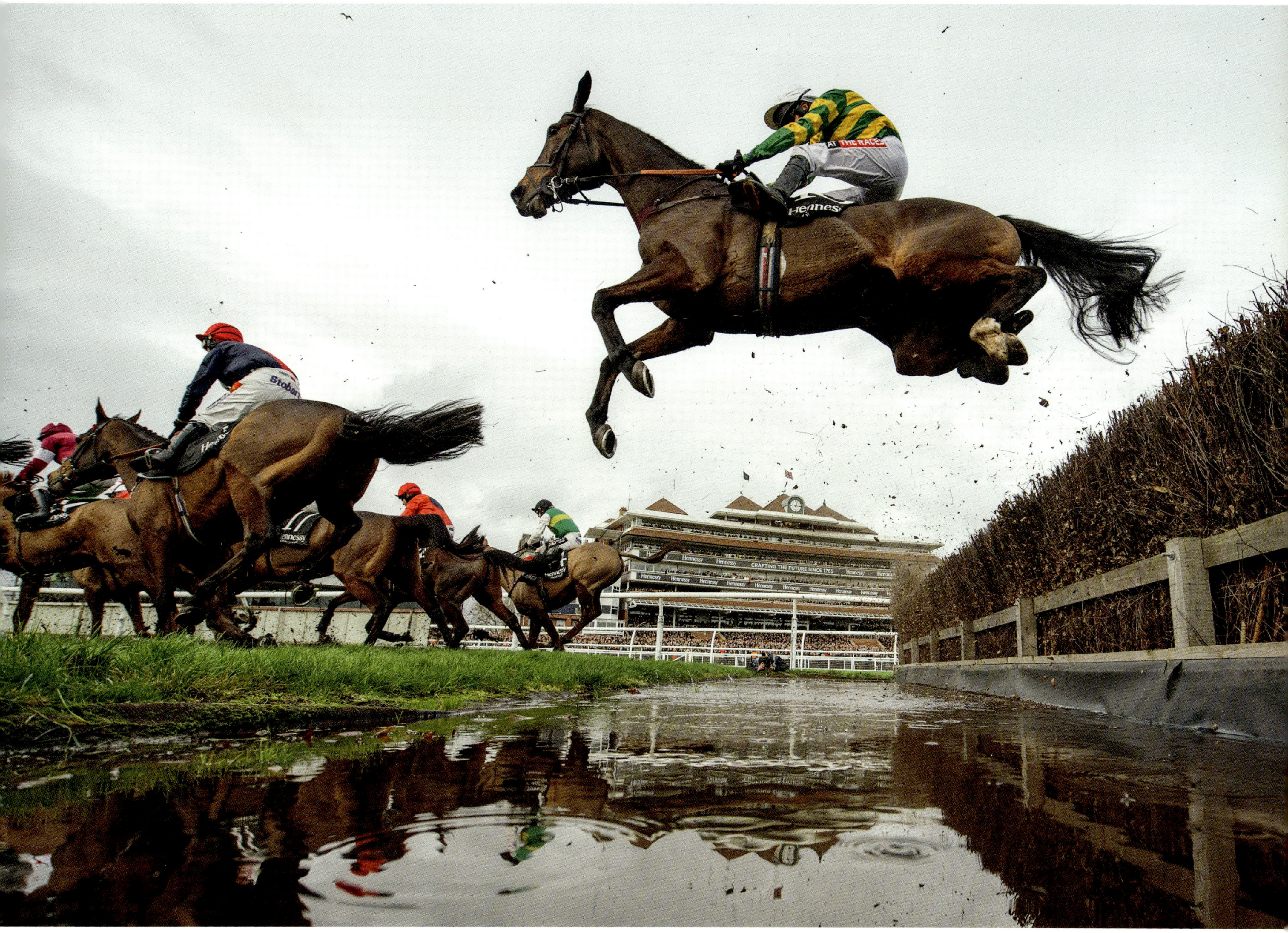

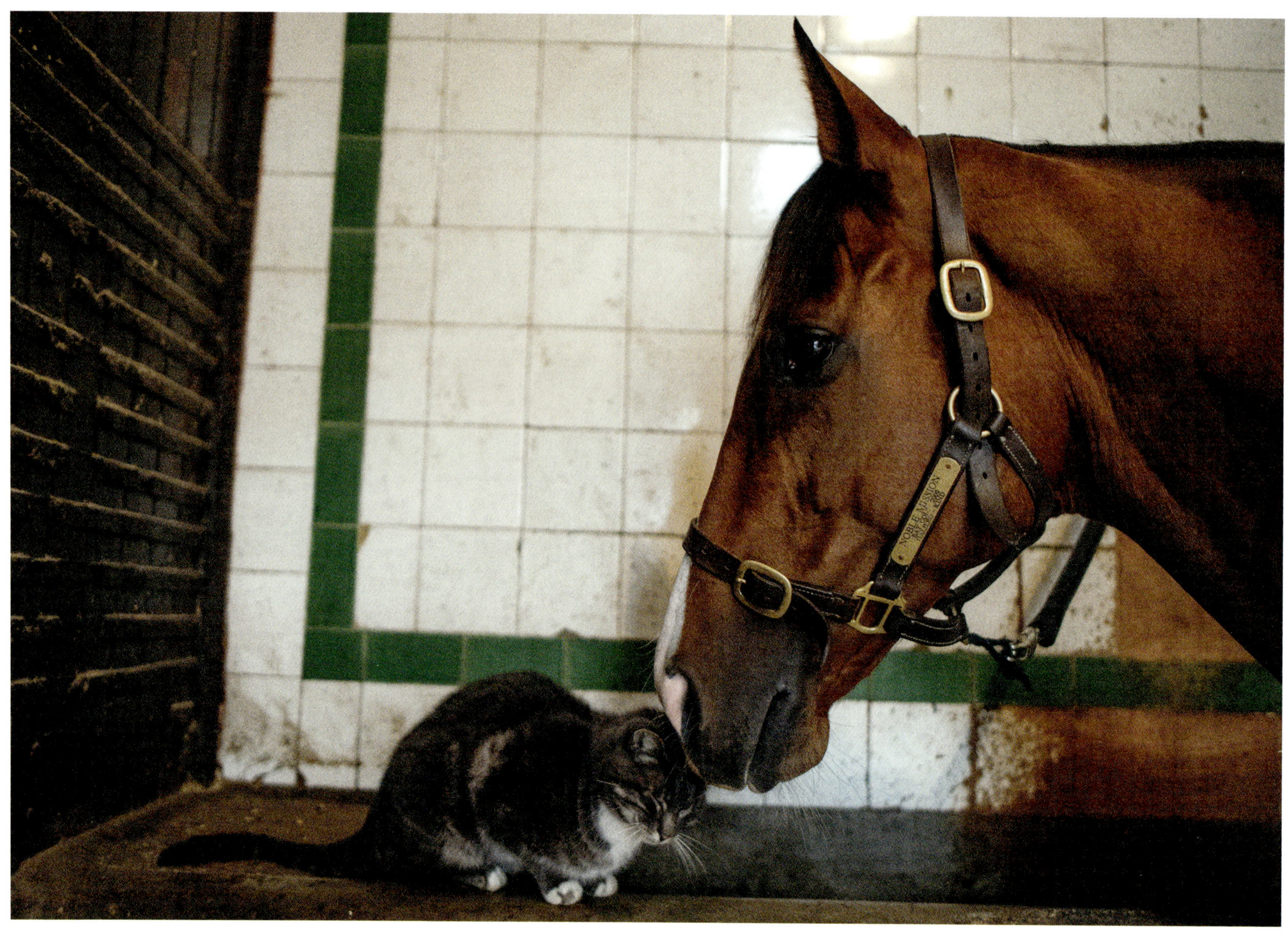

My furry friend
Frankel's full brother Noble Mission
became a top horse in his own
right before he left Warren Place
for stud duties in Kentucky. No one
would miss him more than Felix the
stable cat.

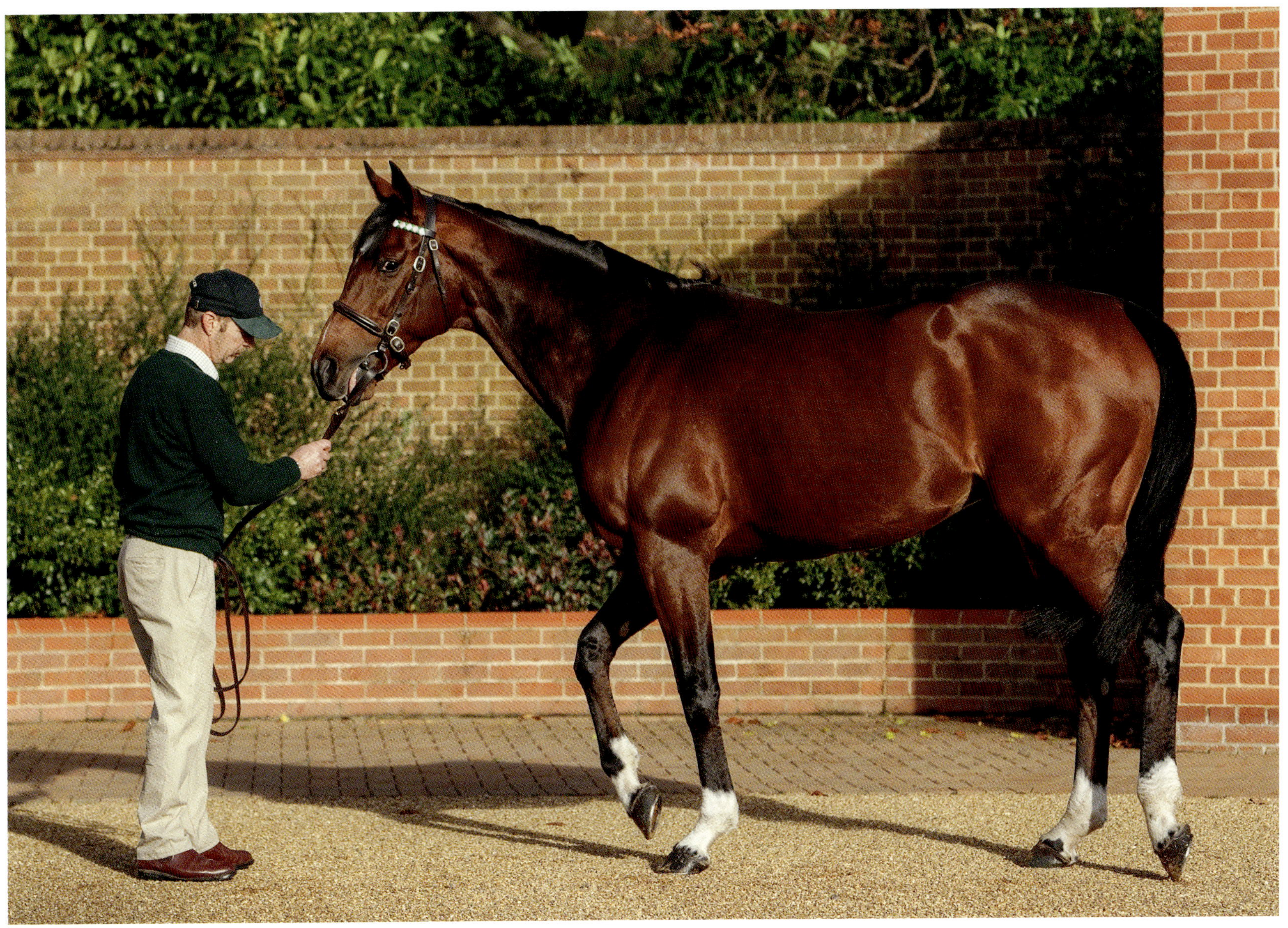

Ready for the new career
Rob Bowley holds Frankel as the
superstar arrives at Banstead
Manor to be unveiled as a stallion
in November 2012. Five weeks after
his final triumph he still looked much
more of a racehorse than the burly
potentate many stallions become.

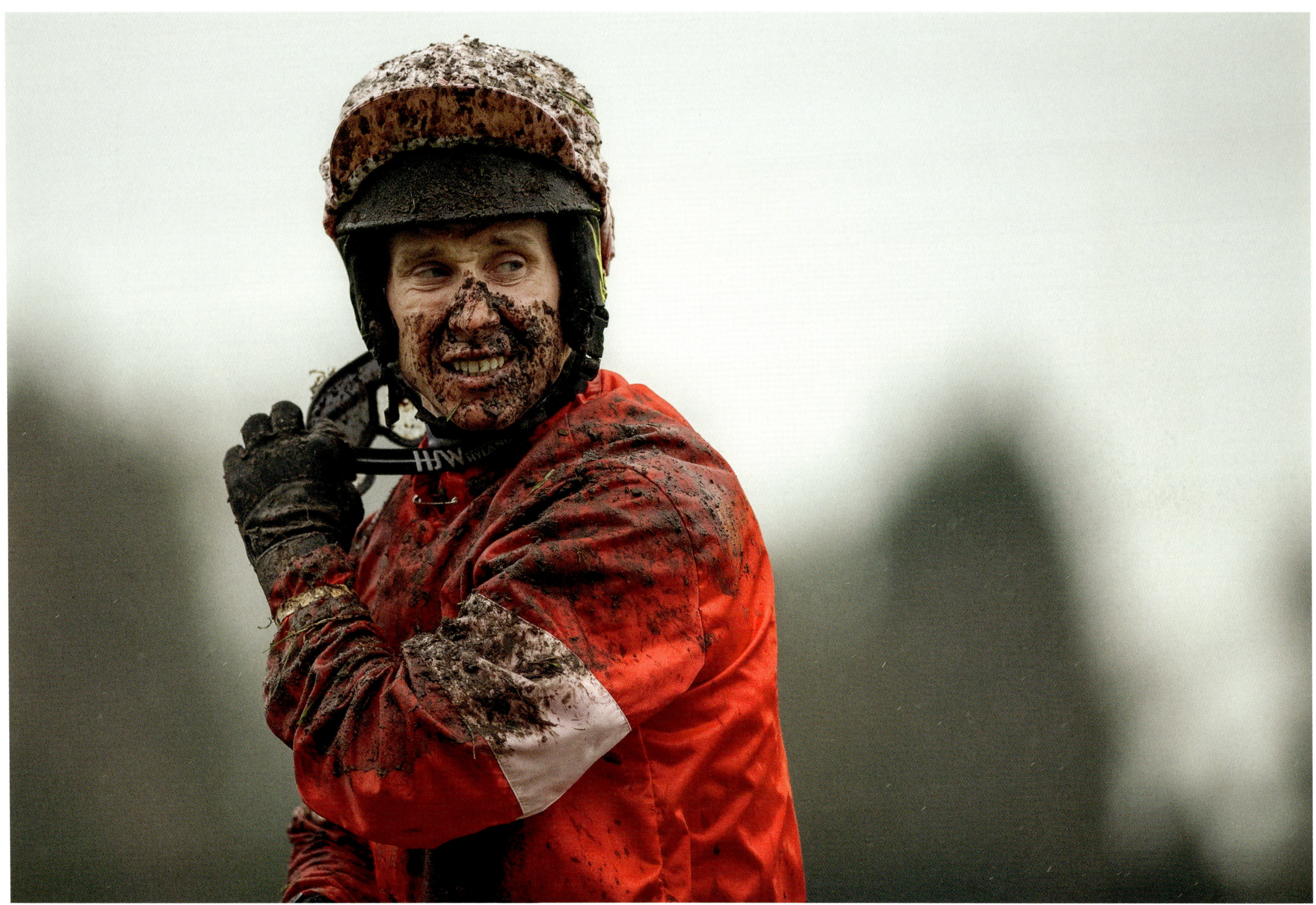

Tough mudder
Richard Johnson is the very opposite
of the fair-weather sportsman.
For more than 20 years he has
battled away in wind, mud, sun and
rain. Into his 40s he still soldiers
magnificently on.

The ground is always waiting
Richard Johnson knows the score.
Springtown Lake had cleared the last
hurdle at Wincanton only to buckle
up two strides later.

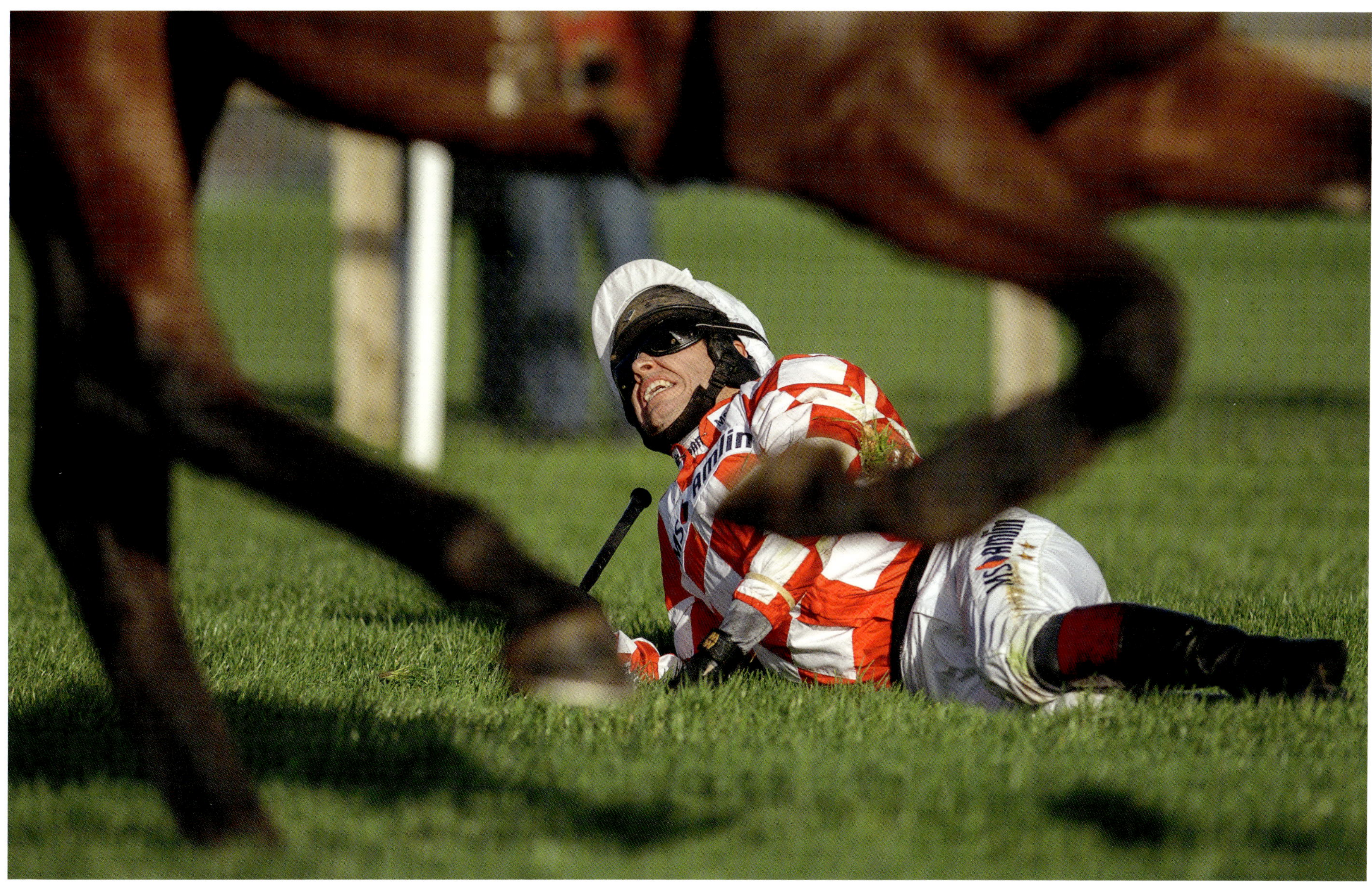

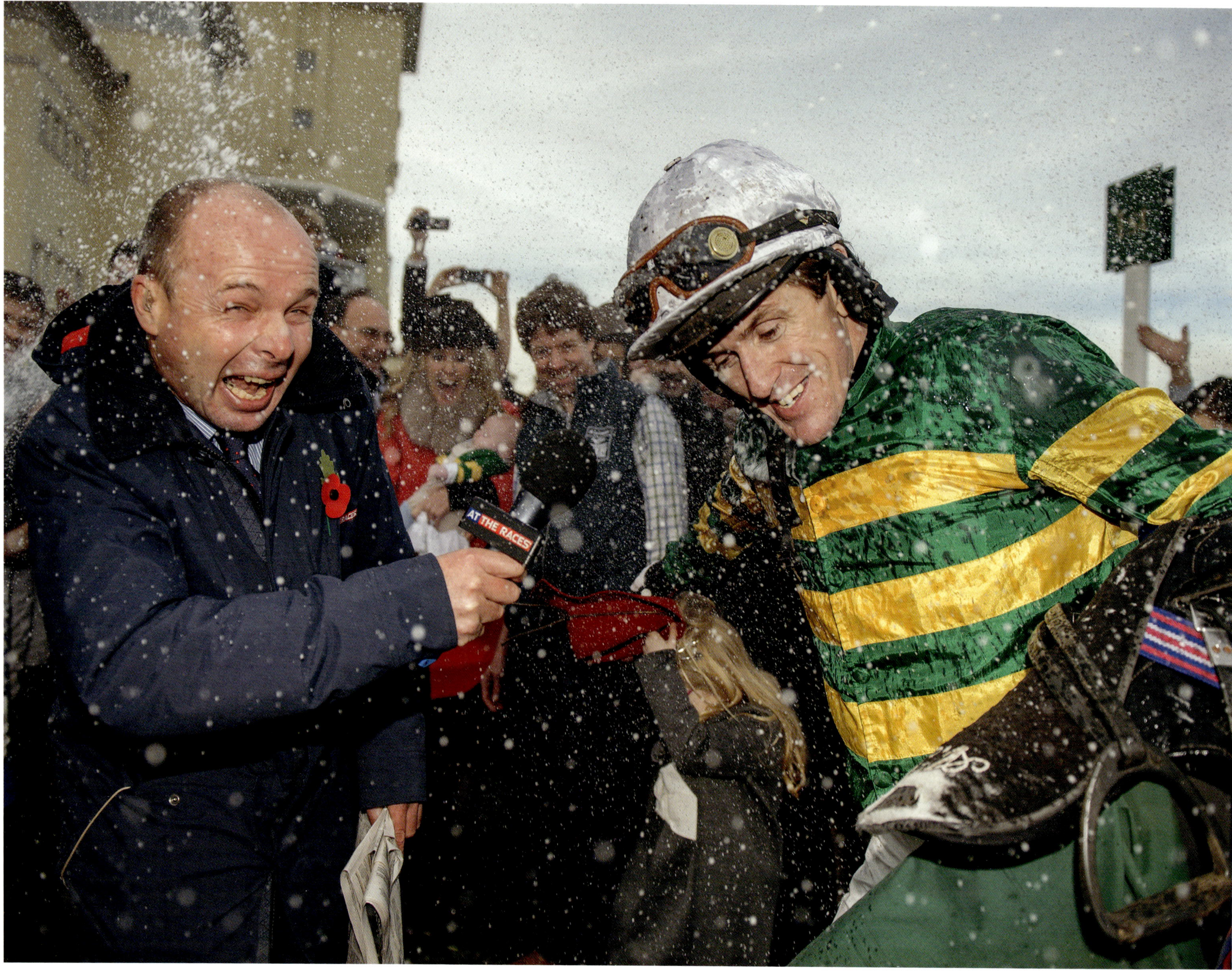
AT THE RACES

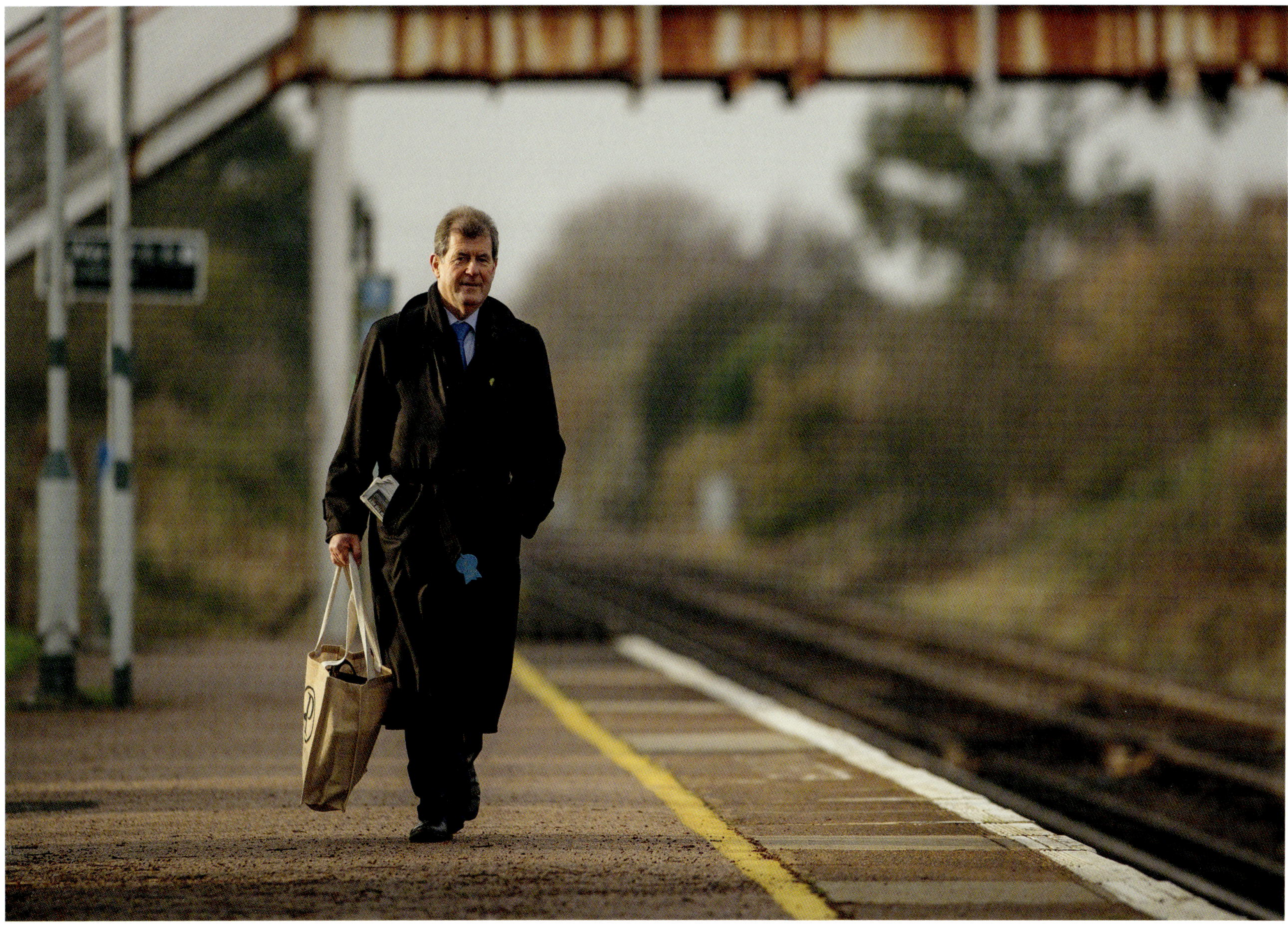

4,000 bubbles!
AP McCoy is hit by a champagne
storm as Luke Harvey tries to
interview him after his 4,000th
winner at Towcester on Mountain
Tunes. McCoy is a teetotaller but
must have absorbed half a bottle's
worth in spray alone.

Solitary passenger
JP McManus had travelled down
from London to watch two of his
horses win at Plumpton. The bag
contains the prizes.

San Gabriel backdrop
A fisheye lens view across Santa
Anita racetrack to the San Gabriel
Mountains that stretch from the
Pacific Ocean to the Mojave Desert.
Normal images only show a part of
them, but with this we see the whole
track and full range.

California sunrise
No one morning is the same at
Santa Anita and even here the sun
is changing from gold to orange to
red to purple. As a photographer
you cannot have enough of it.

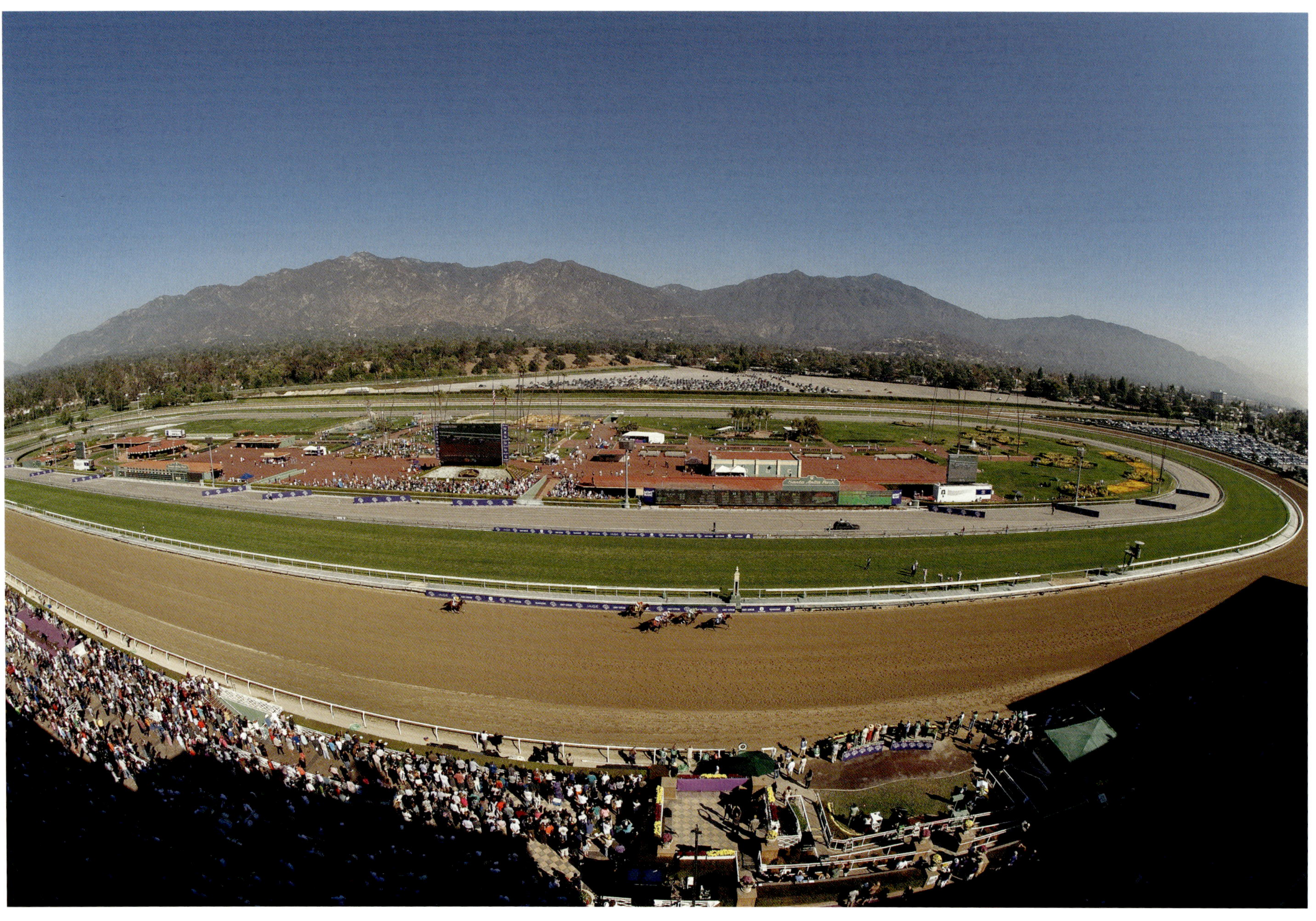

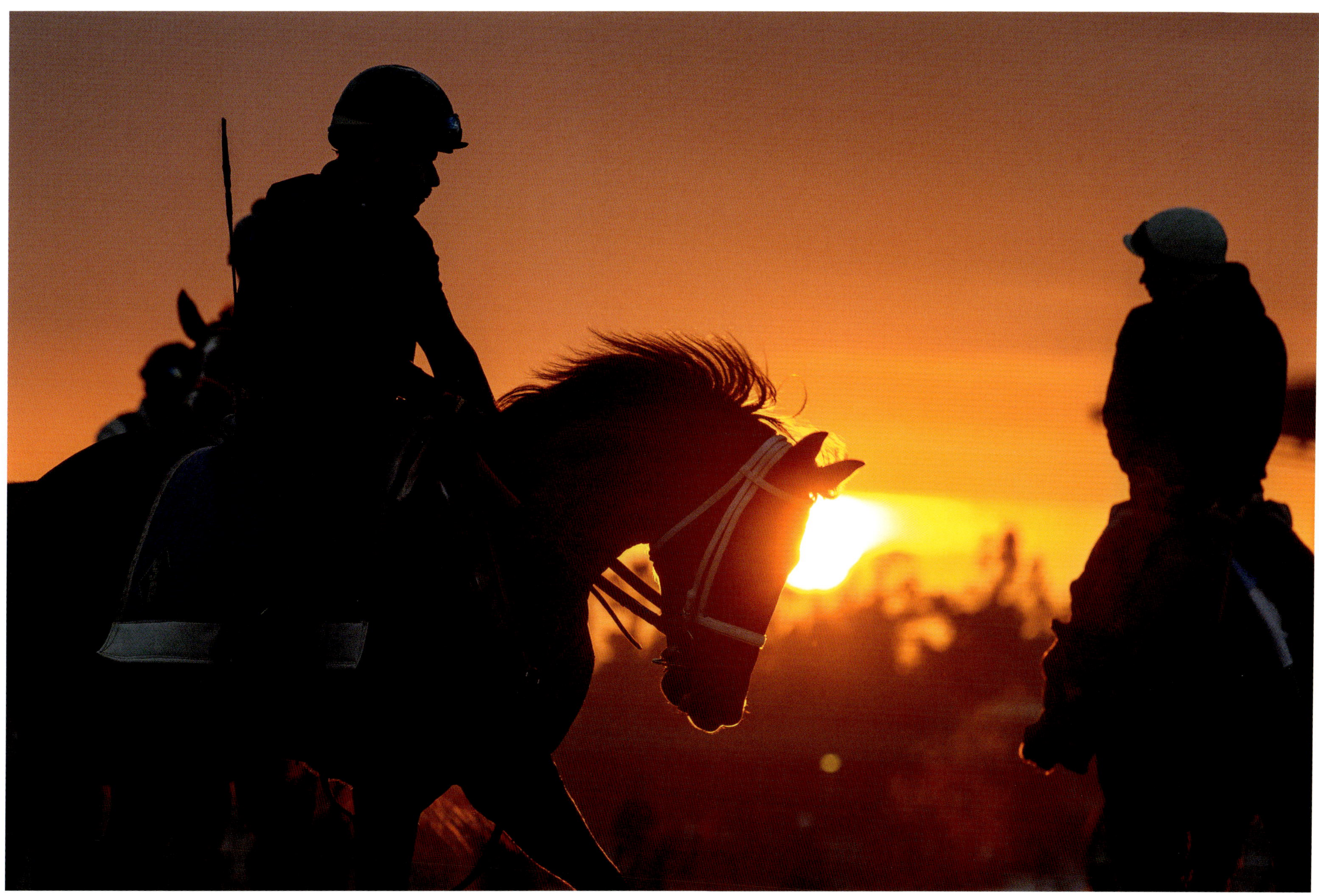

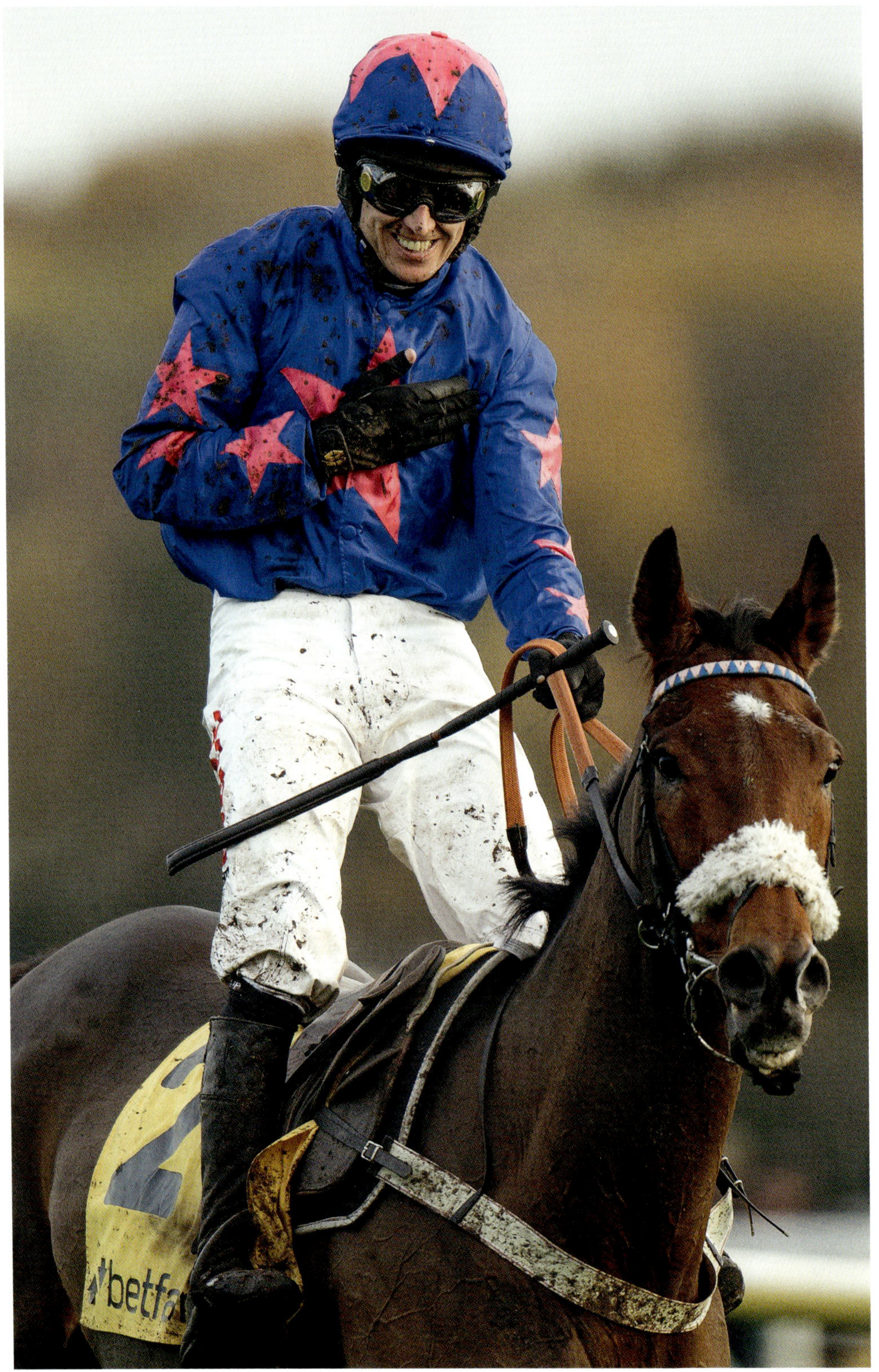

Hand on heart
Paddy Brennan hugs himself as
Cue Card pulls up after winning
Haydock's Betfair Chase in
November 2016. That March the pair
had thrown away a victory chance
in the Gold Cup. The hug was one
of redemption.

A perfect rainbow
We quite often see rainbows
on racetracks but I have never
photographed one as perfectly
framed as this at Haydock. The
centrepieces are Brio Conti and
a young Harry Cobden with silks
to match the image.

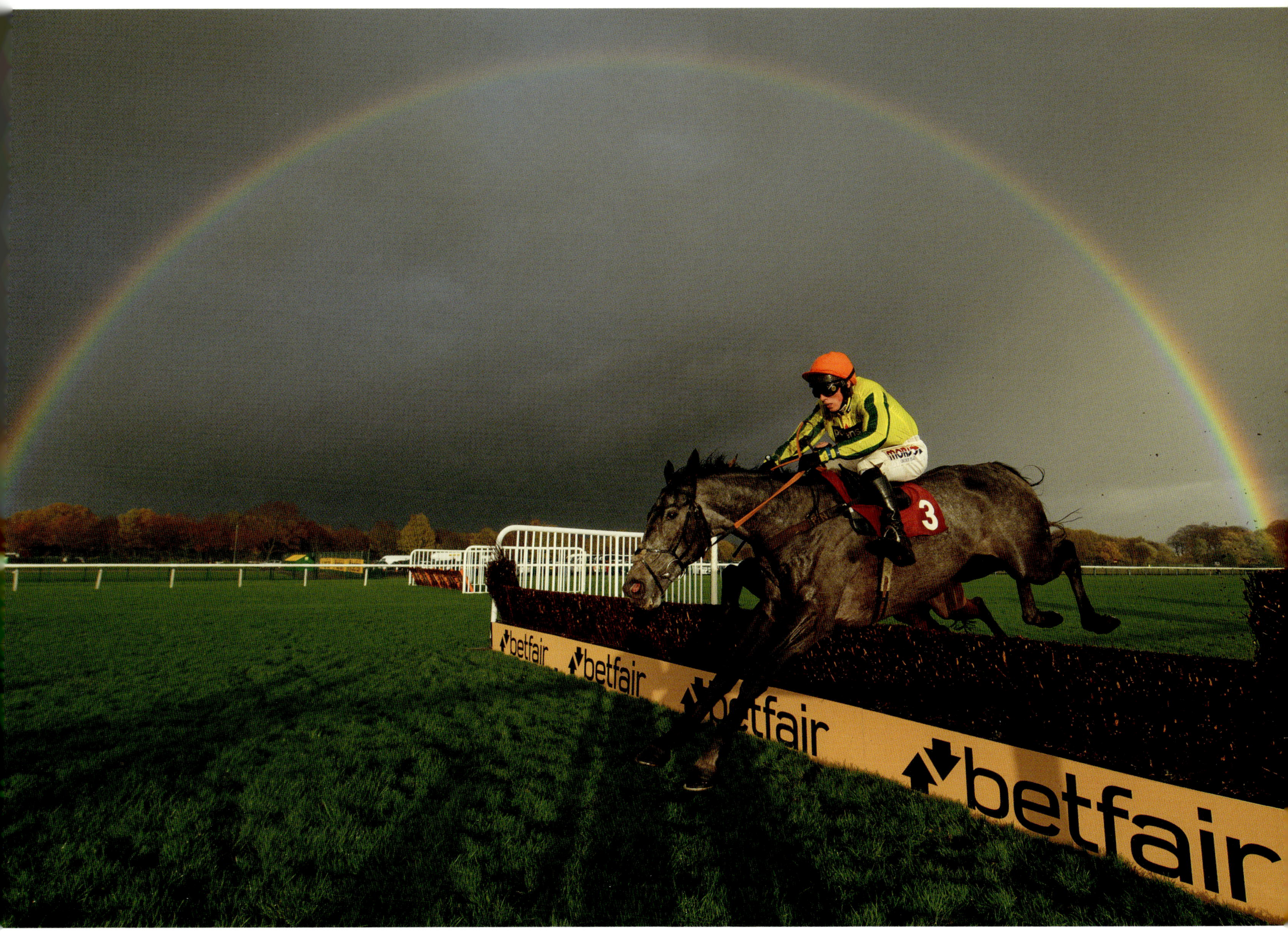
betfair
betfair
betfair
betfair
3

December

Spraying the birch
The grey Vibrato Valtat and
Noel Fehily power through the last
fence before winning the Henry
VIII Novices' Chase at Sandown.
The worm's eye effect comes from
a remote camera at the foot of
the fence.

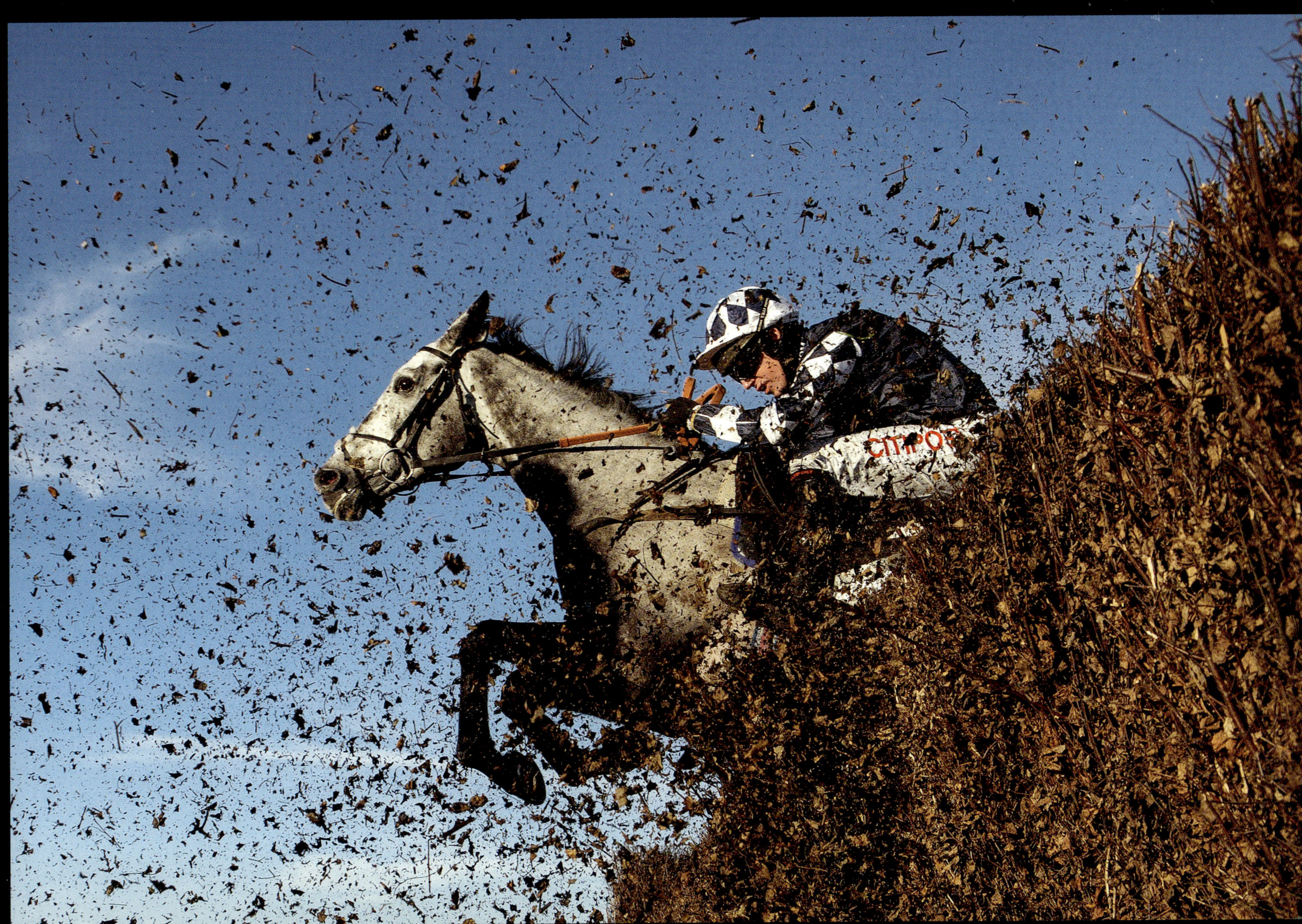

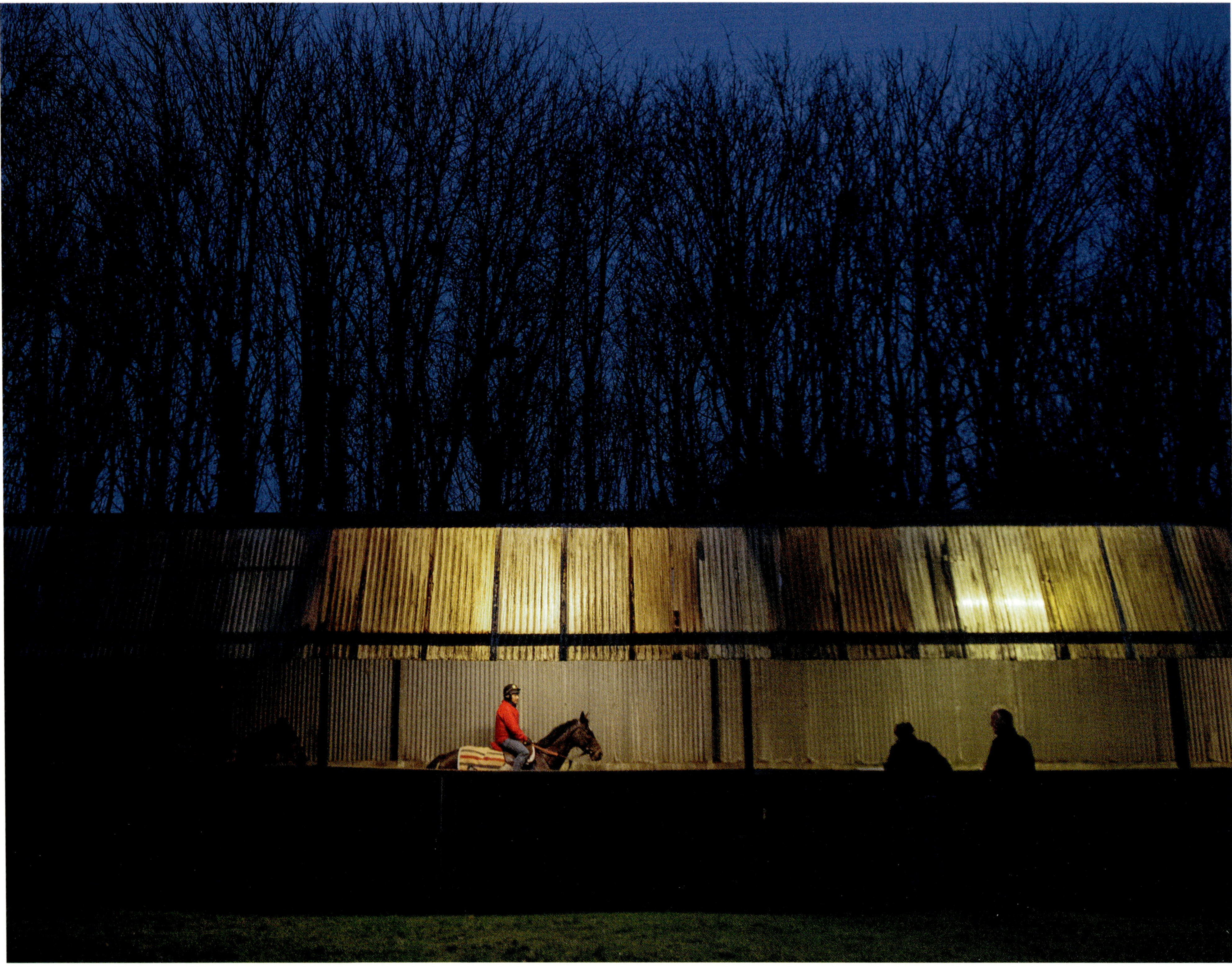

Lamplight at Lambourn
The covered ring at Seven Barrows
does more than protect horse and
rider. It gives the chance for this
great visual effect with gold and
scarlet before the dawn.

How it went
Paul Moloney (left) on Buywise
shares thoughts with young Charlie
Deutsch on Aso as the pair trot back
after the Caspian Caviar Handicap
Chase at Cheltenham. Aso had run
on to snatch second on the line, but
Moloney's was a more distant look.

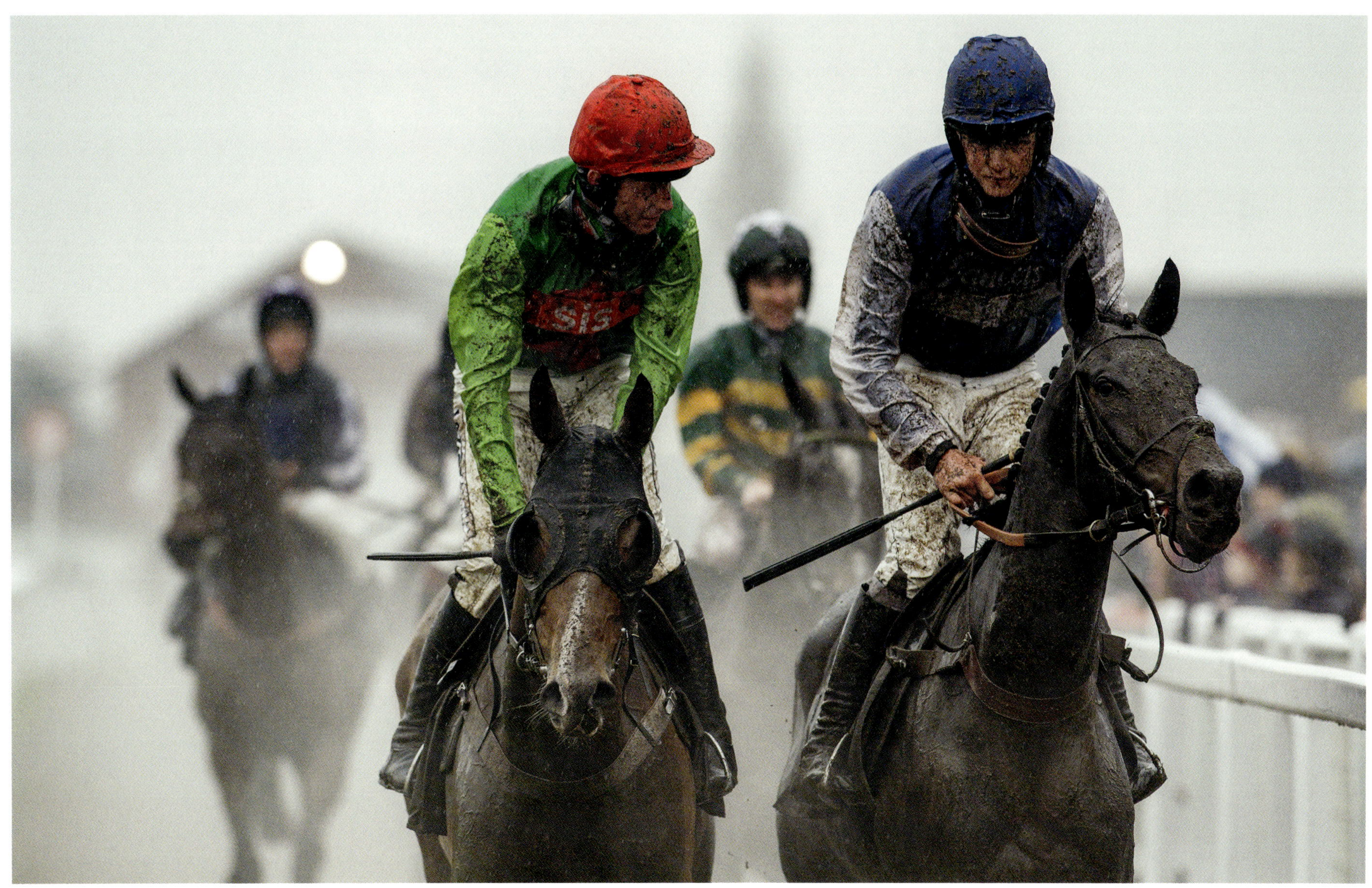

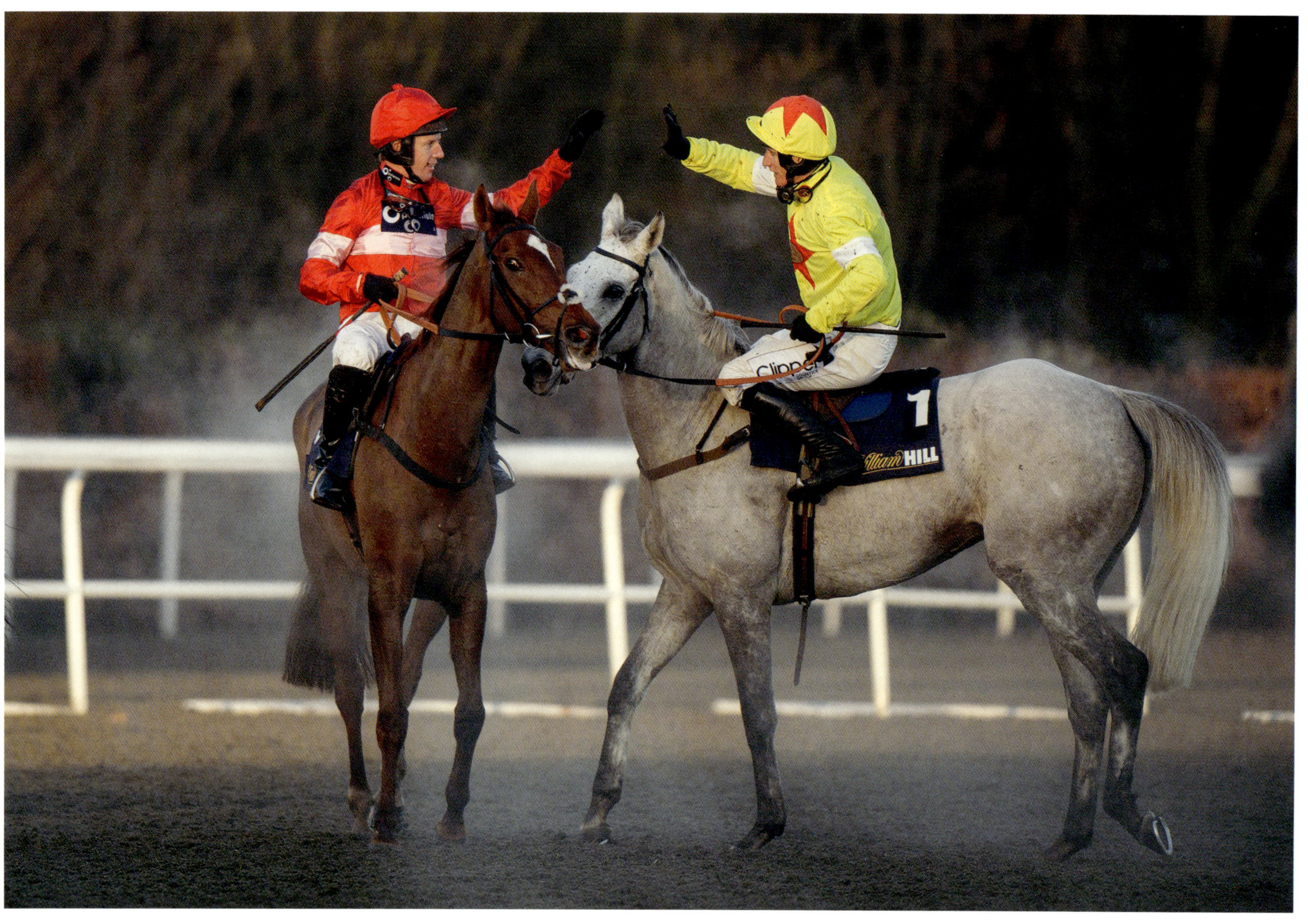

High five
A red-silked Noel Fehily is
congratulated by Daryl Jacob after
winning the 2013 King George VI
Chase at Kempton on Silviniaco
Conti with Daryl close up third on
stablemate Al Ferof. Camaraderie
ousts competition once the post
is past.

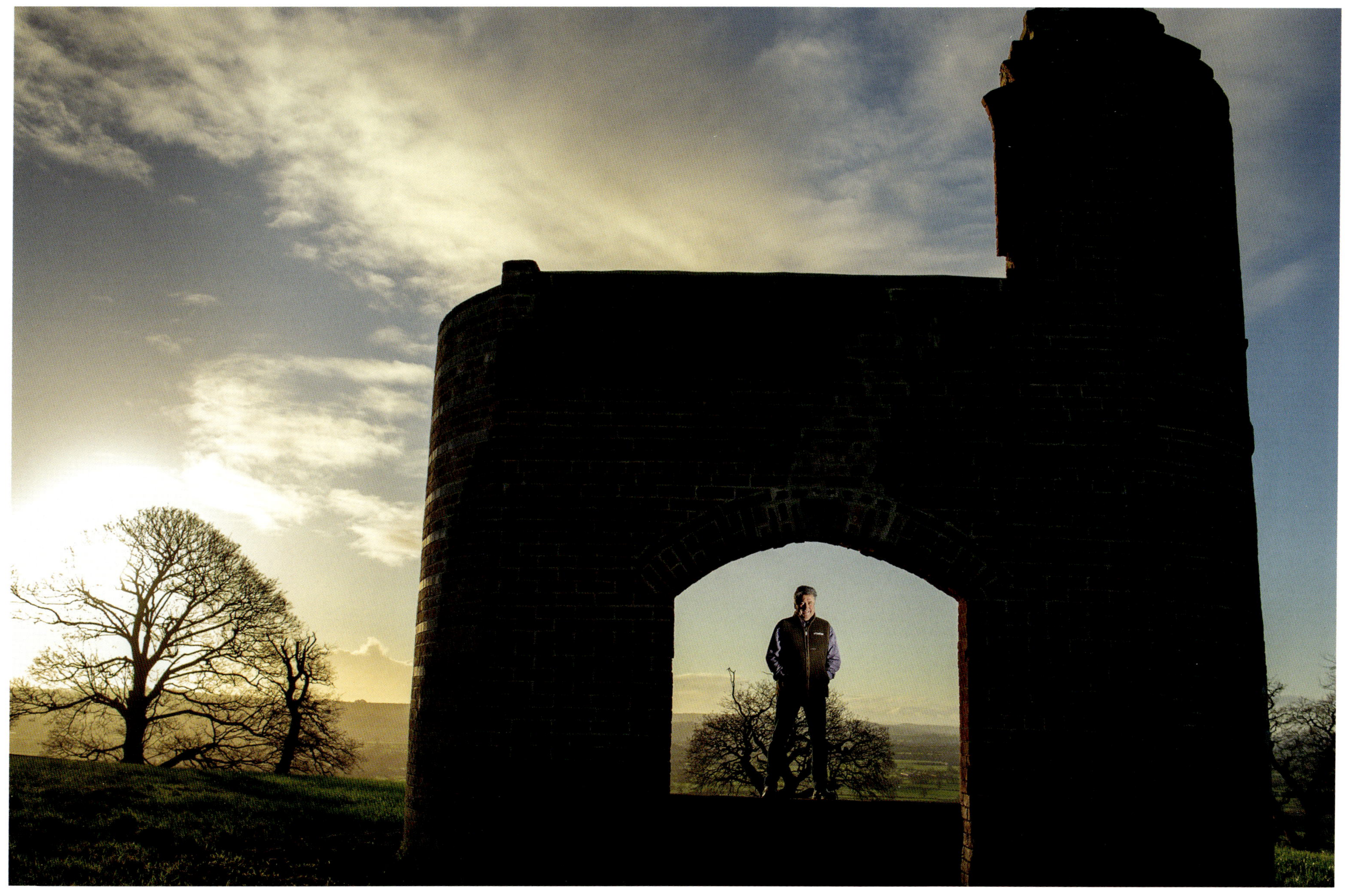

Ancient frame
A view of Paul Nicholls through the
red brick folly that tops his gallop
up Ditcheat Hill. A cold, clear
view, a perfect frame and a sunrise
morning in Somerset.

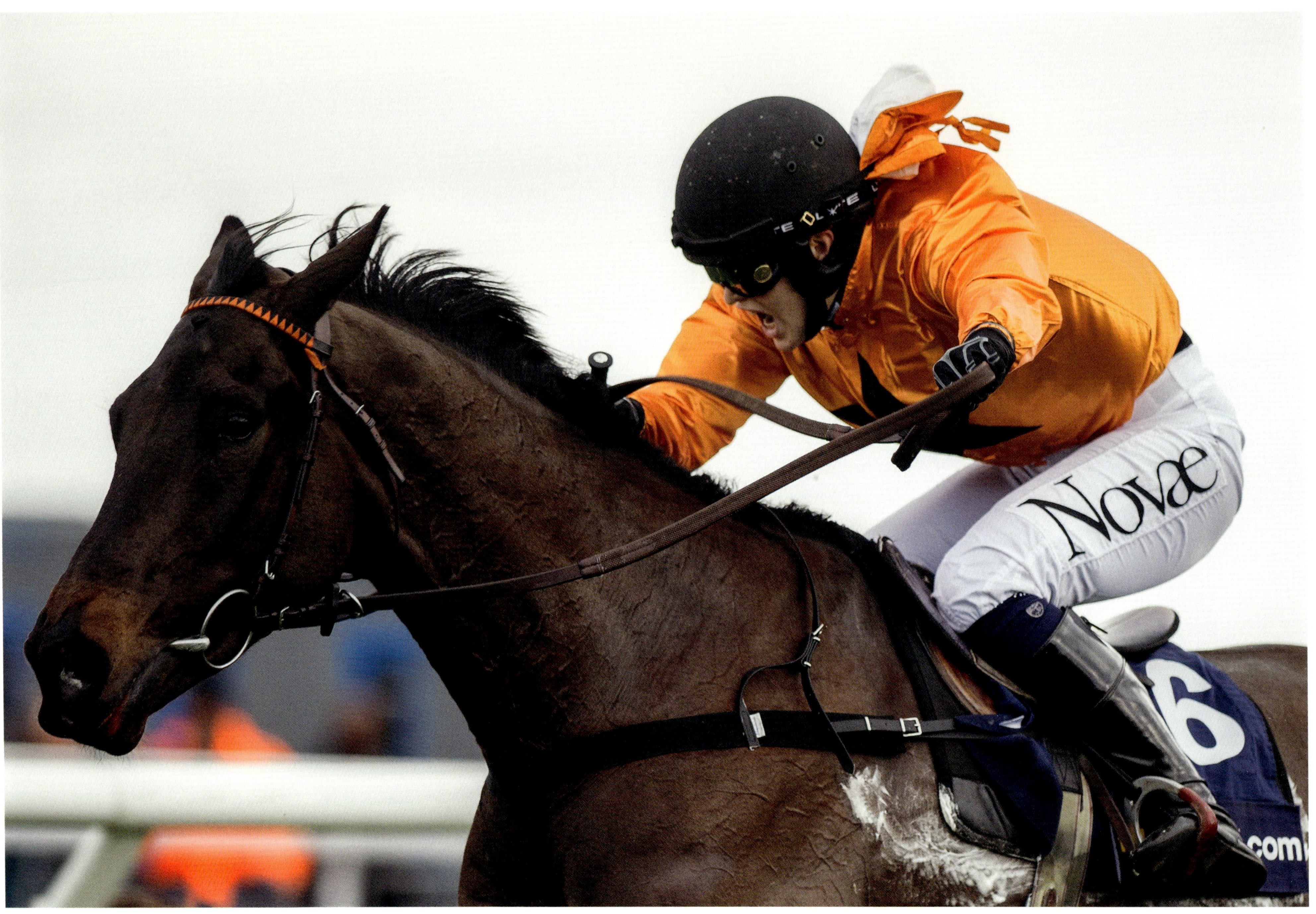

Girl power 1
Lizzie Kelly on Tea For Two in full
cry as she wins the Grade 1 Kauto
Star Novices' Chase at Kempton
on Boxing Day in 2015. She was
becoming the first woman to win
a race of this category in Britain
and wasn't likely to forget it.

Girl power 2
Bryony Frost drives Black Corton
home to win the same Kauto Star
Novices' Chase at Kempton two
years later. It was one of eight races
the pair took together in the 2017/18
season and was to put Bryony firmly
on the map.

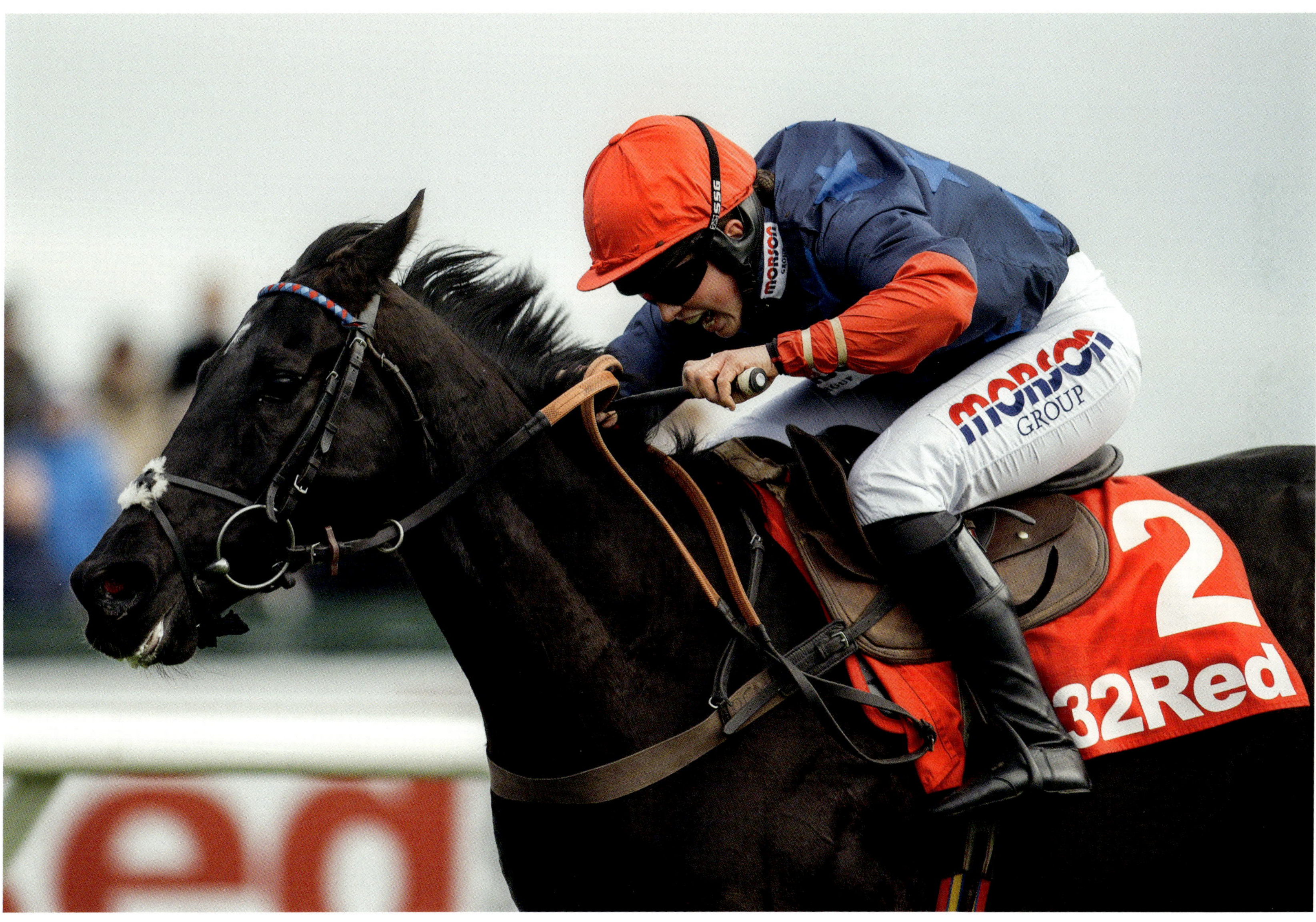
morson
GROUP
2
32Red

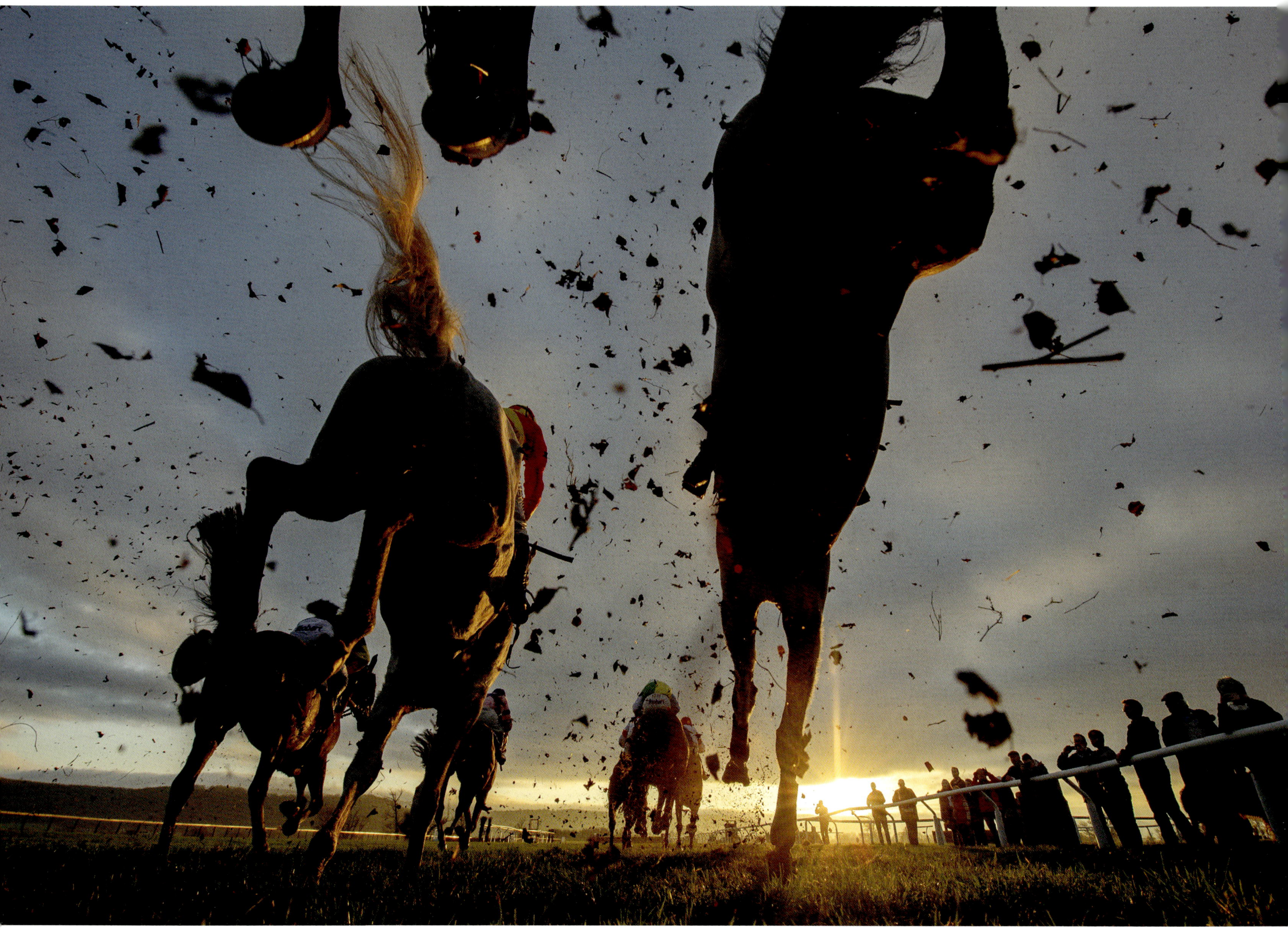

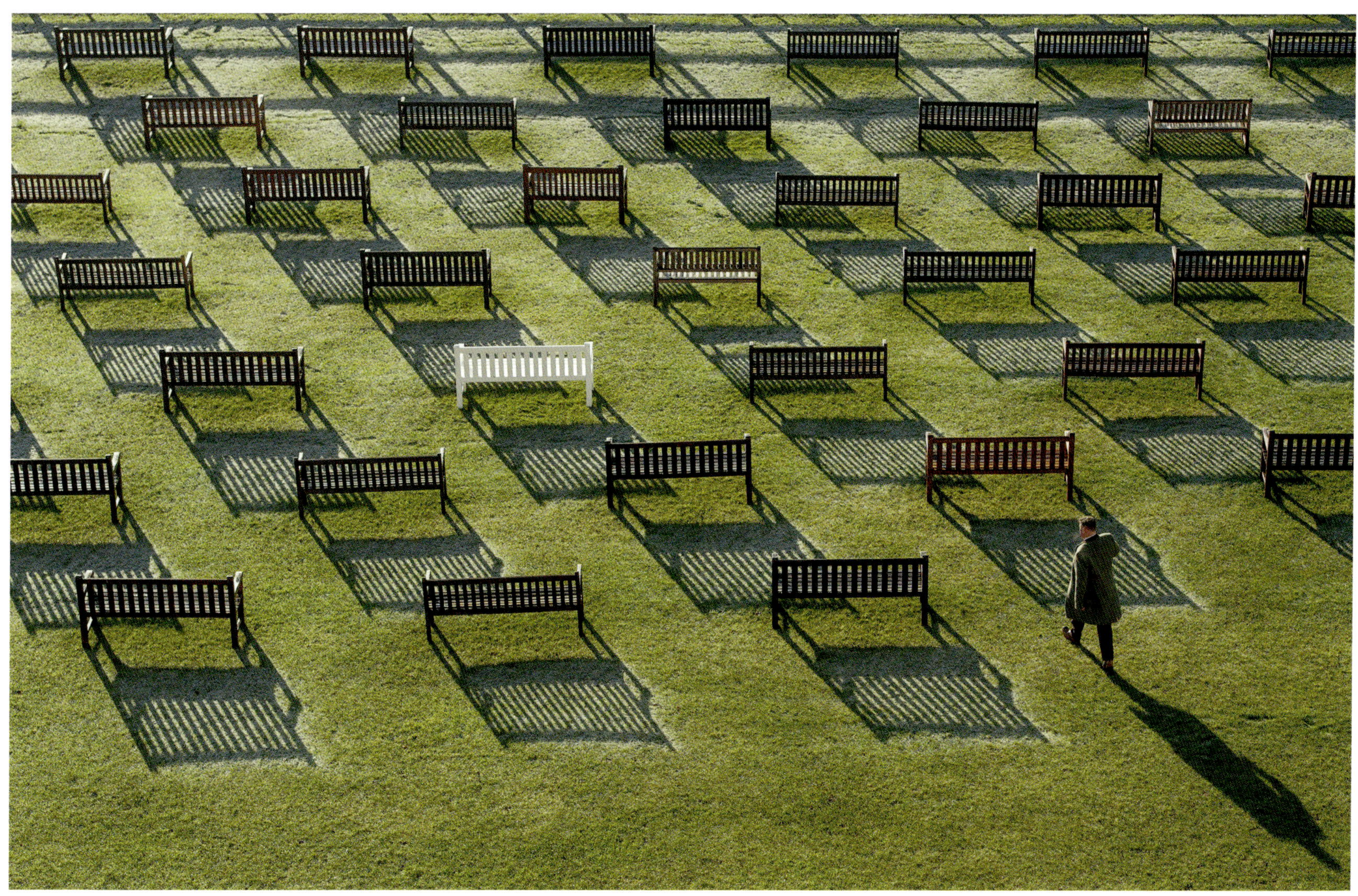

To the setting sun
Thundering towards the setting sun.
The open ditch at Taunton still leaves
two more fences to take before the
final three in the straight. But even at
this stage you can sense the urgency.

Newbury benches
The shadow benches make frozen
patterns across the members' lawn
at Newbury. A solitary spectator
adds the human dimension and an
even mightier shadow.

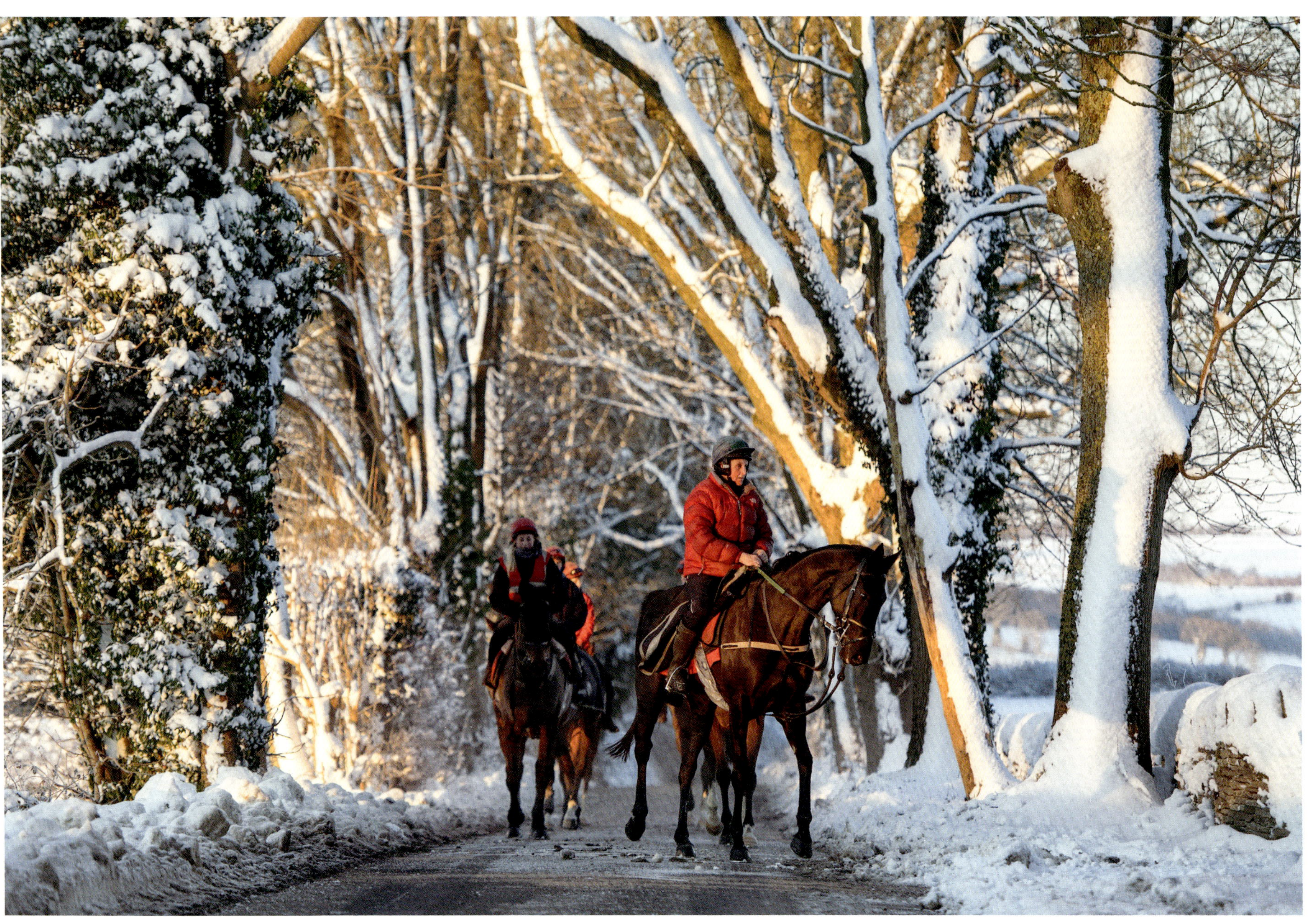

In the deep midwinter
Fergal O'Brien's first lot return
to their stables at Naunton in
Gloucestershire. It was minus seven
as I lay in the snow to get pictures on
the gallops and nearly died with cold.

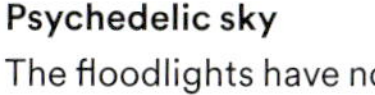
Psychedelic sky
The floodlights have not yet won their battle at Kempton but many races stretch ahead.

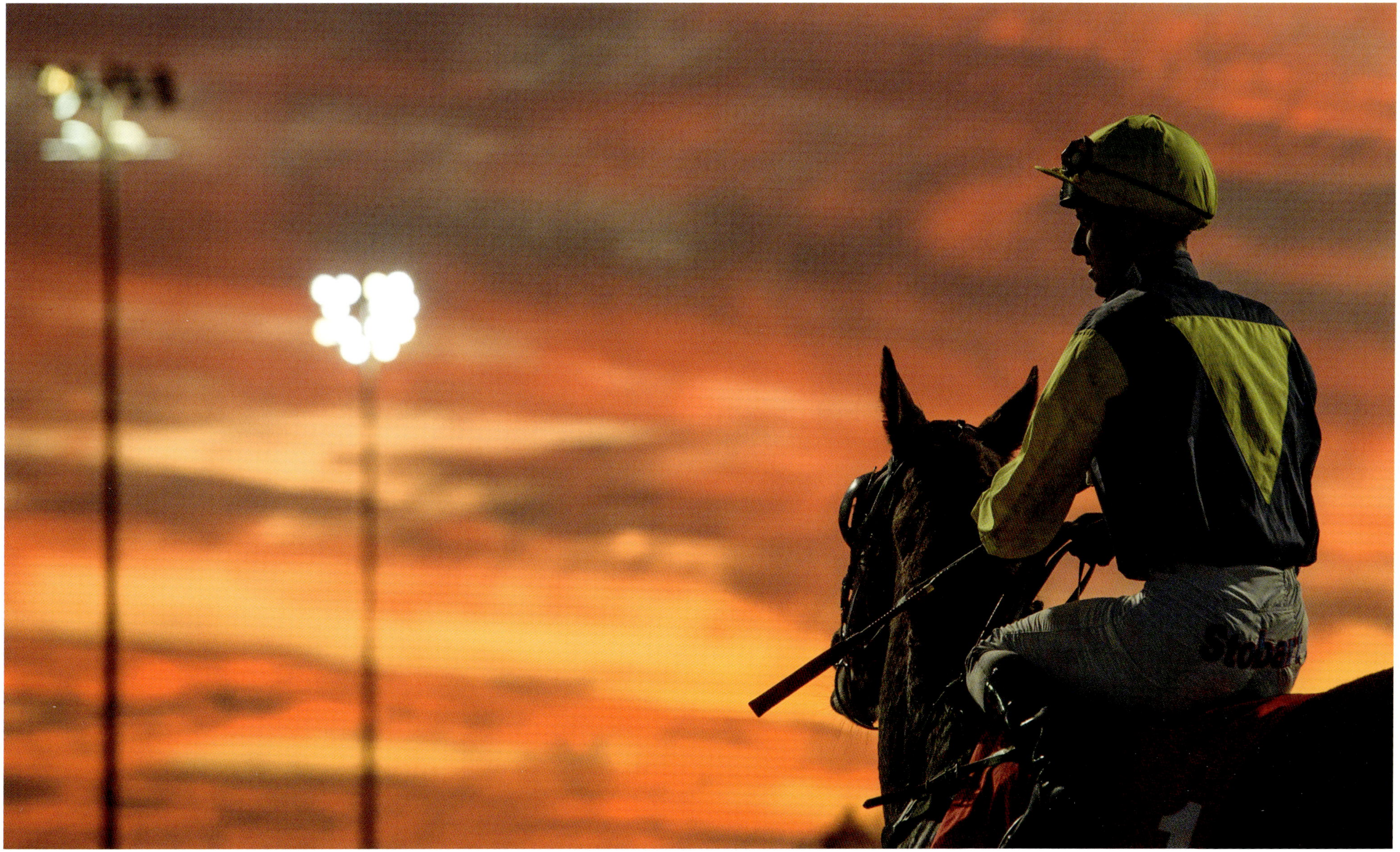

Freezing delight
This is a very ordinary race at
Kempton but the blue and pink frost
in the trees gives an almost Winter
Palace feel to the picture.

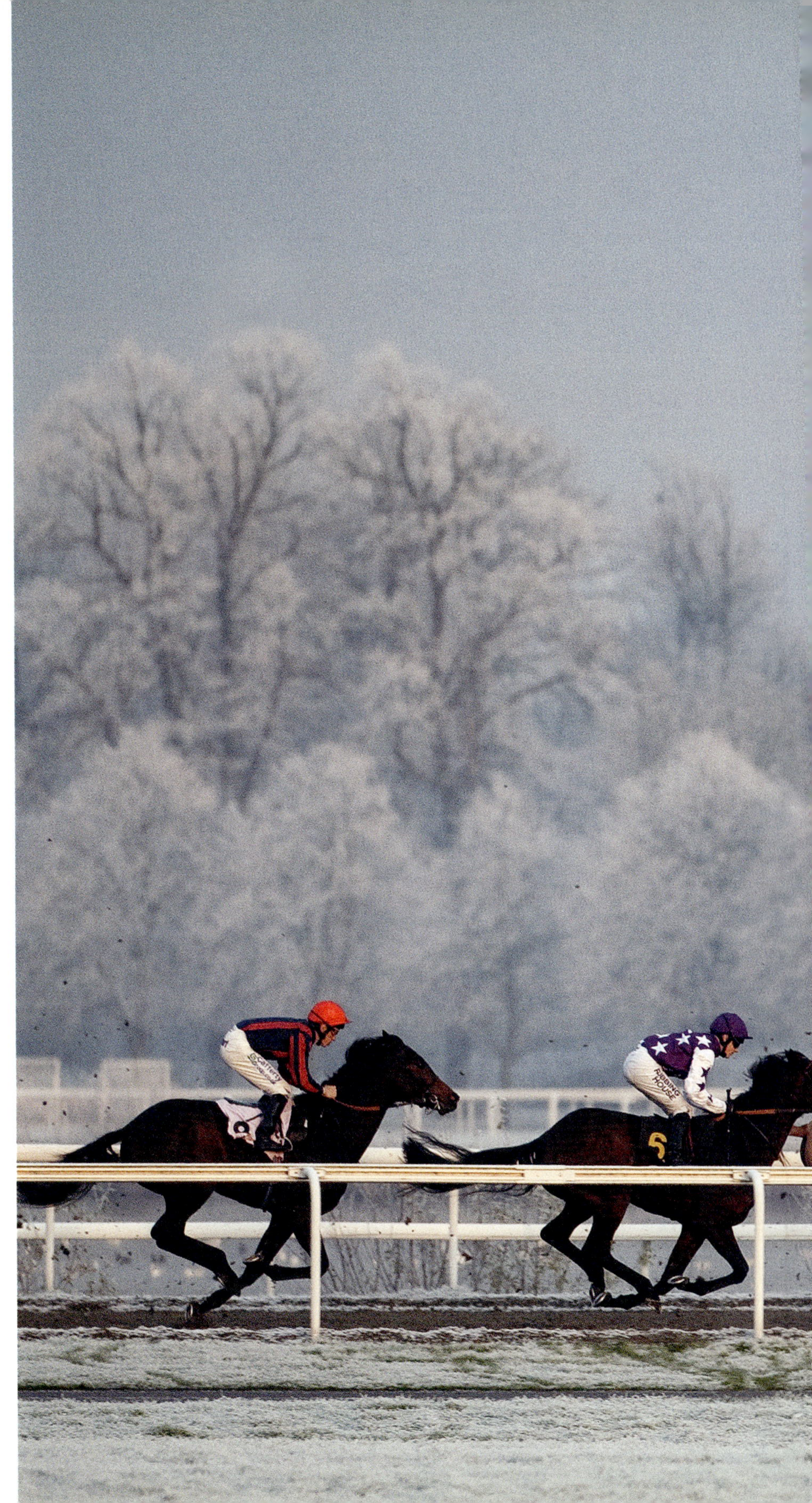

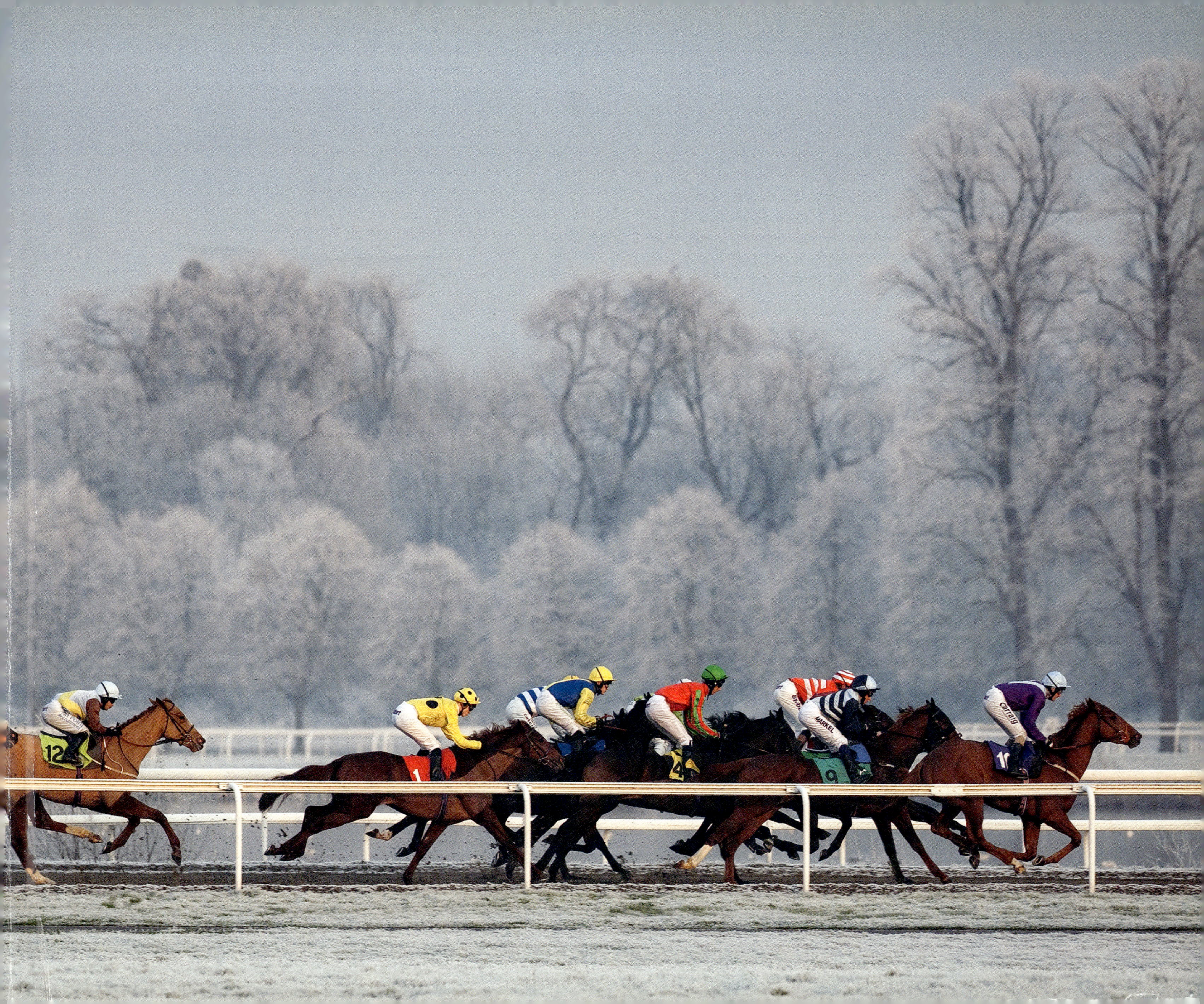